EYE TO EYE

MEMOIRS OF A MAYO CLINIC-TRAINED EYE SURGEON

John S. Jarstad, MD

ISBN 978-1-63903-664-6 (paperback)
ISBN 979-8-88616-323-0 (hardcover)
ISBN 978-1-63903-665-3 (digital)

Christian Faith Publishing
832 Park Avenue
Meadville, PA 16335
www.christianfaithpublishing.com

Printed in the United States of America

To my parents, teachers, coaches, and mentors who lovingly guided me to where I am today

*The author acknowledges the kind help of
Kristi Boudreau
in editing the manuscript.
The following ideas and opinions are solely the author's
and do not reflect official doctrine or policy of the
Church of Jesus Christ of Latter-day Saints.*

Yea, and now behold, O my son, the Lord doth give me exceedingly great joy in the fruit of my labors;

For because of the word which he has imparted unto me, behold, many have been born of God, and have tasted as I have tasted, and have seen **eye to eye** as I have seen; therefore they do know of these things of which I have spoken, as I do know; and the knowledge which I have is of God.

And I have been supported under trials and troubles of every kind, yea and in all manner of afflictions; yea God has delivered me…and I do put my trust in him…

And I know that he will raise me up at the last day, to dwell with him in glory: yea, and I will praise him forever. (Alma 36:25–28 Book of Mormon, Another Testament of Jesus Christ)

And the King shall answer…them…in as much as ye have done it unto one of the least of these my brethren, ye have done it unto me. (Matthew 25:40 KJV)

No blame lies on the weak, nor on the sick…and for him who asks, chide not. (Holy Quran 545)

CONTENTS

INTRODUCTION

Everyone has a story to tell. I suppose my life may seem extraordinary to some and rather boring to others; but in recently studying the life stories of many great and famous men that I admire (Dr. Russell M. Nelson, Thomas S. Monson, the Mayo brothers, Sir Winston Churchill, Dr. Jose Rizal, Sir William Osler), one thing strikes a common thread—they all kept journals.

Inspiration to write my experiences came after reading the fascinating story of one of my ancestral relatives, James Oliver, a civil war surgeon who published a book right before he died, at age eighty-five.* Hopefully my story will be as exciting as Dr. Oliver's and I'll live almost as long.

It is the desire of my heart that the inspiration to proceed with this book will encourage my descendants, family, and friends to higher levels of spirituality, faith, perseverance, and kindness to others. My greatest dream would be that this work creates a love for, and appreciation of, the greatest physician who ever lived, our Lord and Savior, Jesus Christ.

John S. Jarstad, MD
September 7, 2022
St. Petersburg, Florida, USA

[1]

---

[1] **James Oliver**, *Ancestry, Early Life and War Record of James Oliver, M.D.— Practicing Physician Fifty Years*, The Athol (MA) Transcript Company, 1915.

PROLOGUE

He was way too talkative. Always asking questions…questions…questions, and he would never eat all his dinner. Mother was fed up with K.J. She loaded him into the wagon and together they drove up the Valdres Valley (one hundred kilometers west of Lillehammer) into the mountains, ostensibly to look for firewood and to check the traps for food. She had reached the end of her rope. Food was scarce that winter and it was time to teach K.J. a lesson. Was she the wicked stepmother? Or just a dedicated Viking Mother trying to keep her family alive?

After they had climbed from the valley floor several miles from the river crossing, she dropped K.J. off the wagon into the soft snow. "Gather as much of the dry wood as you can find, and I'll be back in an hour or so to pick you up. I'm going further up to check the rabbit traps." "Okay Mama," answered K.J.

She'd check the traps and circle back on the other side of the draw and make him walk home. That would teach him a lesson! After checking the traps and placing the few rabbits into the leather sack, she started the wagon for home.

After ten kilometers, Ingrid Knutsdotter Nordtorp senses returned and she decided to go back for K.J., but it was too late. It was getting dark, and her ten-year-old stepson was nowhere to be found. Maybe he had walked or run home? The boys were all fast runners. But when she reached the farmhouse he wasn't home! "Everything okay?," Pops asked. "Ummmm…K.J. decided to run back," said Ingrid.

"He's not here?" Pops had a panicked look on his face. Now he was angry! "How could you leave K.J. in the woods! It's below zero. He won't survive the night in this weather!" Word went out quickly in the village. K.J. was missing and it was getting dark. Everyone grabbed their lanterns and torches with all the warm clothing they could find to go look for K.J.

For three days the townspeople scoured every place they could think of. Near evening of the third day a neighbor heard K.J.'s muffled calls and he was found! Huddled in a bear's den, a mother bear had heard the boy's cries and taken him in and kept him warm during the nights until K.J.'s neighbors found him—tired, hungry, and barely alive—a miracle!

As the reader may imagine, K.J. did not want to stay in the village near Vestre Slidre with his stepmother after that experience and as soon as he turned seventeen, worked his way to America on a steamship.

It was a hard life in the new world and when K.J. (Knute) and his new young wife Anna moved from Decorah, Iowa to find their own land up further north, an unscrupulous land agent at the land office in Chicago sold the Jarstad family one hundred acres of farmland "just a little northwest of St. Paul," which they found out all too soon was closer to Minot, North Dakota. When my great-grandfather Knut's son Otto was 7 years old and a few years after Knut Jarstad had moved the Jarstad family into their first home—a sod hut—they fell on hard times one year and Knut and Anna couldn't afford to feed all of their six children. Otto was tall and wiry strong for his age. He was "farmed out" and taken in by a neighboring family to work on their farm in exchange for food. Otto was so upset about leaving the family that the neighbor brought seven-year-old Otto back after just one week. "Your boy wouldn't eat anything this whole week, so he's not much good to us," the dryland farmer said. "I'll work hard Papa. I won't eat very much. I'll do anything, just don't send me away ever again!"

A few years later, just as the Jarstad family was beginning to make it in their new world and had moved out of their sod hut into a large white framed house, a drought brought a notice from the bank to foreclose on their home and land. As the bank and sheriff arrived, so did all the neighboring farmers with their pitchforks and shotguns, preventing the eviction. Just a few weeks later, Knut was found on the side of the family home by his son Otto with a gunshot wound to the head. The killer was never found.

The family soon moved on to Medicine Lake, Montana, and then during World War I, brother-in-law Christian Smestad, also a carpenter-machinist like Otto, sent money for Otto to visit Bremerton where the U.S. Navy was hiring all the machinists they could find. Otto called Western Washington "Beulah land" and sent money for train tickets for his wife Ida and the entire Jarstad family to move out west.

Otto met Ida Smestad in North Dakota while he was working as a carpenter on the railroad and as the last stagecoach driver on the route from Culbertson to Plentywood, Montana. Ida was the company cook and also from Norwegian parents. Ida's mother Christina packed salt onto a donkey and traveled each week from the Smestad family farm in Eidsvoll to Oslo to sell the salt. An attractive but impulsive 17-year-old, one day Christina had heard enough romantic tales about America to pique her curiosity and on her next trip sold not only the load of salt but also the family donkey and booked passage to America, eventually settling in Twin Valley, Minnesota, near the Dakota border.

After arriving out west, Otto Jarstad soon was placed in charge of the Bremerton watershed and pump station which pumped the clean fresh water supply from the 1000-acre watershed in the lakes and hills above Gorst, Washington, northward into the city of Bremerton. He kept the station running and the pumps maintained, while he and the family lived in a small 3-bedroom home on the site.

Each year about one hundred Bremerton citizens died of cholera. Otto had heard of a process to chlorinate water and attended a symposium in Kansas City, Missouri to learn how. As he presented the idea to the city leaders a protest erupted because during WWI chlorine gas was used for chemical warfare in Europe with devastating effects and there were veterans in town who were blinded or scarred from the chlorine gas during the war. Finally convincing the city leaders of the safety of this new technology, Otto Jarstad became the first person west of the Missouri River in the United States to chlorinate city drinking water. There was never a case of cholera after that. Otto Jarstad Park at the site of the original pump station is today a beautiful monument to my grandfather, which has preserved his legacy and even has a salmon spawning stream and fish hatchery on the manicured grounds. It is also the site of the Jarstad family Easter Egg hunt and annual Jarstad family reunion.

In a visit to the village of Jarstad, Vestre Slidre, Norway—just North of Fagernes, in 2004 with my son Robby, we reconnected with our beautiful and talented Jarstad cousins Ragnhild and Bjorg-Marie, along with their father and our oldest living Norwegian Jarstad relative, Halvor Oystein. I asked my eldest cousin two questions: 1. How do you pronounce our last name? "It's Yar-schta," he corrected me. "The -d- is silent in Norwegian." 2. What does the name mean? "It means the people vaht help others to cross over." "Oh, like savage Vikings sending them to the afterlife?" "No," he chuckled, "Vee are those vaht help others to cross over the Slidrefjorden (or you might refer to it as a river) here. It is the only place where one can walk over to the other side because there is a hidden sandbar just under the surface which makes it the only safe place to cross for twenty kilometers in either direction. We Jarstad's were the guardians of the escape route for when the Danes, Swedes, or Celts attack. We were the ones who pointed out the only safe place to cross to save our people during an attack."

When I asked my cousin where we Jarstad's originated and moved from prior to settling in the beautiful Valdres Valley. Halvor had a perplexed look on his face. "Vhat do you mean?," he asked. "Vee have always lived here."

CHAPTER 1

MY CHILDHOOD

I was born in Seattle, Washington, the most beautiful city in the world, on September 7, 1955, on a Wednesday. My mother, Barbara Stokes Jarstad, was twenty-three years old. My father, John Otis William Jarstad, thirty-five, was a TV sports announcer broadcasting a baseball game on Ladies' Day at the ballpark. Sick's Seattle Stadium is no longer in existence but was located in the beautiful (now economically challenged) Rainier Valley just three miles south and east of downtown Seattle where the current Mariners and Seahawks professional sports stadiums are located. Mom was under general anesthetic when I was born at Seattle's Catholic Hospital near Capitol Hill, just east of Interstate 5. Little did I know that thirty-four years later, I would start my teaching career in medicine as an instructor in ophthalmology with the same teaching hospital. I was the second child, having an older sister by two and a half years, Kristi.

My trials began at birth. Immediately after arriving in this world, I contracted a severe case of staphylococcal infection, and the medical staff believed this was life-threatening. A frantic call to my maternal grandfather, Marcus Stokes of Port Orchard, to administer a priesthood blessing was made since I was not expected to live. He immediately left his work as a machinist at the Puget Sound Naval Shipyard, caught the Bremerton to Seattle ferry, arrived at the hospital, anointed my little head with consecrated olive oil, and administered a priesthood blessing, promising me that I would live. At the conclusion of the blessing, it is reported that I rose up my head slightly and gave a weak little smile, and for the first time, there was hope I would survive.

When I was one year old, another trial occurred, as I slipped on the bathroom floor and sustained a skull fracture. Early photos show me in a football helmet, which protected my head for the entire second year of my life.

A few other experiences of my infant years can be remembered by me and my family. We had a cocker spaniel named Jet; and we lived in a two-level house on Queen Anne Hill just north of downtown Seattle, where my dad was the first man seen on ABC affiliate KOMO TV channel 4. The original black-and-white newscast shows Dad sitting in front of a camera, behind a desk, reading the news from a legal pad. There were some happy times imitating my dad by crawling inside an old TV cabinet and entertaining my sisters.

When I was three years old, I announced that I was going to run away from home. Mom said, "Okay, honey. Go ahead." After packing some underwear and a teddy bear, I headed down the front stairs to the sidewalk. A few minutes later, under the watchful eye of my older sister Kristi, I turned around and returned home, too homesick to go very far.

When I was five, my dad moved us to Tacoma. He had an opportunity to help start a new TV station (now KCPQ-13) as station manager for a Mr. J. Elroy McCaw (Mr. McCaw's sons Craig,

Bruce, and John were a little older than me; and we went fishing one weekend together at Neah Bay, the northwesternmost tip of Washington state). The McCaw brothers would become billionaires developing one of the very first cellular telephone companies in the United States. I remember that they were all very fun loving yet very well-mannered and told me they weren't allowed to swear or use bad language.

In addition to being channel 13's TV star, my dad also managed the station, edited film, shot commercials, and read the teletype machine for the evening news stories. In those days, television was so new that there were very few people seen on the black-and-white box. Everywhere we went, Dad was a celebrity with everyone asking for his autograph and wanting to shake his hand. He had press passes for parking and the best seats for all the big athletic and sporting events in Seattle and all over the Pacific Northwest.

My school years began as I left our 1,200-square-foot, three-bedroom rambler house at 4812 South Eighteenth Street, in Tacoma's central district. I didn't like school at first and went so seldom that I had to repeat kindergarten. It used to be a joke that it was because I couldn't get the hang of finger painting, but it was probably homesickness and immaturity since my birthday made me one of the youngest kids in my school class.

In the winter of 1961, I made the front page of the *Tacoma News Tribune* with the headlines "Tacoma Tot, 6, Saves Pal, 5, from Drowning" (February 28, 1961).

JOHN S. JARSTAD, MD

Front page: *Tacoma News Tribune*, February 28, 1961

Page 2: *Tacoma News Tribune*, February 28, 1961

My good friends Mike Koester (a retired fire chief, now living in Vallejo, California) and Ricky Rupp (now a food service executive) took me exploring in the woods near the back of the 4812 house. Near the corner of Mullen and South Nineteenth Streets, before the land was filled in and a dental office erected, was a depression of considerable size which would fill with water creating an immense pond, about fifty yards in diameter and up to fifteen feet deep, after the heavy rains. As we were clambering over a large tree stump, I lost my footing and fell into the water, way over my head. I remember reaching up with one hand and having the sure, steady, and strong grasp of my good friend Mike Koester, pulling me up and out of the deep water. After returning home, wet and scared, my mom found out what a hero Mike was and made him a hero's medallion and called the newspaper.

Having played semiprofessional baseball with the Bremerton Blue Jackets of the Western International League and broadcasting baseball for the Seattle pro team and also being the voice of the University of Washington Huskies football and basketball teams, my dad always assumed I would grow up to be a professional athlete. He was certain I would be a major league shortstop. Many hours after work, he would hit or throw me ground balls so I could improve my fielding skills. Soon I began playing organized baseball at the earliest possible age in the Tacoma recreation league—eight-year-old softball. I was small for my age usually the second or third smallest kid in my class, but I did have some innate hand-eye coordination, so I played shortstop that first year. The highlight was hitting a grand slam home run to right field on a ground ball that made it all the way to the fence. My sports career was born, and I knew my dad was proud of me.

Little did we realize that it would end in baseball almost as soon as it had begun. Unbeknownst to my parents or me was that, after age eight, I became progressively nearsighted, so that I could never hit a baseball after that one glorious year. It wasn't until about three years later that I had my first eye exam and found out I was in need of eyeglasses. I can still remember the thrill of seeing the detail of leaves on a tree for the very first time.

Now that things written on the chalkboard could be seen, I began to enjoy school, and about this time, my interest in music was born. My mom always loved the sound of the French horn, one of the hardest musical instruments to play. When De Long Elementary School announced that band would be offered, she immediately went out and leased a French horn from Ted Brown music store. I was going to play the French horn. It was a challenge just to make sound come out, but eventually, I was playing at De Long and joining the big kids once a week at Hunt junior high school since there was a real shortage of French horn players.

In the fall of my fourth-grade year, my best friend was Dennis Good. He lived two houses away on Eighteenth Street. We were inseparable as best friends are. We especially liked to play "COMBAT" in our backyard and in the dense woods south of our homes. We loved to watch the TV show by the same name, pretending we were on the lookout for German troops and saving each other. Dennis was Lieutenant Good or Major Good, while I was Captain Jarstad. We would use our parents' old expired checkbooks and write each other checks for our combat pay of sometimes fifty imaginary dollars. We finally talked my mom into taking us to the Army surplus store to buy "camo" fatigue shirts. These were our prized possessions that we changed into immediately after we came home from elementary school each day.

On Halloween night 1965, my best friend, Dennis Dwaine Good, died of pneumonia (obituary on November 2, 1965, *Tacoma News Tribune*). We had been trick-or-treating in the rain in our combat fatigues, and I had just left his house after we finished counting our loot. I remember he had some sniffles and a little cough. but I was totally unprepared for my parents sitting me down on the sofa the next morning before school and telling me, "Dennis was real sick last night. Then he went to the hospital, where he died." I was in shock. It was so hard not to cry. A few days later, Mom insisted that I go talk to Dennis's father. Mr. Good wanted to talk to me, she said. I didn't want to go. I finally went up Eighteenth Street, two doors, and talked to him. He cried and said how much Dennis loved me and how sorry he was. I started to cry then and couldn't say a word. He gave me a hug and held me for a long time, and very soon afterward, the Good family moved away, and I never saw any of them again.

During this same time, I was to meet one of the teachers who had the greatest impact on my young life—James Dewey.

Mr. Dewey was a family friend whom my mom knew from Bremerton. He came to our home right before he moved to Tacoma to begin his teaching career since our families had known each other in the Church of Jesus Christ of Latter-day Saints. One of the sailors stationed in Bremerton during the war was James Dewey's father. I learned that my grandfather who was the first branch president for the Church of Jesus Christ of Latter-day Saints branch in Port Orchard was instrumental in fellowshipping Mr. Dewey's father during the war years in the 1940s. Mr. Dewey was my sixth-grade English teacher. He was an outstanding teacher, the kind who motivates you to do more than just the minimum job to get by. He was special. If you could get an A on any paper from Mr. Dewey, that was like a trophy. (Brother Dewey later became president of the Tacoma Washington Church of Jesus Christ of Latter-day Saints Stake).

Mr. Dewey noticed in sixth grade that I was beginning to hang out with a couple of funny kids named James and Curtis. They were always laughing and pulling pranks on some of the girls. One of the girls complained they were teasing her unmercifully, and I joined in. Then Mr. Dewey called my mom. He wanted to meet with me before school. He gave me a long lecture about how these boys had bad habits and came from broken homes. That both boys had family members in prison or were involved with drugs. He told me I couldn't hang out with them anymore or I would end up in jail. I respected Mr. Dewey and from that very day avoided James and Curtis. I think Brother Dewey saved me from a life of drugs, legal, and other troubles I would have been quite naïve to.

After making the school baseball team in seventh grade at Hunt Junior High as a shortstop, I sat on the bench with the JV and varsity. In eighth grade, over two hundred kids tried out. While taking two consecutive ground balls on the rocky surface of the tryout field, I booted both and was immediately cut from the team. It was devastating. Mom offered to talk to my school counselor and the coaches to get me reinstated, but I said no.

With this latest humiliation, I turned out for the track team and ran the 880-yard (half-mile) run, the longest distance allowed in junior high track-and-field. A classmate, "Ren" (Randy) Loth (rhymes with both), was also a distance runner and one of the quietest, unassuming, and hardest-working people I'd ever met. I ran extra workouts with Ren (we would do exactly double everything the other track team members did); and I made the team, eventually placing fourth, just a few steps behind my friend Ren, in the final event in the junior high championships in my ninth-grade year.

One day, toward the end of track season, my coach (and science teacher), Mr. (Bob) Malyon, noted that my practice mile times kept getting slower and slower. He called me into his office. "Hey, Jarstad, let me take a look at those feet," he said. He took one look at the bottom of my right foot and felt a tumor about the size of a medium-sized marble. "You need to see your doctor right away," he advised. A week after school let out, I had surgery to remove a tumor from the second toe on my right foot. It was growing out of the bone and was worrisome for cancer. Surgery was done under a local anesthetic. As I watched the large anesthetic needle go through my foot and come out the other side, I imagined what Jesus must have suffered, right before I passed out.

Shortly after that, I saw a podiatrist who noted that I had completely flat feet, and he fitted me with orthotic arch supports. "You'll never amount to anything in athletics with feet like those," he predicted. "Maybe you should consider something like chess or tennis where you don't have to move around so much." That was the last I ever saw of the podiatrist, but I vowed to prove him wrong.

Determined to be an athlete, I next tried wrestling in junior high, earning a varsity school letter. It was in wrestling I met my future brother-in-law, John Kingston. John wrestled 130 pounds, and I was trying out for 120. Gary Hall, John's close friend, wrestled the weight between us. John really liked my sister Lisa, who would become a cheerleader the following year. The three of us became close friends. I was the second-best wrestler in my weight class, so close to making varsity, with really close challenge matches every week. John and Gary sensed my predicament and each dropped down a weight class. They beat out the kid in my weight class so I could have varsity all to myself, after he quit. I enjoyed wrestling workouts and became close to John and Gary. In our sixteen-man double elimination district championship bracket, I placed fourth in the finals.

Wrestlers Ted McCoy (#168) and John Jarstad
(#141) were LDS team members.

Football was one of my great loves as a youth. I tried out for the junior high team as an eighth grader, in the fall of 1969. The first thing the coach asked us to do was to run a lap around the practice field, so we could warm up. I was so miserably out of shape that I only made it halfway around and collapsed. Seeing that I was lying on my back gasping for air, the coach came running over and said, "Son, you better hit the showers. Try again next year."

Humiliated and depressed, I was told by my friend Bruce Slingland about a recreational park league team at Fircrest Park about a mile from my house that was forming as part of the Pierce County Bantam League. I made the team as an end or wide receiver. Coach Frank Montalbano, a former NFL lineman, who attended my church, told me I had good, soft hands; and it was the first time any coach had expressed confidence in me. Payback came by my catching three touchdown passes in the league jamboree and helping our team to the district championship in 1969.

My most unusual game was when we played Fort Lewis with the tough Army kids. I beat their deep back on a flag pattern and scored a touchdown, but this kid was so mad he kept chasing me clear out of the end zone and onto the running track where he tackled me and received a fifteen-yard penalty for unsportsmanlike conduct. I was so mad and so scared that without thinking I jumped to my feet and hit him in the back of the helmet with the football and incurred a penalty of my own.

The next year in ninth grade, I made the junior high varsity team as a second-string wide receiver. I played in eight varsity quarters and started every junior varsity game, often as cocaptain. I scored several touchdowns as #33. Our varsity team had an outstanding season of championship-caliber football. As the head coach was getting ready for the varsity awards dinner, he asked a couple of us who were on the bubble how many quarters we had played.

The going thought was that you needed nine or ten quarters to be assured of a varsity letter; otherwise, it was up to the coach. A buddy named Greg told Coach Sonntag he had ten (when he only had six), and Coach asked him what name he wanted on his varsity letter certificate. Then Coach Sonntag asked me for my totals. It was so tempting. "Eight," I replied. "Are you sure?" he said. "Yes, Coach, I only had eight. "It was my last chance to earn my varsity football letter in junior high school, and I wanted to get a letterman's sweater so badly, but I was honest and didn't get the school letter in football.

Wrestling and track were coming, and I would earn my school varsity letter in both sports. I received my letterman's sweater in time for the school athletic awards assembly for track season in the spring. I enjoyed wearing my school colors for all the track meet dress-up days. One of the least-worn school letterman's sweaters still lives in my closet.

CHAPTER 2

OLYMPIC HOPEFUL

The author competing in a Giant Slalom race at Ski Acres, Washington

As a teenager, my dad owned a ski and motorcycle shop called Ski Hut/Honda at Highland Hill Shopping Center at 5915 South Sixth Avenue in Tacoma's west end. I loved to go there. It started out as a sporting goods shop. Later, Honda motorcycles were added. At age twelve, I began working after school in the ski shop, putting bindings on the rental skis and repairing the metal ski edges. There were also tune-ups with hot wax and P-Tex base repairs. I worked under the supervision of a nice man, Art Overman, who was a skilled carpenter.

Art taught me to use the metal jigs to line up the holes for the ski binding screws and to attach a piece of masking tape as a safety sign to the drill bit to avoid going too deep through the ski. After a good job, he taught me to pat myself on the back and say, "Oooh, you do good work"—a practice I affectionately still use to this day in his honor, after performing an especially good laser eye operation.

My working hours, at the ski shop, were after school from 3:00 p.m. until closing at around 10:00 p.m. I would ride home with my dad or my older sister Kristi. One of my fun duties was to manage the soda pop machine. This involved purchasing bottles of Fanta and Coke for about eleven cents and selling them for a quarter dollar. In this way, I could make a profit of fourteen cents per bottle. This gave me spending money, and I was learning to be a businessman.

I learned the difficulties of working for the family, however, as I never did receive a regular paycheck for my work in the ski repair shop. Later, I presented my four hundred hours in time cards to my aunt Elva McFadden, Dad's bookkeeper. She stuck up for me and got me about a dollar an hour for all my past work.

My other fun job was assembling motorcycles each summer, out behind the shop. The Honda motorbikes would come from Japan in wooden crates with Japanese writing all over the outside. The assembly instructions were in Japanese, too, so one of the senior mechanics would have to show me how to put each model together once, and then it was up to me. My favorite part was the wiring harness assembly (and, of course, the test-ride in the back parking lot, before hooking up the speedometer). My popularity at school was assured by picking several of my fifteen-year-old friends to help me assemble the bikes and test-ride them. One day, between shipments, we made the mistake of riding a customer's bike and put about ten miles on it. When the customer found out, he was so upset he insisted on having Dad buy him a brand-new motorcycle, and that was the end of the test-rides.

Speaking of motorcycle rides. When I was ten, my dad brought home a mini bike from the shop that someone had traded in on a new Honda. It was a little Italian bike with lots of zip and a 50cc engine. I would ride it with my friends in the backwoods behind our house.

One day, when my bike was in the shop, Dave Lamont, a kid in my class at elementary school, brought his Cushman trail bike over; and we took turns riding it in the woods. On my turn, the throttle stuck wide open, and I went halfway up a large tree and came down on my head. It started bleeding profusely. A nice neighbor man, Mr. Blatz heard my screams and came running toward me as I ran toward his house. He knew exactly what to do with pressure and a clean white handkerchief. Mom took me to Dr. Sam Adam's office where I was on the receiving end of about twelve stitches. So much for the motorbike antics.

Owning a ski shop meant that Dad gave us all the very latest skis, boots, and accessories every year. He also traded ski equipment for ski lessons and racing classes. About age eight, I began racing in the annual Bremerton Ski Cruiser races held each Easter at Stevens Pass. It was fun to win a cowboy hat full of Easter candies or a rare trophy.

Later about age twelve, I began racing seriously, and by junior high, I was on a racing team called Alpine Athletic Club based at Crystal Mountain Resort. Gary Effinger was my coach along with a chain-smoking assistant named Walt Waggoner, whom Dad must have paid to drive me each Saturday up to the practices and races. Gary, I was told, was a former US Olympic Women's Ski Team coach. He told me and my dad that he thought I had the determination and drive to become an Olympic caliber downhill ski racer.

At age fifteen, I was competing all over the Pacific Northwest in ski races. My biggest competition was twin brothers whom I could never beat, Phil and Steve Mahre from White Pass. They later won gold medals at the winter Olympics. Perhaps my greatest and one of my last competitive ski races was a downhill event at Mission Ridge in Eastern Washington in the winter of 1972.

I ran the race of my life cutting each gate perfectly and getting airborne just before the lip of each rolling bump to keep my speed up before going down the back side, imitating the downhill racers on

ABC's Wide World of Sports. I can still remember crossing the finish line sitting back on the tails of my skis like the Olympic ski racers I'd seen on TV and beating a kid I thought was Bill Johnson (1984 Olympic Downhill Champion) by 1/100th of a second. I remember a delay in the starting chute before my run and later found out that the racer directly ahead of me failed to prejump the biggest bump on the course, went airborne, and had crashed into a tree running a tree branch through his heart, killing him instantly.

Now that I was sixteen, schoolwork, high school sports, and girls were pulling me away from competitive skiing. Later that year, my dad sold the ski shop, and the free skis and money to travel and compete were no longer available. I remember the difficult decision to give up my Olympic ski racing dream to concentrate on school, work, and preparing for a church mission.

In 2001, I was able to visit Kitzbuhel, Austria, the site of the 1976 Winter Olympics and ski the Hahnenkamm downhill course and get it out of my system. It is a terrible course in the fog, and I knew I had made the right decision to go on a mission instead of trying for the Olympics as none of the American men placed that year in the Olympics downhill. I was later able to teach a ski racing class at Ski Acres, Snoqualmie Summit, during the early 1990s to help pass along the torch of one of my greatest loves in sports—downhill ski racing until I competed and won the Eye Doctor's World Slalom Ski Championship just after the Italian Winter Olympics at Cortina d'Ampezzo, Italy (see chapter 32).

CHAPTER 3

YOUNGEST COMMERCIAL FISHERMAN IN WASHINGTON

On my sixteenth birthday, I traveled to Olympia, Washington, to obtain my commercial fishing license. In order to catch more than three salmon per day one was required to pay $100 and submit an application to the Washington Department of Fisheries. Dad wanted me to get a trolling and gillnetting license so that we could sell fish separately and so I could operate a small boat myself.

After working at Westport as a deckhand for a year and fishing in the Pacific Ocean since I was five every summer, my dad decided I was experienced enough to try my own fishing boat. Dad recently acquired a bright-orange nineteen-foot fiberglass dory with a fifty-horsepower outboard engine and had rigged it to catch salmon commercially by adding four detachable sport rods.

"You can pick up a commercial license on the way down to Westport, and we can fish two boats and double our catch each day until the end of the season," was Dad's reckoning.

I drove to Olympia, the state capitol, where, after some prospecting, I found the Department of Fisheries office. After presenting my application, I was told to take a seat. I must have waited three hours. There was no one else in line. The two women behind the counter were discussing their weekend dates in graphic terms, totally oblivious to the sixteen-year-old youth waiting in a chair facing them. Finally, about 4:00 p.m., I came up to the counter one last time.

"Excuse me, but am I going to be able to get my commercial fishing license today or not?" I pleaded. "Oh, guess we forgot all about you, sonny. Here you go." "What a waste of time and state tax dollars," my young sixteen-year-old mind thought. "I'll bet they have state employee benefits too."

Dad worried about what took me so long to get to Westport. I told him the story. The topic soon turned to fishing. There was still a hot bite on, and he'd caught about thirty salmon by himself that day while I was in Olympia listening to the fisheries department women talk about their dates in terms no sixteen-year-old should be subjected to. I'd wasted a day of good fishing and lost probably $300.

Dad was anxious to get me out fishing but also concerned about me going out on the open Pacific Ocean alone, in a nineteen-foot boat, so he asked my cousin Gilbert McFadden to go with me. Gil, who was about twenty-two, had been a star football player in Walla Walla, Washington, but had a near-fatal injury in a college game when he broke his neck. He gradually recovered and would later go on to coach football at Lakes High School in South Tacoma. Gil had never operated a fishing boat before; and on the way back to the harbor after a day of commercial salmon fishing, with a following sea, he took over control of the *Orange Crate* as we crossed the dangerous river bar.

We soon began hydroplaning and increasing speed. Faster and faster, we surfed until we were literally surfing toward the rocks of Westport. I begged Gil to let me take control and back off on the throttle, and as he did, the wave took us in a 360-degree circle and nearly flipped us over. Later that night, I told Dad about the experience, and from that day forward, he let me fish alone.

Some of my fondest memories were of those summers fishing in Westport and the friendly competition between Dad, my uncle Glenn, my cousin Gene Jarstad, and me, seeing who could catch the most salmon each day. King salmon were being sold for $3.00 a pound and coho for about $1.25 per pound in those golden days at Westport. A good day was a hundred pounds of "large" or king salmon. That was each fisherman's goal. The "highliner" each day would pay for dinner at the Islander Restaurant, the nicest restaurant in Westport owned by a Neddie Rose Farrington (a wonderful lady who would come to me twenty years later to restore her vision with cataract surgery).

After a long day on the boats, we took turns showering at the trailer park and, when everyone was ready, walked over to the restaurant and pulled out our fish slips from the fish buyers and compared catches. The fisherman with the biggest catch of the day would pay for everyone's dinner. It was usually Glenn or my dad who would end up buying.

The name of the boat I would operate was called the *Genius*. It was a sixteen-foot wooden boat that no one else was using. After Gene graduated to the charter boat fleet as a licensed skipper, he didn't have time anymore to commercial fish. Instead, he took out the tourists on a big beautiful new fiberglass boat, the *Nauti-Gull*. Uncle Glenn, who was also too busy to fish, kept the *Genius* running for me and gave me the opportunity to use it to help pay for college (he was pretty tied up as the mayor of Bremerton). Later, when I returned from my church mission, I ran the *Genius* one more year before getting my charter captain's license and taking tourists out on salmon fishing tours.

CHAPTER 4

DEFENDING THE COASTLINE

There were many faith-promoting days on the Pacific Ocean before GPS navigation. My technique for finding my way back to the harbor in the fog without radar was often by prayer and a depth sounder and compass. It deserves some mention.

After a day of fishing, the fog would often begin to roll in by three or four o'clock in the afternoon. When it was time to go back to the harbor, I would head directly true east by compass and watch the depth sounder until I was in twenty feet of water (just outside the breakers near shore). I would look for the crab pot marker buoys. If the buoys were painted orange and blue, I knew I was north of Gray's Harbor. If they were brown and red, I knew I was south of Gray's Harbor. As soon as I could determine which direction I needed to run, I would go north or south until the depth sounder suddenly dropped from twenty to forty-five feet where I knew I was in the channel. I would then go east (at that time, the compass heading was exactly sixty degrees), which would take me right to the Westport Harbor. Of course, all this time I was also praying like crazy that I would find the navigation buoys or harbor entrance and not encounter any large ships going in or out of the channel.

One of my strangest trips as a charter captain was when the Club Mona Lisa (a "gentleman's" club) from Las Vegas hired the boat for the day. The night before that charter, a man named Billy, with a feathered hat, appeared at the dock and said, "I want to buy your boat."

"Oh, I'm not sure if it's for sale," I replied.

"No, I want to buy you," he said. "How much?"

"You're going to have to check at the charter office," I told him. "I'm just the captain."

Well, sure enough, the next morning, he arrived with twelve heavily mascaraed girls dressed in a wild assortment of outfits with fifteen ice chests full of hard liquor. Every one of the girls and him got so drunk that the crew ended up reeling in most of the fish. At the end of the day, Billy came to and gave me the first and only $100 tip of my charter boat career.

"We had a great time, and we'll buy you again tomorrow," he said.

The next day, only half of the group came and had a similar day on the water.

"If you're ever in Nevada, look us up," they said as they were leaving. "We'll be sure and show you a good time." I never took them up on their offer.

When one becomes a US Coast Guard-licensed charter boat captain, they must pass a rigorous two-day written and one-day oral examination at the coast guard regional operations center. The test is administered at the commandant's office and requires knowledge of navigation problems, safety, international and local rules of the road, identification of lights and shapes of vessels, and chart and compass navigation problems. After passing the exam and meeting with the commandant, the successful applicant then is sworn in as a US merchant marine officer. Raising his right hand to the square, he takes the same oath as those in the United States Military "to defend the laws and Constitution of the United States of America against all enemies both foreign and domestic." Little did I know that I would ever see action in this regard before my days as a charter boat captain were completed.

In the summer of 1980, during the Soviet occupation of Afghanistan, I had a rare opportunity to defend the United States of America, as captain of the MV *Rebel*, owned by Don Pugh of

Bellevue, Washington. The vessel was a forty-six-foot twin-diesel-engine charter boat that would accommodate twenty passengers and a crew of two or three. It was one of the faster boats in the Westport fishing fleet (which at that time numbered 240 charter boats).

As we left for a day's fishing, we ran north through dense early morning fog to an area near Copalis Rock, about twelve miles north of Ocean Shores. We were fishing in forty feet of water just a mile from the beach when suddenly without warning, out of the fog, appeared a tall red building, coming right toward us. As it materialized out of the pea-soup fog of the early morning Washington coast, I soon realized that it was not a building, after all but a ship. A red-painted fishing trawler with a bright-yellow hammer and sickle on the bow—and it was coming right for us! A Russian trawler was near our beach less than a mile from the US shoreline? I worked the *Rebel* around to hem him in as I made an urgent call to the US Coast Guard Station at Westport.

Captain Jarstad said, "SECURITY, SECURITY, SECURITY, Westhaven Lifeboat Station… Westhaven Lifeboat Station… This is the MV *Rebel* calling…"

Westhaven US Coast Guard Station said, "Go ahead, *Rebel*. This is Westhaven Lifeboat Station."

Captain Jarstad said, "Yes, this is the MV *Rebel*. I have a Russian trawler in forty feet of water near Copalis Rock with gear down taking our fish, well inside international waters. Please advise. Over…"

Westhaven USCG Station said, "Stand by, *Rebel*. What is your status? Over."

Captain Jarstad said, "I've got him hemmed in, but I can't hold him for long. Can you send anything up here to catch him in the act (of stealing our fish) or get him out of here? Over."

Westhaven USCG Station said, "Stand by, *Rebel*. We will advise the commandant… Over …" (They waited for what seemed like an eternity.)

Captain Jarstad said, "Westhaven, I can't keep this guy from getting away. Please advise. Over."

Westhaven USCG Station said, "Stand by, *Rebel*…"

About five minutes later, the trawler headed right for us and started to pull up his stainless steel fine mesh gear, nearly cutting the

Rebel in two as I gunned my throttles to get out of his way. Just as I was frustrated by the thought of the Russians taking our fish and getting away scot-free, we began to hear the thunderous roar of a jet airplane engine.

Out of the fog, which was now beginning to lift, came two Navy fighters swooping low over the water. They made a quick pass overhead and then circled around and returned. One of the planes fired cannon shots (*Poof! Poof!* The water exploded!) across the bow of the trawler, which was now heading out to sea at full speed.

"WOW! That was cool!" one of the tourists exclaimed. "Does that happen every day on these fishing tours?"

"No," I said, "that was a first for me."

Little did I know, when I became a charter boat skipper, that I would ever defend the US Coastline against foreign intruders.

Gene Jarstad, Robby Jarstad, and John Jarstad, MD,
with two king salmon and a large lingcod

CHAPTER 5

BAPTIZING MY FATHER

One of the most significant events in my life was the baptism of my father, John Otis William Jarstad, in 1972. My mom owned a rental house where the missionaries for the Church of Jesus Christ of Latter-day Saints lived, so there were frequent interactions with the missionaries.

During this time, my dad was the victim of a dishonest store manager at the Ski Hut, who, along with a slick attorney, conspired to wrest the successful business away from my dad. The store manager embezzled funds over several months, thereby making the business look unprofitable. A secret bank account was established by this individual, and $60,000 was diverted away from the business in a fairly short time.

Dad became discouraged, and the store manager and his "business partner" attorney made an offer to buy Ski Hut/Honda. Dad, in his discouragement, sold the store to this dishonest pair, but the new owners never paid him a cent after their first monthly installment. After three years in the courts, Dad won, and the judge had to order a writ of execution to liquidate the attorney's properties because he still refused to pay Dad. The case made legal history in Jarstad v. Tacoma Outdoor Recreation (519 P. 2d 278, 10 Wash App. 551). The dishonest manager fled to somewhere in Australia and later settled in California, where he built a hotel with Dad's money. Needless to say, these were very discouraging times for my father.

At this same time, he was also serving on the Tacoma City Council when half the council—including the mayor (but not including my dad)—was recalled for corruption. One night, Dad, who was honest but not religious, came into my room and sat on the end of my bed.

"Johnny," he said, "my life just isn't turning out exactly the way I'd planned." There was a long silence. What do you say as a fifteen-year-old kid in that situation? I prayed for inspiration: "Dad, don't you think it's about time you joined the church?" There was a longer pause.

"Well, I guess you're right." I couldn't believe it!

"So does that mean we can call the missionaries?"

He gave the okay. After about six weeks of lessons and discussions, as a sixteen-year-old priest in the Tacoma Fourth Ward, I was asked to baptize my father, the deputy mayor of Tacoma Washington, into the Church of Jesus Christ of Latter-day Saints.

I'll never forget that day.

The stake center was filled to overflowing. I think many people who knew my famous father came out of shear disbelief. My three sisters sang "I Am a Child of God," and the cultural hall and gym was opened to accommodate the overflow. Years later after Dad had served with Bishop Dewey in a ward bishopric, I asked him about his conversion.

"I was obviously humbled by the business situation and ready to listen, but the key for me was Joseph Smith. He had to be a prophet of God, and that I was sure of. I had a hard time accepting the *Book of Mormon* because of the story about the angel Moroni delivering it, but I was so certain that Joseph Smith was a prophet and that both he and his brother Hyrum were men of integrity and men of God, that I could accept anything else they were involved in."

My first baptism as a prospective missionary was my own father. I'll always remember standing in the baptismal font at the Tacoma Stake Center as a trembling sixteen-year-old newly ordained priest, hoping to do everything right in baptizing my dad. He made a promise twenty years earlier that one day he would join the church if Mom would marry him. We later joked that it only took him twenty years to keep a promise.

CHAPTER 6

THE STATE CHAMPIONS

Washington State cross-country champions in 1973 (Curtis High School): Coach Burt Wells, Mark Mowry, Rick Johnson, Mark Walls, Doug Twitchell, Don Nelson, John Jarstad, Mike Alexi, Mark Bascom, Mike Thomsen, and Keith Parker

S ports was always important at my house and an increasingly frequent topic of both conversation and television viewing. This was especially true on the weekends, as I entered junior high school. When Dad wasn't out broadcasting TV sports events, he was at home practicing his running color commentary on each pro football or basketball game, honing his skills and his golden voice.

During the summer after ninth grade, I was approached by a good junior high friend, Mike Levenseller, who, like me, lived on the border of the Tacoma and University Place school districts.

Mike would later go on to an amazing career in football, setting records as a wide receiver at Washington State University, playing in the NFL for the Cincinnati Bengals, and later coaching his alma mater Washington State Cougars. "Hey, John," he said, "how about coming over to Curtis High with me? It's a smaller 2A school (now 4A), and I think we could both make the football team and maybe even start on the varsity."

That sounded good to a kid who narrowly missed a varsity letter at Hunt Junior High, and I petitioned the district for a transfer. Since I lived a good three miles from the boundary, a transfer would not be easy. I remember meeting with Tacoma Public School superintendent, Dr. Angelo Giuadrone, and explaining with my parents why I wanted to go outside the Tacoma District (overcrowding, smaller classes, making the sports teams). Then Dr. Giuadrone said, "Now tell me the real reason." I didn't want to mention it, but Mom insisted. There was one other factor.

During the previous year, my dad easily defeated a nice neighbor man who was the first Black man to run for city council in Tacoma (interestingly, Dad would later appoint this same man to the city council to fill a vacancy, and Dad would suffer severe persecution, including death threats at this time of racial tension for appointing his Black opponent to the council).

His son was a year older than me and was very angry about the outcome of the election.

One day, as I was waiting for my school bus on the corner of Twelfth Street and Firlands, he came up behind me and pushed me as hard as he could right into the path of an oncoming city bus traveling at about forty miles per hour. I flew off the sidewalk toward the speeding bus but somehow bounced backward, right back onto the curb, instead of down in front of the bus. It was a miracle, but I was unhurt. I could easily have been killed. There were several witnesses.

Dr. Giadronne had heard enough and signed my transfer. I was in at Curtis High!

With fall football finding me on the junior varsity practice squad, I had a strong desire to prove myself. Levenseller and I were ineligible that first year as transfer students, so the coaches put us in, as what my dad called "cannon fodder for the varsity." This meant we would run the plays of the opposing teams as halfbacks, and the varsity guys would use us as tackling dummies. Mike and I both had our "bells rung" several times, and it was a long season but a fun one, getting to know each other and our future teammates.

The next year, we were both eligible and made the varsity team. Mike as a receiver and running back and me as second-string line-backer (or monster back) on defense and also as a member of the kickoff team. I was only five feet nine and 145 pounds but could hit hard and was above average in foot speed. I got quite a bit of playing time on the kickoff team since we scored so often. We had an unde-feated season and won the state title in football that year.

The best part, for me, was playing two games a week (Seamount League policy was that if a player participated in the equivalent of two quarters or fewer in a varsity game on Friday night, he was allowed to play in the junior varsity game the following Monday afternoon). In addition, the coaches selected me defensive captain of the JV team. In one game, I made two interceptions and twenty-eight unassisted tackles against Foster High School's varsity. At the end of the year awards banquet, I was given a trophy for **"Most Improved Defensive Player Curtis High School 10-0."** My football career was taking off. Little did I know what was in store for me my senior year.

That senior year began with hot, sweaty two-a-day football practices. I was excited to see exactly where I would fit in on the returning state championship football team. I started the intrasquad game as first string linebacker and was in tight competition with a larger, mature, strong sophomore kid for the starting middle line-backer job. The first league game was coming up.

One night, after practice, Coach Bagby called me into his office.

"Jarstad," he said, "I've decided to put you down with the junior varsity." JV as a senior? I was stunned. I couldn't.

"Coach, why?" There were no answers. "I can't do it, Coach," I said. "I can't play on the JV as a senior."

"So you're turning in your gear?" he asked.

"Yeah, I'll go get it right now."

I handed in my pads and helmet and made my way out of the locker room. The coach from the cross-country team, Burt Wells, was waiting for me just outside the football coach's office.

"How's football going, Jarstad?" he asked.

"Not so good," I replied. "I just turned in my gear."

"I thought you might," Coach Wells responded. Then he pulled out a brand-new "Curtis blue" cross-country runner's uniform. "You know we have our top three varsity runners down right now with knee injuries. You could be our number one runner." I looked back at the football coach who kind of winked at either me or Coach Wells.

"You guys planned this, didn't you?" I was mad, but I wouldn't go back to football. "Okay, I'll run cross-country for you."

Coach Wells had a string of nine consecutive league championships in boys' cross-country that was the envy of the Seamount conference. More importantly, he knew just how to motivate and get inside the head of fifteen- to eighteen-year-old kids to coax out their very best efforts. He also led by example. He was an outstanding runner in his own right and could beat any cross-country runner on the squad except for perhaps the top three varsity boys each season. He was proud of this and would get in your face just a little to rub it in if he could still beat you in a run.

For me, he didn't need to. After "getting cut" in football, I ran with something to prove every meet. As soon as I joined the varsity runners, I began to win races and even set course records at Tyee, Mount Si, and our home 2.6-mile course at Curtis High School (thirteen minutes and thirty-one seconds). Finally, just before the end of the regular season, we were facing Sumner High School.

Sumner had a notorious runner named Rex Nequette. Rex was strongly built and intense, even mean, when it came to cross-country—barking, elbowing, and yelling at anyone in his way from start to finish.

As I followed him up the first hill, he was elbowing and pushing our Curtis runners, knocking two of the younger guys down. "Stay with Nequette," Coach Wells told me before the race. "He's your rabbit." So as he passed me on the first hill and shoved and elbowed me hard, I got a little mad. I started to chase him. It was vengeance now, and it was personal.

We emerged from the woods with Nequette having a hundred-yard lead. There was about a mile left to go in the 2.6-mile race. There seemed to be no way I could catch him now. I was in a comfortable position in second place with no one fifty yards or closer behind me from either team. Just as I was about to concede the race and stride it easy on home, the football coach blew his whistle.

"Jarstad needs our help guys," he yelled. "Two lines." So in the middle of football practice, the players all lined up along the back stretch of the final quarter mile perimeter; slapped me on the back; and yelled at me to "Catch him," "Don't give up," "You're a Curtis Viking," and "GO GET HIM!" With that inspiration, I started my kick with just over a thousand yards to go. I caught up with Nequette just as we entered the finish chute and just beat him to the tape.

We finished in a dead heat tie, according to the Sumner coach. Our coach, Wells, insisted that I had won since Nequette had been run into the finish pole and fallen while I remained standing. (Later, I learned, in a bit of irony, Nequette had broken his wrist during this fall at the finish.) After a few moments of heated deliberation with the Sumner coach, Coach Wells announced that it was a tie and that the time of thirteen minutes and thirty-one seconds for the 2.6-mile cross-country course was a new school and course record, beating Mark Eddington's old school mark by thirteen seconds.

The small crowd cheered, and my teammates were elated, assuming I had won. It was poetic justice for them, especially the ones Nequette had shoved down at the start of the race. The last image I had of Nequette was seeing him a few weeks later at the state championships running behind me with a white cast on his wrist.

One momentous day in November 1973 I will never forget was the Washington State boys' high school cross-country championships. We boarded the shiny yellow University Place School District bus with our team of seven varsity cross-country runners—along with the JV members of our team and some die-hard supporting fans and cheerleaders—for the state meet at Evergreen High School in White Center (near the Sea-Tac Airport). We were in a jovial mood, and things were very lighthearted on the bus ride north.

The guys had me doing imitations of TV cartoon characters like Tudor the Turtle and Mr. Wizard. Then my teammates were raucously telling jokes about the sports section of the *Tacoma News Tribune* from earlier in the week.

"It says here your mom made bacon for your breakfast last week, John." Another quoted the newspaper as saying, "Jarstad, who set a school record earlier this year, experienced severe stomach cramps and finished a below par 16th at Saturday's West Central District Cross Country Finals."

"What did your mommy feed you for the state championship race today, Jarstad?"

"How much bacon did you eat this morning, Jarstad?" Yeah, yeah, yeah. (I ate cold cereal.)

We arrived at the course early on a crisp, overcast November day. It had rained earlier in the week, but the forecast was for cool, dry weather. We jogged the course as we strategized, as only high school cross-country runners can, about whether to go out fast or slow and in a pack or individually, when to start our final kick, and which runners to be on the lookout for. The pressure of the final meet of our high school careers was building up to a boiling point, and those of us who were at our first state final were feeling the butterflies churning inside.

As we finished our warm-ups, about twenty minutes before the start of the race, one of our senior runners, Don Nelson, suggested we get away by ourselves for a team meeting. Then one of the group suggested we have a prayer.

My teammates knew I was planning on a mission (I was the only member of the church on the varsity squad.), and I was surprised they all asked me to pray. We knelt down, and I began to pray, "Heavenly Father, we thank Thee that we have made it to state. We've worked just as hard as any other team, but we pray that Thou

30

wilt help us to each run our very best race today. That if it be Thy will, we will win the state championship today. Bless and protect us we pray, and we thank Thee for allowing us to be here. In the name of Jesus Christ. Amen." Then we went to work.

Fellow Senior, Don Nelson, was our top runner, when his knee was healthy; he'd been to state three times before. "We need to go out fast," he counseled. "There's a real bottleneck after the first hundred yards where it's hard to pass people, and everyone pretty much settles in to a pace behind the guy in front of him."

It was an inspired and proven winning race strategy. We were in good shape after the first turn and could see each other near the front. We panicked a little as ten to twenty runners began to pass some of us, and some of us slipped back, but our fans encouraged us. A few runners from other teams slipped and fell and dropped back out of contention as we dodged around them and paid them no heed. Our fans and classmates from Curtis were strategically stationed along the course and would yell our names at the top of their lungs as we came within shouting distance.

As we entered the track for the final four hundred yards, we all began to sprint. One report counted me passing over twenty runners on the four-hundred-meter track to finish twenty-second overall and fourteenth in the team competition, out of nearly two hundred runners. Don Nelson and Doug Twitchell were in front of me; and Bob Walls, Mike Alexi, Rick Johnson, and Mark Bascom were within shouting distance behind us as we crossed the finish line.

We won! We were the 1973 Washington State High School AA Boys' Cross-Country Champions! A former JV football player and a trio of guys with bad knees had won it all. We finished with one of the lowest team scores in Washington State history (in cross-country, the runners are scored by giving a number to each runner in the position they finish, and only the top five runners scores count in the team competition. A perfect team score would be 1+2+3+4+5 = 15). We dunked Coach Wells in the lake in a traditional victory splash after we received the team trophy and had our pictures taken.

Later that night, we all rode the pep bus up to Marysville to support our football team in the first round of the first Washington State high school football playoffs. Our cross-country team was honored at halftime during the football game and introduced as the Washington State AA Cross-Country Champions. Unfortunately, our football team lost that night to Stanwood, and their season was over. I never felt bad after that about missing my senior year on the football squad. We were state champions in cross-country!

Not everything my senior year was a triumph. I quit the wrestling team to spend more time with my girlfriend and to work more hours at the gas station to save money for my mission. My girlfriend D'Neen was interested in the church and coming with me to early morning seminary, where she was steadily developing a testimony of the gospel. Soon after the missionaries began teaching her, her alcoholic stepdad put his foot down and forbade her to have any more lessons or become baptized. It was a difficult time. She wanted to know if she should wait for me on my mission. I didn't feel like I could ask her to do that since I would be gone for two years, even though she was a wonderful girl of whom my dad approved.

The other highlight of my senior year was in track. I ran the mile in four minutes and twenty-six seconds and just missed qualifying for state; but in the two miles along with my teammates Don Nelson and Mike Alexi and running a personal best the week before with a 9:47 at the Shelton Invitational, I was able to qualify for the state finals with a third-place finish at West Central Districts on the Federal Way High School track.

Unfortunately, while running in third position at the state finals a week later, my right shoe came untied on lap number three. As I pulled out into lane 4 to tie my shoe, one of the officials who knew my dad as the college sports announcer at Husky Stadium thought I was quitting the race and yelled: "Don't quit, Jarstad! Jarstads never quit! Keep going!"

So instead of tying my shoe, I tried to get back in the race with my right shoe flapping. I ended the race in a tie for dead last at ten minutes and five seconds, well off my personal best time. A humiliating defeat in what started out to be such a race full of promise. My family was there along with my home teachers from church all trying to console me and look on the bright side. It would be the last time I would compete in track spikes.

Following my disappointing state track meet, at that weekend's senior graduation party, I ran into my sophomore-year girlfriend Elaine, whom Dad encouraged to go into radio and TV (which she did, succeeding as a radio DJ, a "weather girl," later a news anchor, and *PM Magazine* TV star). Dad was so impressed with Elaine. "She is a natural for TV," he would always say. "Not only is she beautiful, but she has a brilliant mind and a good heart."

Elaine was my first real girlfriend. We met in geometry class. As we began dating, we both agreed not to kiss until after the braces came off my teeth. It was a great day when I drove over to her house on the afternoon my braces were gone. I asked her if there was any-thing different about me. She looked at my clothes and then my face; and when I broke into the biggest cheese-eating grin, she finally had an "aha" moment and yelled, "You got your braces off!" Then it was time for our big first kiss. It was great!

During homecoming week, it was announced that the school would be having a "kissing contest." Probably could never get away with that today? Each class would compete at noon; and like musical chairs, as soon as a couple broke suction or broke the "lip lock" and daylight was seen between the two contestant's lips, the judges would tap them out, and they had to sit down.

The competition was held in the courtyard just outside study hall and the lunch room. Elaine and I came up with a plan. We would tap each other on the shoulder when it was our turn to breathe. That way, we wouldn't be breathing at the same time through our noses. It worked! We won the sophomore class competition. We both received a one-foot-tall glass jar of Hershey's Kisses chocolates. The next day, they announced the winners over the school loudspeakers and then the surprise that at the homecoming assembly in the school basket-ball gym, there would be the finals of the school kissing contest with the winning couple from each class competing for the grand prize. We were stationed in the middle of the gym on the "C" (Curtis High School Logo) with the junior class winners and the senior class win-ners on each side of us. As the countdown began, we reminded each other of our winning strategy, and soon the competition was on. The assembly went on with various awards, skits, and homecoming information; and after forty-five minutes of numb locking lips, the other two couples dropped out, and we were crowned champions of the Curtis High School Kissing Contest.

Years later, at our forty-year high school reunion, I mentioned that event to Elaine and she claimed that she could not remember having participated. Funny what time will do. I remembered it as one of the most triumphant highlights of high school.

As my dad neared the end of his life, fighting a discouraging battle with cancer and multiple medical problems, I wrote Elaine asking if she would mind sending Dad a letter of encouragement to tell him if he'd had any influence on her successful career. She wrote Dad the nicest note, crediting him for encouraging her successful career and thanking him for getting her started in radio and television.

CHAPTER 7

A NEAR-DEATH EXPERIENCE

The summer after high school graduation, while working as a salmon and tuna deckhand at Westport to earn money for a mission, my stake president Ludene Snow, who grew up in my grandfather's Church of Jesus Christ of Latter-day Saints branch when Grandpa was the first branch president, asked to have me come home the next Saturday night for a stake priesthood meeting. I was curious, and the reason was to receive the Melchizedek Priesthood. He interviewed me and asked if I considered myself worthy. Then he asked me whom I would like to ordain me. I thought about my seminary teacher, Brother James Dewey, but President Snow suggested my dad. I hadn't even thought about Dad. "He *is* an elder in the church," President Snow explained, and "that was the usual way things are done." That made sense. So on August 18, 1974, I was ordained to the Melchizedek Priesthood office of an elder in the Church of Jesus Christ of Latter-day Saints by my dad.

I went immediately back to the ocean to complete work on the charter boats. I remember telling people who asked that I was saving money to go on a church mission. This was strange to some but endearing to other tourists, who gave me food and better tips than I was accustomed to.

After being ordained an elder, I sacrificed trips to the "Playpen" video arcade and pool hall with my friends and skipped going out to restaurants (our major source of food since we had no cooking facilities) to maximize my mission savings account. I guess I overdid scrimping and saving, because the first week of September, I got sick. I felt achy all over and started to run a fever. I just couldn't go in to work; so I remained at the "shack on stilts," as we affectionately called our little room in the back of Sea Charter's office, holed up in my sleeping bag. Finally, Mrs. Nyhus, whose family owned Gull Charters, and her daughter Lee Ann visited. Since Sister Nyhus was a registered nurse, she knew I was really sick and insisted on taking me back home to Tacoma. The trip home was pretty much a blur other than Lee Ann cradling my head and stroking my shoulder-length sun-bleached hair and putting ice on my fevered brow.

I was sick with a high fever; and after two days, Mom called our family doctor, Sam Adams, MD, who gave instructions to put me in an ice-filled bathtub and give me aspirin. The fever would break, and then I would be overcome with shaking chills. My temperature would bounce from 96 to 108 degrees. Finally, my liver began to swell, and it became difficult to breathe.

About this time, I had my first near-death experience. I rallied a little, sat up in bed, and yelled, "I don't want to die." My sister Lisa came into the room and told me I wasn't going to die. My older sister Kristin later came in to sit at the bedside with me.

I could feel death coming on. The buzzing of my ears, the pulsating, grainy vision, and the pleasant rose-scented smell—the warmth of death surrounding me in a pleasant embrace. I looked to my sister and said, "Isn't it wonderful? I don't have to breathe anymore." I felt my soul retreating to the top of my head and, like a candle, slowly flickering out.

Then I remember hearing my sister yelling and watching the room from the upper northwest corner and her friend Doug coming in who was a paramedic and giving me CPR. I came around and was taken to the hospital. After several days and procedures, including a painful spinal tap, it was determined that I had contracted infectious hepatitis from polluted water after falling into the harbor at Westport. I turned a dark-tan brown due to my pink sunburned skin and yellow jaundice.

My mom recalls waiting outside my hospital room one afternoon hearing me talk to someone she assumed was my doctor. Then, as she eavesdropped, she was amazed to hear me speaking to my grandfather Marcus Stokes, who had died over ten years before. After two weeks in the hospital, I returned home and, for the next four months, to continue my convalescence.

At this time, I also remembered a vivid dream that occurred three years earlier. Before this particular dream, I had begun to take church pretty casually and remember missing two Sundays in a row and failing to fast on fast Sunday for the first time in ages. (The first Sunday of the month, all congregations in the Church of Jesus Christ of Latter-day Saints fast without food or drink for twenty-four hours and two meals and donate what they would have spent on food to the poor and needy). That Sunday night, I had a vivid dream that seemed so real.

While gill net fishing, after pulling in the nets, I was untangling the long cork line at Owen's Beach in Tacoma. It was just before dawn, and the stars were incredibly bright. Just then, I looked up from my nets and saw a large star getting brighter and brighter. It looked like a comet coming right toward me. Then I realized that was no star. It was the Second Coming of Jesus Christ.

From the scriptures, I remembered that, in "the Rapture" at the Second Coming, the righteous would be caught up in the air to meet the Savior. I remember running along the beach and jumping up to get into the air, but no matter how hard I tried, I couldn't get off the ground. My sins were weighing me down, like a backpack full of weights; I just could not get off the ground to get caught up in the air. The dream ended as I woke up in a cold sweat. I never missed another Sunday church fast meeting.

CHAPTER 8

MISSION TO ENGLAND

By the time I recovered from hepatitis A, I was too sick and weak to accept my cross-country and track scholarship to Weber State College in Ogden, Utah. I enrolled instead at Tacoma Community College and prepared for a mission. In early December, I was called to the England Birmingham Mission with an entry date of February 8, 1975.

During these few months before my mission, my dad was less than fully employed, and finances were tough. My uncle Glenn

Jarstad (mayor of Bremerton, Washington, at the time) loaned us his nearly new Cadillac for the trip to Utah, and away we went. We stayed with Elder Workman, a missionary who taught my dad the missionary lessons, in Centerville, Utah. The morning before going to the mission home in Salt Lake City, my dad told me he loved me and gave me a father's blessing for the first time. Then at the Salt Lake Temple, we were united and sealed forever as a family before I entered the mission home.

It had been difficult to change into a missionary. Not only did I have to shave my full beard and lop off my golden-blond, sea-bleached, shoulder-length hair (there were no barbershops in Westport), but I had to wear a suit for the very first time. Money was tight, so I went thrift store shopping for my first suit. I did finally get one new, very inexpensive, off-the-rack suit before I left and would buy several tailor-made suits once I arrived in Great Britain.

The Salt Lake mission home was kind of like a boot camp (or so I was told) or two-a-day football practices (which I did have experience with). I remember the first day being called out of the group meeting by a baldheaded man and told I needed a "missionary" haircut. That seemed so ironic since I had just received my shortest hair shearing in the past ten years only a week before (remember these were the '70s, and long hair and, in my case, curly "Afros" were "in"). Nevertheless, I complied.

Learning the missionary discussions, for the very first time, was thrilling; and I remember thinking, *Do we really believe this? WOW, that's cool!* Even though I was a four-year early morning seminary graduate and scripture mastery champion in my Tacoma Stake, there were obviously still things I needed to learn about the gospel. There were wonderful spiritual experiences in the Salt Lake Temple. One of the spiritual highlights was a meeting of several hundred missionaries in the upper assembly room of the Salt Lake Temple, listening to Elder O. Leslie Stone speak to us about the significance of the temple covenants.

By the time our group of six missionaries arrived in England, I was excited and ready to go to work. I loved England the moment I could see through the early morning February 15, 1975, fog. *It is so GREEN!* I thought, *And so much like home.* I don't know what I was thinking it would be like, but it did surprise me being so similar in climate to my native Seattle. Yet the land seemed somehow neater and better organized than the forests of Washington State. Hedgerows and fences were everywhere, and there were lots of sheep.

We were met at the Birmingham New Street train station by the APs (assistants to the mission president) and driven to the England Birmingham Mission home at 185 Penns Lane, Walmley, Sutton Coldfield, Staffordshire, England. There we met our mission president, Reed L. Reeve, and his family. He interviewed each of us individually and told me he enjoyed reading the letter I sent to him just after my mission call came. My letter to President Reeve mentioned that it rained so much in Washington during the winter months that we had to make our own sunshine. He liked that and told me I would feel right at home in England.

We next had a meeting where we would be assigned to our senior companions. I felt impressed immediately who mine would be, and I was right. Elder Jay Durtschi from Centerville, Utah. He looked a lot like how I envisioned my grandfather Marcus Stokes would have looked as a young man. Durtschi was very upbeat and positive. He was already engaged and would return to the USA in about a year to marry his high school sweetheart. I had no one writing to me of the female persuasion, at least not seriously. Elder Durtschi and I worked hard in Stoke on Trent but did not baptize anyone into the church.

My second companion was Elder John Ford. Years later, I would see him at a high school track-and-field meet in Federal Way where our kids would compete against each other. He was also a very hardworking, dedicated missionary, and it was with him that I would have one of the most spiritual experiences of my life.

I had just finished memorizing the "Our Relationship to Christ" discussion. We would ask our investigators to pray to have a personal relationship with the Savior. I thought, *How can I ask them to do this if I haven't done it myself?* So I prayed fervently to come to know the Savior and to have a personal relationship with Him. I also prayed to know why I had suffered the near-death experience earlier that year and why I had not felt that there was anything after death that I could remember. I also fasted and prayed to know what else I needed to know.

That night, I had a marvelous dream that has stayed with me throughout my life. I know we are not to reveal certain sacred experiences, so I will only say that this dream was so real that Elder Ford asked me what had just happened when we woke up. I can honestly say that the Relationship to Christ discussion is true. There was no longer any doubt that Jesus Christ was real, nor would there ever again be any doubt about certain aspects of the gospel the rest of my life. I will always be grateful for this choice spiritual experience.

There were many choice experiences with faithful, fun, and dedicated members and nonmembers of the church in England. Excellent companions like Elders Wells, Farnsworth, Johnson, Jones, Griffith, Potter, Francom, Stokes, Deets, Madsen, Thompson, Devanny, Cox, Durtschi, and Ford. Many I have kept in touch with over the years; and Durtschi, Johnson, and Potter have become life-long friends. Potter is my stock broker and has been an investment partner.

It was soon after transferring from Stoke on Trent to Walsall in Staffordshire that in the fall of 1975, I had another near-death experience.

While tracting one afternoon on splits with Elder Smith, from Salt Lake City, we were both hit with bricks from a passing lorry (large dump truck). Apparently, someone was not happy with our success in Walsall and sent a truck filled with guys out after us. Elder Smith was hit in the stomach and had the wind knocked out of him. I wasn't so lucky. My brick hit me directly on the upper-left side of my head and knocked me out cold for about six minutes. While bleeding profusely, I came to hearing the Mormon tabernacle choir singing in my ears, and Smith said I was quoting scriptures. Almost immediately after coming to, I noticed Adrian Beech, a nineteen-year-old local young man that we were teaching the gospel to, standing above me (Adrian would later join the Church of Jesus Christ of Latter-day Saints; serve a mission to Ireland; emigrate to the USA; marry a beautiful, brilliant returned lady missionary; and become an outstanding bishop, now living in Oregon City, Oregon).

"Elder Jarstad, are you all right?"

"I think so. Can someone call an ambulance please?"

It was soon on its way, and I was taken to the Walsall General Hospital where I was on the receiving end of about fourteen stitches. A polite Pakistani doctor told me to take it easy for a few days. I asked him if I might have had a concussion.

"Oh yes," he said, "most probably."

"Can I work?"

"No. You must not do anything for three or four days."

"So can I ride my bicycle?"

"Oh yes, most probably."

I was a little confused but determined not to let this setback slow down the work. We had a busy teaching schedule, so after resting at home for an hour, Elder Johnson and I went out teaching on our bicycles. I wasn't much help that first night with a splitting headache, along with concussion confusion, but the Lord soon rewarded us for our efforts.

There were places of extraordinary success like Walsall Ward (where we helped build a chapel and had fourteen baptisms in a six-month period in 1975). There were also some very challenging places like Redditch-Bromsgrove, where we worked incredibly hard and baptized only one person, a seventeen-year-old girl named Glenys Griffith, who is now Glenys Horton.

Glenys was able to find my name on the Internet in the summer of 2001 and wrote a letter asking if I was the same John Jarstad who was a missionary in England in 1975–1977. I wrote back, and in the summer of 2002, she visited with her family; and we had a wonderful reunion with Elder Potter, who helped teach and baptize Glenys when we were companions in Redditch, England, in 1976.

Glenys served for many years as a registered nurse and operating theater supervisor at Brighton Hospital in East Sussex, England. She and her husband, Brian, are parents of two brilliant sons. Glenys has the most incredible vocabulary of any human I have ever known, is an accomplished artist, and is one of the hardest-working nurses I have ever seen. I tried to recruit her to work for my eye center in 2002 and 2003, but her heart belongs to England.

It was in Bromsgrove, England, near Redditch, that I learned the power of fasting and prayer. Elder Robert Potter and I decided that after working without success for several weeks, we would fast and pray until someone let us into their home to teach the Savior's gospel. After three days without eating, we were near panicked. Some of these people were downright mean. One local farmer summed it up: "These people are a bit rough. Some of them wouldn't give a blind man a light."

Finally, at 4:45 p.m., as we were about to finish working for the third day without any success, a door opened, and a couple in their late sixties invited us in. An amazing feast was set up on a sideboard. "Come in. We've been expecting you. We've seen you in the village. Our daughter was supposed to come for a birthday party but cancelled, and we have all this extra food. Please help yourselves and enjoy it." The Lord answers prayers. We taught them a first discussion and finished our fasting with a feast.

Two of the wonderful people we taught and baptized as missionaries in Walsall were Peter and Kathleen Russell, now living in Albany, New York. Peter was a recreational diver and became a successful building contractor. They had a son and daughter who were so cute. Ian would dress up in an Aston Villa football kit, and Debbie had the most adorable nurse's outfit. At five and three years old, they were the cutest kids in England.

Brother Russell helped us build the chapel in Walsall with his bare hands. After Peter was baptized and we were in the locker room area changing out of our wet clothes, we suddenly heard a loud splash. Brother Russell flew back into the font area and found Ian had jumped headlong into the baptismal font, wanting to be like his dad. After the initial terror of a possible drowned child wore off, we all had a good laugh.

Rita and Doris Powell of the Mossley Estate were wonderful people who also responded to the message of the restoration of the gospel. In 1993, on my way back from a medical mission to Zimbabwe, Africa, I stopped by their home (address from memory) to pay them a visit. They were so happy to see "their missionary" and grateful that I had brought along my ophthalmology instruments to examine Doris's eye. She had a mild case of macular degeneration and was relieved to hear it wasn't progressing.

George Farley was an older man who had lived a hard life as a master brick layer. He was also a chain-smoker. Try as he might, he just couldn't pack in smoking. We didn't know what else to try until we heard that Elder Mark E. Petersen of the quorum of the twelve apostles was going to be visiting the Woodsetton Church of Jesus Christ of Latter-day Saints Chapel to give a fireside. We took Brother Farley to the meeting, and he told us on the bus ride home to Walsall that he knew he had just listened to an apostle of the Lord and that he wanted to quit smoking and be baptized. It was a spiritual meeting when Elder George in our district baptized Brother Farley.

In addition to the converts, there were some unforgettable members of the church. One of several active stake missionaries in Stoke on Trent was Margaret Jennings. Margaret loved the Osmonds and would take a *Book of Mormon* with her everywhere she went. Many gospel discussions were given whilst she rode the bus to and from her work at a factory in the "potteries."

Ward Mission Leader Richard "Ken" Burton of Walsall worked as a window display creator for a large English department store chain. His family fed us, took care of us, and just loved the missionaries. His wife Sandra and friend Kathy Baughen (Sister Kath) actually found and taught a gentlemen for us by "telephone tracting" while they were working together as stake missionaries in Walsall.

Bishop Stanley Woods and his wife Margaret and children Stephen and Ruth were another faithful, inspiring family. Bishop Woods would start every meeting with something like, "Welcome, brothers and sisters, you look just marvelous, really great, just fantastic…" A very positive individual. I was able to examine his eye on another trip back from Africa and found he had a retinal vein occlusion. We made a quick trip to the Wolverhampton Eye Infirmary where, after some deliberation and a business card passed to the receptionist, we were finally allowed to use the equipment in the eye infirmary. We got Bishop Woods plugged in to the system by having a registrar (resident) in ophthalmology confirm my diagnosis and help Bishop Woods get treatment for his eye.

One of the fun memories was that of the Ken and Dennis Degville brothers and singing "We Are Sowing" in the Walsall Ward choir. Later seeing Bishop Ken Degville in the London Temple while I was on a layover at Gatwick Airport on my way to Nigeria and having Ken recognize me straightaway and say, "Elder Jarstad! What yow doing here?" "'Ow yow doing, mate?"

Perhaps, my biggest disappointment was not being able to baptize a prominent family in Bromsgrove. Leon was the owner of a large industrial complex. Elder Potter and myself were tracting one Saturday and came upon his palatial mansion (we later learned it had been a large country pub or inn in the 1500s or 1600s).

Elder Potter (at this time, a brand-new missionary who had been an outstanding athlete at Logan High School in Utah and would later go on to become one of the outstanding missionaries in England and serve as an assistant to President Callister) said, "Why don't we skip this one, huh?"

I replied, "Every nation, kindred, tongue, and rich person."

So we knocked on the door. A little girl of about twelve came to the door and said, "Jehovah's Witness! We're not interested!"

As she was slamming the door for some reason, I felt inspired to yell as loud as I could, "No, we're MORMONS!" As we were walking out the long driveway to the road, the girl came running after us.

"Daddy wants you to come back."

"I'm terribly sorry for our rudeness, lads," Leon said. "Only we're having company. Perhaps you could call again."

"When?" I insisted.

"How about Tuesday evening?"

"I'm really quite sorry for our rudeness. Would you, lads, like to join us for tea (dinner)?"

I couldn't believe it. Neither could Elder Potter. We had a dinner appointment with probably the richest man in Bromsgrove. Neither of us will ever forget the reception we had three days later. A seven-course meal was served by a butler on fine English china: leg of lamb with mint sauce, Yorkshire pudding, vegetables, and, for afters, ice cream. Then it was on to the drawing room where two chairs had been set up for us to teach Leon the gospel.

He was very polite and asked several thoughtful questions. Then as he mulled over the implications, he became apologetic. "I've actually got my own religion. But perhaps my sister and her family would like to hear about your religion. They're religious people."

This led to another one of the most spiritual discussions of my mission about the plan of salvation.

We met Leon's sister and her husband, who lived just a mile or so away from Leon. As Elder Potter and I taught the plan of salvation discussion, we were in total harmony, praying for each other and this wonderful family. We knew Leon's sister and husband and two little girls felt the Spirit of the Holy Ghost. There were tears in their eyes and a wonderful feeling of peace and power in the room.

Unfortunately, politically, it seemed impossible for them to join the Church of Jesus Christ of Latter-day Saints in Bromsgrove, England, in 1976. Even the Bromsgrove newspapers had negative editorials about the Church of Jesus Christ of Latter-day Saints, and shortly afterward, I was transferred to the north to become a district leader, and Elder Potter rapidly matured into a spiritual dynamo in the mission leadership.

One of the funniest experiences of my mission was the Jack Russell terrier incident. It soon became a legend throughout the England Birmingham Mission.

As my junior companion Elder Johnson and I would tract door-to-door, we would memorize scriptures on laminated cards that would take many hours to create on our days off to withstand the English rain. These scripture cards became my prized possession.

One day whilst tracting, I lifted up the mail slot in the door of a bungalow to give it a proper loud knock. Because of the bitter cold, we wore gloves and used our scripture cards to lift the door knockers and mail slots. No sooner did I raise the bar with my scripture cards than they were taken from my hand by a feisty Jack Russell terrier. I lifted the mail slot to peek in, and sure enough, the little dog had them by his teeth and was shaking them furiously. I knocked harder, but no one came to the door. I must admit I lost my temper or temporarily my sanity. Weeks of work on the scripture cards, and now they were gone.

In a desperate panic, I took off my belt and threaded it through the mail slot. Sure enough, the dog dropped the scripture cards, but now he held the end of my belt in a death grip. I reflexively pulled the belt as hard as I could, unintentionally banging the little dogs head against the door in a tug of war. Just then the lady of the house opened the door and asked, "Yes?"

"We're missionaries—"

"Sorry! Not interested!"

"Okay, ma'am, but could I please have my scripture cards back?" I humbly inquired. "Your little terrier snatched them right out of my hand as I lifted your mail slot to knock."

"Oh, dear. Very well. He's been known to take the postman's hand nearly off, you know. You're a lucky young man. I should be a bit more careful next time, if I were you."

"Yes, ma'am. And thank you very much."

I was elated to have my scripture cards back again. I heard Elder Johnson laughing his head off.

"What's so funny?" I asked.

"YOU!" is all he could say.

One of the fun and exciting experiences of my mission was playing point guard in two exhibition basketball games against the Birmingham Bulldogs, of what would become a team in the European NBA level league in Central England. Our team was comprised of star high school and a few college basketball players—American LDS missionaries. I was along because Elder Potter had been a high school all-star, and I had played church basketball and pick-up games after wrestling practices. The English players were all over six feet four but very thin, maybe 150 to 175 pounds. I came off the bench and scored eleven points in the first game and nine in the second as we won both games. I even slapped a rebound at the rim in one game that went through so fast off the heel of the rim that all my teammates were sure I'd just dunked the ball. After a trying and yet modestly successful mission, I returned home to Seattle on February 15, 1977.

CHAPTER 9

MY STRUGGLE–A COLLEGE EDUCATION

I returned from my mission and promptly gave a report that first Sunday to the Tacoma Stake high council. One of the physicians on the high council caught up with me afterward. As I was on my way to my borrowed car, he stated, "I enjoyed your report. I just had to tell you this. Never before in all my years on the high council have I ever seen a young man change as much as you have been changed by your mission."

He was probably right. I left in February 1975 as a fisherman with shoulder-length sea-bleached blond hair, a full beard, and a very unsophisticated demeanor (I almost said a foul word in my farewell talk, quoting my football coach who said, "If you didn't give it your best, you weren't worth a chicken spit!).

I had never owned a suit and was rarely seen in a tie or shined shoes. I returned in a three-piece navy blue English pinstriped wool suit, with a pocket watch, in toe cap-spit-shined shoes, and with a leather briefcase; speaking perfect Queen's English; and exhibiting formal manners. I had to agree with the good doctor—I had changed!

My new look soon attracted a job offer. An appointment was requested for "an employment opportunity" by a member of the stake which I soon realized was to sell life insurance. I arrived in my English suit and shined shoes and briefcase and listened to a twenty-minute presentation by the owner of the agency. He concluded our meeting by showing me pictures of him with some doctors and dentists and attorneys that he had sold whole life policies to for over a million dollars!

"Just think," he said, "this could be you. How would you like to see pictures of yourself next to these high-profile people in the community?"

"That sounds great!"

I was thinking to myself, *I'd much rather **be** those people. How do I get there?*

Education was the answer. But no college classes would start for another six weeks. So I began working with my dad on his fishing boat. "There's plenty of work for both of us, Johnny Boy," he said.

"I've got this idea to rig the *Joker* for dog fishing (small sand sharks) in Puget Sound. They're paying four hundred dollars a ton for them right now, and the dogfish are all over the place."

So away we went, gillnetting for dogfish in the freezing rain in the middle of February 1977. After a couple of weeks, I got really discouraged. One day, a dogfish bit my right thumb nearly off, right through my heavy rubber work glove. It wouldn't let go, so I had to break out its teeth with a Billy club to get it off me. It was terribly, cold, slimy, smelly, boring work. Dad couldn't have helped my resolve any better to get me serious about college and a life away from fishing.

Later, I would hang a large color picture of a fishing trawler on my bedroom closet door. It was the last thing I would see before turning out the light each night: the trawler "RESOLUTE" in a storm-tossed sea making way with her gear out. Many nights, as I became too weary to study further, I would see the RESOLUTE on my door, rally, and study for an extra hour, paying any price to avoid going back to the fishing life.

Soon I found myself enrolled at Tacoma Community College, not far from my parents' home in West Tacoma. The classes were small and not too difficult. I also landed a job in the Math Lab as a tutor for all subjects short of calculus (which I was taking, along with English literature and chemistry). I had completed a quarter before my mission while recovering from hepatitis and had a 4.0 college GPA and so applied to BYU as a transfer student.

Later that summer, I was accepted for fall semester 1977 and found a 1971 Fiat 850 Spyder convertible that was for sale because it "didn't start but runs great," according to the ad. I had replaced starters before, so after test-driving it and finding it in good mechanical condition otherwise, I offered $600 ($50 less than asking price) and drove off. I soon had the new $35 starter in and was bidding my fiancée Louann goodbye and driving to Utah.

Soon after arriving in Provo, Utah, I noticed an announcement for tryouts for the varsity football (soccer) team. After playing soccer or rugby just about every Monday on our "preparation day," I decided to try out. I soon found I was one of the speedier players, and when the tryouts were over and the coach posted the list, I was excited that my name was there! The coach thanked those for trying out who did not make the team, then asked all of us who made it to meet with him individually. "Jarstad," he said, "what's your major?"

"I'm premed biology."

"Oh no! That's not gonna work. We had a guy last year that was premed, and he lasted about a month. Classes were too demanding, and he quit right in the middle of our toughest matches. No, son, I'm afraid you can't do both. We travel every other week, so it's going to have to be soccer or premed. Think it over, sleep on it, pray about it, and let me know tomorrow, okay?"

It was a tough decision, but I wanted to be a doctor more than a varsity collegiate soccer player.

A required class for freshman at BYU was a physical education class called Fitness for Life. The joke was if you failed that PE class, you weren't fit to live. The final exam was an indoor mile on the

Smith Fieldhouse Track. As a former cross-country champion and high school miler, I would typically set the pace for the class. On the final exam indoor mile, I sprinted out to an early lead, then began to pass everyone. And by the start of the fifth lap, I began to lap other runners. With 220 meters to go, I began my final lap kick. The PE coach strung the tape across the finish line just before I crossed.

"Unbelievable!" he shouted as he looked at his stopwatch. "Four minutes, twelve seconds! That's a new record for the final exam mile. Come with me, son. There's someone I'd like you to meet."

We soon climbed the stairs up to Sherald James's office where I was introduced. "Coach James, here is the BYU men's track coach. Coach, this is John Jarstad. He just ran a four-minute-twelve-second indoor mile."

"So, Jarstad, have you ever considered turning out for the track team?"

"Yes, Coach, I contacted you during my junior year in high school where I was a record holder in cross-country at thirteen minutes and thirty-one seconds for 2.6 miles and a state qualifier in track in the 2-mile run at nine minutes and forty-seven seconds. I sent you my times, and you wrote back that your athletes were running around nine minutes on the track team."

"Oh, we tell all the boys that. Why don't you consider running track for us here at BYU?"

"Thanks, Coach! I'll give it some serious thought. I'm premed though so—just to warn you."

"Well, in any case, that was a great effort. Congratulations on breaking the Fitness for Life indoor mile record."

Later that year, I competed in the Provo City Freedom Run 10k race and finished third behind two varsity track athletes and ahead of three others. And just like that, my school athletic career was over.

CHAPTER 10

ENGAGEMENT

Louann had written to me the entire last year of my mission. She was a new convert to the Church of Jesus Christ of Latter-day Saints and was introduced to the church by her best friend Marci Wells, at Curtis High School. Louann had seen my picture on the missionary board at church and began writing to me as part of a laurel class project to write to the missionaries.

After writing for about ten months, Louann finally sent me a photo. All the missionaries would joke that she must be really ugly if she wouldn't send a picture. Yeah, yeah... When it finally arrived, everyone was in total shock. She was a knockout! She looked exactly like a young Meg Ryan. We met at church after my homecoming talk, and she introduced herself. We soon became inseparable and talked about marriage.

When we first met, Louann worked part-time after school as a dental assistant. She would trick me by putting numbing gel on her lips before kissing me, and when I would go numb and talk mushy, she would start to laugh. After dating all winter and spring, we began to talk seriously about marriage. I proposed to her in the living room of my parents' home. She said yes.

Now what do we do? Neither one of us had any money. She was working full-time that summer after graduation at Taco Bell, and I was fishing with my dad and going to community college. "Why don't you just go to work for my dad at the newspaper?" Louann volunteered. "They pay about eleven dollars an hour with all the union benefits." It was tempting, but I had a real desire to make something else of myself. I was certain that the only way was to get an advanced degree.

"No… I'm going to college. I really want to be an eye doctor." Louann was perplexed. "Well, if you're going to be in school for the next eight years, don't expect me to wait for you," she argued. And that was it.

After working hard at home for a semester, Louann, who was so opposed to the idea of college, arrived at BYU for winter semester. We met once soon after she arrived, but it wasn't the same. She wanted to see the world of college and date different guys. She eventually married a wonderful spiritual older guy who became a bank president, and they lived happily ever after.

On the rebound, I began to date and date and date. Usually, it was only one or two dates, and then the idea of my years of struggling through medical school was a turnoff, or I didn't have a nice-enough car or something. I did have fun pretending to be from England and using my English accent to break the ice something like this: "'Ello, love, 'ave you got the time?" or "Could you direct me to the nearest kiosk?"

That would invariably start a conversation (in the religion section of the Harold B. Lee Library—you BYU students know what I mean), and soon, several attractive coeds would be trying to bet whether I was or wasn't actually from England.

After amusing myself with all the attention for a while, I would fumble through my wallet and produce my "British driving license," with my name and address in Great Britain and particulars. My goal was to date only girls who were "waiting for missionaries" because they were very safe, and by "saving themselves" for their missionary, there was no risk to my medical career. I did have one scare when a girl named Jane started to get serious and wanted to kiss me. I ended that relationship quickly. About this same time, I was being introduced to numerous potentials by my study buddy from chemistry class Kevin.

Kevin was predental and married, and they had a baby girl. We would study organic chemistry every night in the library or science building and study near each other for moral support before class in the mornings for this insanely difficult class. Kevin was happily married and the institution's most ardent recruiter.

"Hey, there's a nice one," he would interject about fifty times a day, trying to get me to look at a cute BYU coed.

Sometimes, he was serious, and other times, it was laughable. A cute girl who was six feet four (much taller than me) or one who looked like she could be old enough to be my mother or one so young she looked like my little sister Karen (a high school junior).

One day during finals week, Kevin was again up to his old tricks.

"Hey, John, you got to see this."

"NO, Kevin! It's finals week, and I'm not doing this."

"I'm serious, man. This one is really cute."

"I don't care. I'm not looking," I replied, buried up to my eyebrows in benzene ring structures.

"Okay, man, but you'll always regret it if you don't turn around. This could be the one."

"Kevin! You've said that a hundred times at least. I'm not looking! Period!"

Five minutes later… "Hey, Jarstad, she's right behind you. I'll give you five bucks if you just turn around and look. No, make it five bucks if you can get a date with her."

"Ooohhh! Kevin! All right, I'll look."

Kevin was right! She was the best-looking girl he had ever pointed out to me in all our months in the library. She was a brunette with big brown eyes, was a very sharp dresser, and had an edgy attitude. I watched her for about three minutes. Two guys came up to her and tried to flirt.

"BUZZ OFF, YA JERK!" and "LOOK! LEAVE ME ALONE, OR I'LL CALL SECURITY." She snapped.

"I MEAN IT!"

WOW! I thought. *This will be a challenge.* I remember thinking, *If this girl has any kind of spirituality, I'm going to marry her.*

I'd never seen anyone quite like her before. But how would I talk to—much less get a date with—the sarcastic ice princess?

Then it hit me: time for the paper airplane. Yes—that might just work. The paper airplane was a tried-and-true method for meeting women in the library or cafeteria. It was a gentle put-down, too, if things were not going to work out. The message was cleverly inscribed inside a wing and the glider carefully aimed (you did not want to miss the intended target) and fired.

"Excuse me, but this is my semester project for quantum mechanics and physics 988. Would you happen to have an eraser I might borrow?" was the inscription inside the bomber's right wing.

"PS, you're kind of cute!" was the ordinance in the left wing.

She looked at it for a minute and did not throw it away. That was a plus. Next she started looking through her purse. I can't believe it—she's asking people in other study carrels for an eraser. Finally, she tosses the airplane back with a twenty-five-cent eraser. "What, no reply?" I said. She's silent.

Round two.

I wrote a "thank you" in another plane and inside wing two wrote, "Hey! You're kind of cute. Can I buy you lunch?"

She read it carefully and began writing. It seemed like forever.

"Well, okay, but I'm with my roommates. Can they come too?"

So we all went to lunch, and they invited me over to their apartment for dinner. I tried to get a real date with PS, but it's nearly impossible. She was one of the most popular girls in her apartment complex.

Later that week, I began coming over to her apartment and talking to her roommates. We soon found we had something in common. Two of her five roommates are expert skiers. We decided to go up skiing together.

"PS, do you want to come along?"

"No, I have homework," she said.

Racing down the expert runs with her roommates, I got to know them and found out all I could about PS. Camping out on her doorstep many nights, I waited for her to return from dates with other guys.

I did what any other BYU guy would do. Attending her student ward on Sunday and sitting with her roommates helped put a damper on the competition, and soon we began dating. I let her drive my Fiat convertible. She's a good driver. I called her at home during Christmas break. We dated steadily during winter semester.

On Valentine's Day in 1978, I brought over a heart-shaped cake with strawberries and a twelve-foot computer paper sign that I spent two days creating. And I wrote the following message in three-foot-high letters using a crayon: "I WUV WU MISS S." (She was doing student teaching in elementary education at the time.)

Days later, I found her open journal on the couch as I was talking with her roommates. I saw a duplicate drawing of my valentine sign that caught my attention. Then I saw it for the first time in the very handwriting of the ice queen: "When I saw the sign, my heart melted. I think I was in love with Johnny." WOW!

Easter Sunday was coming; BYU would soon be out for the summer. Saturday night before Easter, the thought hit me—propose... TONIGHT!

I prayed, "Really? Is this the right thing to do?"

I was not sure, but it hit again... It's the right thing to do.

I went to the store and bought an Easter basket with candy and a plastic egg. I wrote a note telling her that I loved her and popping the question by placing it inside the plastic Easter egg. I called her up. It's late—about 11:00 p.m. We talked on the couch. I told her I had a surprise and gave her the Easter basket. She liked the candy selections, and I told her to open the egg. She's curious and quickly opened it and read the proposal. Then her big brown eyes got huge.

"Really?" she asked. "Really? You're serious!" She didn't say much.

"So will you marry me?" I asked out loud. A long, long silence. "Well?" Another pause...

"Probably…probably, maybe." (How's that for a definitive answer?)

Then her roommate arrived home, and the screaming began. The other roommates woke up, and suddenly, I was informed that I owed everyone ice cream (a BYU tradition when a roommate got a good night kiss or engaged). I was exhausted and left PS in the capable care of her five roommate sisters and headed to buy gallons of ice cream before heading home to my apartment. My dating days were over.

We went shopping together in Provo to pick out a ring. Then I was off for home later that night in my Fiat convertible with my sister Lisa, who also attended BYU. We got off to a very late start, and I soon fell asleep at the wheel just past the Utah-Idaho border. I wake up hearing a rustling sound that sounded like sagebrush.

"Sagebrush! I must be off the road!"

I opened my eyes and pulled back onto the shoulder, just short of the only concrete overpass in a hundred miles, narrowly missing death.

The next six weeks of the summer were spent doing marine biology research at the University of Washington research facility at Friday Harbor in the San Juan Islands. There, I met up with friends—Bill "William K." Jackson, a fellow premed student (who will later become a General Authority Seventy as a leader in the Church of Jesus Christ of Latter-day Saints); Glen Hunter, from Salt Lake City; and several other biology/premed students. We had a memorable day "Kung Fu" kicking dead trees on a hillside above the research station and many long nights in the lab watching sea urchin cells divide.

Letters to PS and rare phone calls made wedding plans impossible to coordinate. The wedding was postponed until we could get together after the summer. I completed the six weeks of research in Friday Harbor and returned to fishing at Westport, earning enough money to pay for another year of college.

PS and I agreed to move closer to each other, in to different units of the same King Henry apartment complex, near the outdoor pool. I lucked out and had no roommate the first semester.

We spent a lot of time together and got into our first fight when she hurled a shoe at my head while taking laundry to the apartment complex Laundromat (guess I was walking too fast and not listening to her). I was continuing to maintain an A average by skipping many fun activities and holing up in the H. B. Lee Library for five or six hours a day after classes.

I had a regular study carrel on the second floor science library near the south wall of the north wing (today it's a map room). I was there from the time classes were done until 11:00 p.m. each night. Food was prohibited in the library (if one was caught). I brought a sack lunch of peanut butter sandwiches and an apple or carrots and took breaks at the drinking fountain nearby.

There was another student, an Asian kid with glasses who competed with me each night for being the last one out of the library. We met nightly at the south door and gave each other an all-knowing look as our eyes met. No words were ever spoken, only the look of "Another tough day?"

"Yeah, I was going to make something of myself. How about you?" On the last day before finals and graduation, we finally spoke to each other:

"Hey, I got in to graduate school in engineering."

"Nice going! I'm going to med school."

"I'm not surprised."

"Thanks for being there each night for me."

"Yeah, you too. Good luck!"

"Likewise."

Other fond memories of my three years at BYU include the following:

1. Memorizing anatomy charts and drawing them back from memory to reproduce on the biology exams, practicing labeling them with the structures and functions of everything from sea slugs to highly developed mammals.
2. Drawing benzene ring structures and complex proteins for organic chemistry.
3. Physics equations, experiments, and statistical probabilities.

4. Blowing up my chemistry lab trying to extract iron from hemoglobin and getting a glass rod fragment in my thumb while trying to save money on test tubes by cleaning them out for reuse.

5. Religion instructors who were extremely spiritual and humble and obviously paid the price to "know the Lord."

6. Organic chemistry professors with bow ties who give you a B (not an A- or B+) when you were eighth in a class of ninety premed students.

7. Professors who were life rings in an academic storm of loneliness, discouragement, and at times, hopelessness (thank you, Dr. John Green and Dr. Sally Taylor). Some who have more faith in you than you have ever thought possible yourself.

8. A Latin dance professor who told you, "Some of you are very good, and some of you are trying very hard." Teaching dance steps that will one day earn me first place and two million rupiahs in the Indonesian Ophthalmology Association's Annual Dance Contest twenty years later.

CHAPTER 11

MARRIAGE

S hortly after my research elective at Friday Harbor labs in the San Juan Islands, Gull Charters called and said that they knew of a six-to-ten-man boat called the *BIG ZIPPER* that was owned by a man named Ray Zipp. He's looking for a skipper.

Mr. Zipp was preparing to make the trip from Seattle to Westport around Cape Flattery (the northwestern most tip of the continental

USA). I would finish my six weeks in the San Juan Islands just as the charter season was beginning at Westport, and Mr. Zipp was excited to have me help him captain the boat "around the horn" as a wonderful opportunity for us to get acquainted and for me to learn the nuances of the *BIG ZIPPER*. We left Shilshole Marina in Seattle and headed north and west for the Strait of Juan de Fuca.

It was a memorable trip. As we finished fueling at Sekiu and were heading toward Neah Bay, Mr. Zipp began to ask me about the Church of Jesus Christ of Latter-day Saints. As I was explaining the *Book of Mormon*, we both saw a deadhead directly in front of us. It was a log about three feet thick and at least twenty feet long. I stopped the engines immediately and put them into full reverse. Too late. We bumped the log. Next you could hear the *pop-pop-pop* of the log rolling along the bottom of the *Big Zipper*'s hull until it hit the twin propellers with a loud *BANG!* and another *clunk* as it rolled out from beneath the rudders. I carefully put the shifters into forward gear and prayed that we would be okay. We weren't. We had a terrible vibration now and decided to limp back to Port Angeles with the incoming tide for an inspection and repairs.

We made it safely and soon had the boat on the dry dock ramp in the marina. It was worse than we thought. Both propellers and both rudders, along with both shafts, were badly damaged and would need to be replaced or repaired in Seattle. I would remain in Port Angeles, with the boat, while Ray took the damaged parts to Seattle and civilization. I checked into a cheap motel in downtown Port Angeles and spent days down at the marina, bored to death and waiting for word on the parts. I did manage one nice meal at the Old Country Buffet by spending a day helping Julius, a Native American fisherman paint his forty-five-foot ocean trawler, *THE WARRIOR*.

I found solace and mental stimulation at the Port Angeles city library, reading as many medical books as I could find. After two weeks, with no definite date of relaunching the boat, I dejectedly caught a Greyhound bus for home. A week or so later, Mr. Zipp called to inform me the boat was ready, and we were back on our way to Westport. I called my best friend from high school Jeff Malyon (junior high track coach Malyon's son), whom I had introduced to the missionaries after my mission and baptized shortly after I returned from England. I asked Jeff to go with me since Mr. Zipp was now too busy, and the two of us arrived at Westport after a twelve-hour ride down the Washington coast. It was exciting to finally get going as a licensed charter boat skipper.

During this busy time, I would attempt to limit the boat early and spend all available afternoons observing Dr. Redman and Dr. Lush, the Westport town doctors, as part of my BYU premed clinical observation course. In my "spare" time, I filled out medical school applications. I was in great financial shape as I headed back to BYU for my junior year.

Junior year of college went quickly by, with PS either taking my car home to her place after school and bringing me something to eat or going with me to the Cougar eat for some student fare. We talked about when and where to get married. I suggested a December Christmas break wedding; PS was adamant about always wanting a June wedding. We compromised and decided on May 25, about a month after school was out. PS invited me to spend the holidays in Silver Spring, Maryland, with her family. Her dad was sick with metastatic colon cancer and was still working full-time as chief auditor for the US Veterans Administration Canteen Services.

Two days before Christmas, shortly after we arrived, PS's father died. I was outside helping PS's brother Scott with some roofing chores when PS and her sister called us inside to give us the sad news. The funeral was held shortly after Christmas. It was a horribly bleak, sad time.

The night before Brother S. passed away, I had a dream. I dreamed he appeared to me. and I don't recall all the details, but I remember him asking me to promise to take good care of PS. I woke up, saying, "I will, sir. I promise I will." By 10:00 a.m. the next morning, he had passed away.

We decided that since PS's mother would be all alone and since she also needed to plan the wedding, it might be a good idea for PS to enroll at the University of Maryland for the semester before the wedding. Four months apart would be a challenge but safer that way too. I packed up PS's things and shipped them out to Maryland after I returned to Utah.

It was a lonely semester, and I poured myself into my studies. There were lots of letters and phone calls and wedding plans to consider. I returned home in April and began to prepare for the summer fishing season at Westport. I studied for and passed the charter boat captain's exam through the US Coast Guard office in Seattle. It was a three-day test on safety, navigation, and operating of a ship at sea and on the inland waters. The studying paid off as I was able to pass the exam on my first attempt (about 10 percent of applicants would do so annually). I began to put the word out around Westport that I had my "big license" and was looking to run a full-size charter boat. Within a couple of weeks, I received a telephone call from Gull charters with an offer to run an eighteen-passenger boat the *REBEL*, owned by Mr. Don Pugh of Bellevue.

The *REBEL* was a fast twin-engine-diesel boat made by Youngquist cruisers of Seattle. It was forty-eight-feet long and had a covered fly bridge and all the latest electronics including Loran and radar which was quite helpful in the fog, along with an excellent fish-finding sonar system and an upgraded, clean, and roomy cabin. It was a dream come true.

Soon I would be known on the citizen band radio airwaves as "Johnny Rebel" captain of the MV *Rebel*. With the increase in passenger capacity from ten to eighteen, my summer earnings would be boosted considerably. I captained a few weekend trips and then, on May 23, boarded a flight with my parents and best friend, Jeff Malyon, for Washington, DC, and my wedding.

We arrived and met PS's family, and my mom and dad stayed with PS's mom while Jeff and myself were put up at PS's good friend Elinor Hennessee's home. It was a little disappointing that Jeff could not accompany me into the Washington, DC, temple for the session before the wedding or the sealing, but the rules were that he had not been a member of the Church of Jesus Christ of Latter-day Saints long enough yet to qualify. Still, he would be part of the wedding party for the reception and my best man.

My journal entry for the night before the wedding states,

> Tonight is my last night as a free man.
> Tomorrow I will be married in the Lord's temple.
> I'm thankful that I can be married, knowing that
> I have a testimony of the importance of eternal
> families and the sealing power of the priesthood. I
> also consider myself fortunate that my best friend
> Jeff can be here with me to be my best man and
> share in the experience. Also I'm a little nervous.
> I feel especially fortunate that I have been able to
> reach this important day without having the guilt
> or burden of moral mistakes that would detract
> from the spirit of this sacred experience.

It was a wonderful, spiritual experience to go to the DC Temple, which looks like a castle right out of a fairy tale, and kneel across the altar in the presence of my parents and PS's family, and with my best friend Jeff Malyon nearby, to be married to one of the most beautiful women in the world. I remember the counsel of L. Morgan Bates, who married us, imploring us to always remember two little words, *please* and *thank-you*, and to always strive to be considerate.

The rest of the day was a blur with photographs outside the temple and checking in to our hotel and then picking up the tuxes for the evening reception. We held it at the Silver Spring Stake Center and over four hundred people attended. PS and her mother auditioned several local bands and chose a very good group called FURY for the evening's festivities. We received boxes and boxes of gifts, and even US Senator Henry "Scoop" Jackson sent us an official US Senate ashtray/candy dish with the senator's seal delivered to the reception by office courier.

After saying our goodbyes, we left the reception to return to the hotel. We drove about a mile in a car filled with balloons and dragging pop cans behind us when we both suddenly heard giggling coming from the backseat. Shocked, we pulled over and stopped the car and then began laughing. Elinor Hennessee had stowed away in the backseat under the balloons and was giggling away after listening to our conversation. We all had a good laugh, and I made a U-turn and returned her to the church.

We spent a few days in Williamsburg, Virginia, and then packed up all our gifts and flew to Seattle where the fishing season was in full swing.

CHAPTER 12

THE CHARTER BOAT CAPTAIN

I t was my first full summer as a charter boat captain, and it was a seven-day-a-week job. I'd wake up at 4:00 a.m.; pull on my long johns, thermal top, and down vest; and run over to the pier at Gull Charters, on dock street. Since my cousin Gene Jarstad also captained a boat and lived near us in the same trailer park, we would often run over together, stopping at the corner grocery store for supplies.

A typical day's food supply would be a butterhorn and carton of milk for our breakfast, followed by picking up an apple, orange, and banana, along with a package of thin-sliced ham or pastrami for lunch out on the boat. We checked with the office and picked up our bait (about twenty dozen freshly electrocuted four-to-six-inch herring) along with a bag of ice and our customer manifests.

We would start the coffeepot and warm up the engines with a blast of #2 diesel smoke, while the deckhands would begin rigging the eight-foot fiberglass salmon poles with twenty-five-pound test line and twenty-pound test monofilament leaders with two 4-0 barbed salmon hooks. After a short talk on safety at sea along with seasickness instructions (holding tightly on to the side railings while vomiting over the side if one was so disposed) and the location of the life jackets, I gave orders to cast off the lines, and we were on our way.

The Westport Harbor in the late 1970s had as many as 240 licensed charter boats carrying an average of fifteen people each daily across the Grays Harbor bar of the Chehalis River out to fish the Pacific Ocean. The season ran from April 15 to October 30 each year. A three-fish-per-fisherman limit was in effect at that time, and it was not uncommon to hit a school of silver or Chinook salmon and limit out occasionally before noon.

The deckhand or bait boy would cut the heads off the herring bait and place the two hooks through the bait in series, with the lead hook determining the spin of the bait and the trailing hook often catching the salmon as it struck the bait. The philosophy of salmon catching could fill volumes; but in essence, a good spinning bait with sharp well-placed hooks, the right mooching speed of the boat, and fishing at the correct depth as seen by the orange secondary blips on sonar guaranteed a successful "hookup."

Then it was up to the captain to help coach the novice salmon angler, reminding him or her, that it was unlike trout fishing, where it is unnecessary to set the hook and in fact just the opposite. When a salmon first bites, one should peel off about ten quick strips of line and wait for the fish to hook up and then, once the line goes slack, reel in like crazy to keep the fish on, all the while keeping the tip of the fiberglass rod pointed up to keep pressure on the hook in the fish's mouth.

At times with eighteen anglers and their inevitable tangles, we would hook a nice salmon, only to have it turn and run under the boat emerging on the other side with several lines tangled.

One of our favorite stunts, as a crew, was to pick up the customer's line with an empty hook on the opposite side of the boat and have the deckhand tell the customer, with the fish on his line, to tighten his star drag and toss his fishing pole overboard. After repeating the command several times and reassuring the patron that we would replace his custom rod and reel if it deep-sixed to Davy Jones's locker, the deckhand would toss the pole into the water whereupon it would soon emerge on the opposite side of the boat where, as captain, I would pull it up by the fishing line, promptly loosen the drag to an acceptable level, and summon the amazed angler to the railing where his fish was now free of tangles and jumping in the air twenty to fifty yards from the opposite side of the boat.

After several fire drills by the crew often netting three or more salmon in the same net and quickly rebaiting the lines, we soon caught our limits and began the run for home.

Not every day was a limit out by noon affair. On some days, fish were hard to come by. Many days at sea, there were long hours spent listening and talking on the Citizen's Band radio to other captains trying to find the best spot for their crew and where the hot bite was that day.

About 3:00 to 4:00 p.m. each day, whether we had our limits or not, it was time to clean the fish and head for the dock. Most customers understood when we hadn't achieved our limits, but some would plead for us to stay out just fifteen more minutes or try one last spot to catch a big one. At last we'd say, "Okay, we're going in," and that was it. The *REBEL* with its twin-diesel supercharged V-8 engines really flew, doing about twenty-five knots fully loaded. The superchargers would whistle as they sped up to cruising speed, and the combination of the whistling superchargers and the big V-8s gave each charter boat a characteristic sound distinct from the smaller pleasure craft or one lung sailboats in the fog.

Upon returning to the harbor and docking at Gull Charter's pier, the customers gathered up their belongings, and the deckhand and I placed their fish in heavy plastic fish bags with what was left of the ice and said goodbye. Occasionally, after a great day with early limits, some of the passengers would offer to buy the captain dinner or tip the skipper and the deckhand. It was always welcome but not necessary since as captain, I was paid 35 percent of the total charter fee, with 10 percent going to the booking office and 55 percent to the owner. With fees of $40 per person, I could net 35 percent of $760 on a full boat each day. Great money for a college student in 1978!

During this same time, PS was working at a small local restaurant and coffee shop called Dee's Café. She would often work the evening shift, starting about three in the afternoon and finishing around midnight. We joked that we often passed like ships in the night, literally—living out of the same trailer but not seeing much of each other except when I came to the café for dinner after fishing all day. PS enjoyed sleeping in and going to the beach during the day before work and shopping at some of the tourist traps, a practice she still enjoys today when on vacation. As the summer wore on, we realized that we were saving a considerable sum of money. With my charter fees and PS's tips and wages, we would be in excellent financial shape for the coming year, our last as undergraduate seniors.

CHAPTER 13

MEDICAL SCHOOL

UNIVERSITY OF WASHINGTON
School of Medicine
June 2, 1984

THE PICTURE MAN

J uly was the deadline for most medical school applications, and it was unusual to hear of any interview invitations until September at the very earliest. After arriving back at BYU, I received an interview offer from the government medical school, USUHS

(Uniformed Services University of Health Sciences) in Bethesda, Maryland. It was a brand-new medical school, and when I had visited PS's home during the previous winter, we had made it a point to visit the school and take a tour.

Mrs. Joan Crotty was the admissions officer at the school and gave us a red carpet tour of the facilities. I did a little research on my own and found that the school had attracted some of the leading professors in the area to teach there.

To my surprise, Joan Crotty called and told me I could interview at Letterman Army Hospital in September near Stanford University, and we arranged the interview.

I flew to San Francisco and stayed with my sister Kristi, who was working as a civilian contractor for the navy at Lockheed in Santa Clara. She took me to Stanford University Medical School, where we spent the day in the medical library researching anything we could find on the professors at USUHS. Kristi grilled me with mock interview questions until I told her I'd had enough. I was ready.

The interview at Letterman was a blast. It began as a group interview. About half wore military uniforms, and the rest of us were in suits. The military folks were intimidating in their spit-shined shoes (glad I learned that art as a missionary in England) and starched collars (ditto). To my utter amazement, a woman walked in and introduced herself:

"Ladies and gentlemen, good morning. I'm Joan Crotty, director of Admissions for Uniformed Services Medical School."

"Oh, hello, Dr. Jarstad."

"John Jarstad is an applicant that visited our school in Bethesda last winter. Good to see you, John."

I was amazed. Everyone else was green with envy.

"How do you know her?" a guy next to me asked.

"I took a tour last winter," I replied rather triumphantly.

After explaining the interviewing process and the day's events, Joan opened it up for questions. One kid asked a dumb one about the obligations of military service and if there was a way to pay his way out of it after graduation or something, and I could see the displeasure registering on Joan's face.

Another tried to belittle or question the facilities and reputation as a brand-new medical school. It was time to jump in. Up shot my right hand.

"Yes, Mr. Jarstad."

"Joan, I've read about the school and visited the beautiful campus in Bethesda, and I noticed that you have attracted some of the most brilliant professors in areas of medicine like orthopedics and neurosurgery with several big-name professors like Dr. Malcolm Carpenter, who pretty much wrote the bible on neurosurgery and neurobiology. Are these professors we would actually get to meet and take classes from?"

Joan lit up. "Why, of course, John. You will have Dr. Carpenter for neurobiology, and he will teach the lab—excellent question."

I had just hit a home run! The entire tone of the group changed, and the excitement was suddenly palpable. Questions shifted immediately to "What qualities are you looking for in successful applicants?" "How can we indicate that USUHS is our first choice?" and "How many positions are allocated for the West Coast as opposed to the Midwest or South?"

I sailed through my interviews with an Army colonel and Air Force major who mainly wanted to know what my family tradition was with the US armed services. After I mentioned my dad had nearly graduated from pilot school until bone cysts ended his career, my uncle Glenn Jarstad was with the occupation troops in Germany in WWII, and all three of my uncles on Mom's side were in the Pacific Theater with the Navy in WWII, I was in!

Three days after returning to Provo, I received a telephone call from Joan Crotty.

"Dr. Jarstad," she said, "I wanted to be the first to tell you. You've been accepted into the entering class of 1980 at Uniformed Services University Medical School, and I'm authorized as one of our first accepted new doctors to offer you any branch of the service you select, including public health."

"That was your first choice?"

"Thank you, Joan. I can't believe it. I'm going to be a doctor! An MD!"

"I'll be sending you a confirmation letter out this week. If you do decide to change branches of the service, we can accommodate you for about three more months until our class is filled. Congratulations again, Dr. Jarstad."

I was on cloud nine! I was in! And it was only September. I knew I had applied at several other schools, and yet the first offer was so attractive. All educational expenses would be paid by the government. No debt. A lieutenant's pay all during medical school, the finest facilities of the US government, National Library of Medicine, Bethesda Naval Hospital (maybe even help treat the president), Armed Forces Institute of Pathology, George Washington University, Georgetown University, and Howard Medical College.

As our thoughts went to PS's home and all the plans we had for our newfound wealth ($20,000 per year plus all-expense lieutenant's pay while going to medical school), we went to the temple to escape our noisy neighbors. A very early session in the Provo Temple of the Church of Jesus Christ of Latter-day Saints, and as we returned home, we opened the mail (it was my birthday, September 7, 1979).

A letter in the mailbox was waiting from the University of Washington in Seattle. *If this is a rejection letter, I'll know I'm supposed to go back east*, I thought.

"Dear Mr. Jarstad," it began, "you are commended for your fine academic preparation. The University of Washington Medical School would like to extend an invitation to interview for the entering class of 1980. Please call our admissions office at your earliest convenience to schedule a date and time. Respectfully, Dr. H. Camacho, Dean of Admissions."

Now things got complicated. I thought, *What if UW accepts me too?* Still it was exciting to have an acceptance and another possibility. I arranged the trip, and it was exciting to come home and talk to my excited parents and family.

The interview at Seattle was weird. I arrived in my three-piece English suit. There would be four students interviewing together the same afternoon—two women students from UW Seattle who were dressed very casually and a tall guy with long wild hair in a burnt-orange corduroy suit and tie-dyed necktie from Whitman College, in Eastern Washington.

Our difference in shoes said it all. I was wearing my spit-shined toe caps from my recent interview in California, and he was wearing worn-out Hush Puppies khaki loafers that looked like he'd used them for intramural football that semester. Talk about confidence boost. Thank heavens for the mission again! I was warned about the UW being a liberal school and to be careful with the abortion question. The interview panel consisted of Dr. Warner Sampson, a noted cardiologist; another physician who was an obstetrician; and three medical students. Then the questions flew.

Socialized medicine (I thought it might be a good idea since it was affordable and everyone was covered, but I had actually experienced it in England for two years; and I had a story or two to tell about take-a-number scheduling, two-minute exams, and come-back-tomorrow stories); specialization versus primary care (I didn't know exactly what field I wanted to be in but admired the fact that UW turned out excellent primary care and specialist MDs and had a world-class reputation); research (I thought I would enjoy it and valued the contributions medical research made to the quality of life for Americans).

Then it came: "Mr. Jarstad, please tell us your views on abortion."

"Okay." *Here goes.* "I had spent my days off during the summers observing an OB-GYN doctor in a small rural town along the Washington coast. I held abortion to be a private matter between a woman and her doctor. I thought that those skills should be taught and be available to treat women especially when it became a matter of saving the life of a mother. I did not personally agree with abortion as a method of birth control or convenience, but that was my opinion."

They seemed almost satisfied, and then one student chimed in: "Would you personally ever be able to perform an abortion?"

"That's a hypothetical question and assumes I would be going into OB-GYN or family practice. But as I said before, if, for example, I decided to work in a small town like Westport or Raymond, Washington, where I did my preceptorship, I think it would be essential to be able to have the training and skills to be able to perform that procedure in an emergency."

That was the best I could do without compromising my beliefs.

The interview ended shortly afterward, and I had a sinking feeling like I definitely didn't get accepted. I spent a little time with the family and caught my flight back to Utah. I called and spoke to someone at UW who told me the acceptances would go out at the end of each month until the class was filled. But to not get my hopes up about hearing anything soon since it was unusual to be selected in an early month and that most successful applicants heard about Christmastime.

Already having a medical school acceptance in hand provided me with an inner calm and confidence that must have been transmitted to the committee, I received an acceptance letter from the University of Washington School of Medicine two weeks after my interview advising me of my acceptance into the entering class of 1980. Also advising me to maintain my current level of academic success and that the acceptance would be withdrawn if I failed to maintain my current standards of academic progress (whatever that meant—generally don't fail any classes).

UW also strongly encouraged me to graduate with an undergraduate degree as 98 percent of entering students received their bachelor's degree prior to matriculation. I had actually applied a year early to gain experience with the application and interview process and so that, in the event I didn't get in the first time, I could reapply the next year and have an equally good shot.

My good friend Bill Jackson had done this and was accepted a year early to UCSF (he was from Ojai, California). Now it was late September, and I needed about forty-five credits to graduate. I immediately enrolled in two home study religion courses and signed up for an evening American history class (this could be challenged before the second test, and if one passed the course final with 80 percent or higher, they could test out and not be required to attend classes the rest of the semester). I crammed the syllabus and scored a 92 percent, giving me an A for the five-credit class. That left me with twenty-two credits to go for winter semester, and if I took a full-load spring term, I would make it. That's just what I did completing spring term just after Jessica, our first child, was born, May 14, 1980.

Jessica was born during my final term at BYU. PS had stopped attending college after fall semester and was working part-time as a waitress until the last two months of her pregnancy. We moved for spring term to a two-bedroom apartment in a married student ward just one block south of campus. There were no cell phones in those days, believe it or not, so I called between classes frequently each day to see if she was in labor. On the fourteenth, she told me the doctor would induce her since she was two weeks overdue and hadn't gone into labor yet. I remember coming home from class to take her to the hospital since they were going to start inducing her labor that night. We checked my wife in to Utah Valley Hospital in Provo, and after everything was ready, some of the nurses told me to prepare for a long night and that I might want to go home and shower and come back.

Feeling pretty nervous, as most first-time fathers probably are, I thought I would drive to upper campus and collect my thoughts in the parking lot of the Provo Temple. Shortly after arriving, I was too excited and nervous, so after placing PS's name on the prayer roll, I returned home. Immediately the phone rang, and a nurse said to come right back now, and PS was yelling in the background, telling me to hurry. So I drove right back to the hospital.

What was anticipated to be six to eight hours of labor ended up being about an hour and a half. Jessica was born, and I held in my arms for the first time our very own child. It was an awesome experience. I remember calling everyone with the exciting news. I even misdialed my parents' number at about 2:00 a.m. Eastern time with a 201 area code instead of 206. A nice couple wished us well anyhow.

After Jessica was born, we only had about two weeks to pack everything up and head home to Washington State. We would spend the last two months of summer with me working on the charter boat and PS working as a waitress once again. Because of the late start, we didn't save as much money as previous years, and finances were tight.

We left for Pullman, Washington, and Washington State University with two cars: a Jeep Cherokee and a Ford Fairlane. Both were about eight years old. The Jeep had problems, and we somehow got rid of it. Then I found a Honda scooter in the newspaper for $300 that was a year old. I rode this to campus every day and even drove it occasionally the seven miles to Moscow, Idaho, when our first-year classes were held there on Tuesday and Thursday.

Memories of Moscow and Pullman included rafting down the Okanogan River, flag football games at the University of Idaho in Moscow and in the Kibbe Dome (I played quarterback). My first mechanical bull ride. Being the only student with a child. All-night study sessions with Paul Parker and Scott Rice in College Hall (the same building my dad had attended classes in forty years earlier while editor of the WSU *Evergreen* student newspaper). Meeting Babe Hollingberry the WSU baseball coach and having him overhear a classmate say my name and him turning around and saying, "Did you say Jarstad? Are you related to John Jarstad?" And then him asking me if I'd like to come out for the varsity baseball team (Dad had played for him years before and has kept in close contact with him over the years since Dad graduated).

Other first-year medical school experiences included the following:

1. The long six-hour drives to and from Tacoma for the holidays.
2. The drive to Eastern Montana we made during Thanksgiving break to visit PS's sister Gayle near Wolf Point (I think it's just a couple of hours farther).
3. Watching BYU football with George Stephens, Neal Clinger, Richard Groom, and Craig Howell, the other Church of Jesus Christ of Latter-day Saints med students who were from Idaho (I was the only LDS medical student at WSU).
4. Buying Cougar Gold cheese and milkshakes from the Cougar dairy.
5. Running out of money the last month of classes and qualifying for food stamps and the WIC (Women, Infant, and

Children) Program to get through the school year (we were not allowed part-time jobs). Being poor but happy.

The second year of medical school involved moving back to Seattle. Also a full season of charter boat fishing at Westport. With my longer availability in the summer of 1981, I was able to earn more money. The *Rebel* was geared up and ready to go. This year, I was paid a flat 40 percent of the charter fees with 50 percent going to the boat owner and 10 percent to the charter office Gull Charters. In those days, a day on the ocean would run the tourist fisherman $40-plus bait and tackle, so my cut was $16 per person. On a full boat, that meant $320 plus tips. I paid my deckhand $2 per passenger, and he received about $50 in tips and could sell salmon eggs from cleaning the catch for another $10 to $20. We worked seven days a week but were not always full, except on weekends. With PS working again at Dees Café and "baby passing," we saved almost $7,500 that summer for medical school.

We were blessed in being able to rent a mobile home from close friends who just happened not to be at Westport for the fishing season. Don and Jane Rogers one year and Bill and Lucille Adams the next.

In the fall, we were fortunate to move into Seattle's brand-new married student housing at UW Blakeley Village just north of the University Village Shopping Center. The units were condo-style two-story townhouses with ample storage and a playground and common clubhouse for gatherings. Our last year there, we arranged an all-Church of Jesus Christ of Latter-day Saints-medical-and-dental student potluck. There was great camaraderie, and it was only five minutes by bike along the Burke-Gillman Trail to the medical school campus.

Other memories of medical school include the following:

- Taking Jessica as a toddler to class on a Saturday lecture series and having her get fussy and start talking so loudly disturbing the lecture that I had to take her outside.

- Watching *All My Children* soap opera in the Waterfront Center over lunch and telling other students the background from fifteen years ago on some of the characters.
- The difficulty of PS's narcissistic brother-in-law staying with us for fourteen months when he could not find work.
- Taking call every third night and staying up all night at the VA Hospital starting IVs and drawing blood from the forgiving, patient veterans.
- Going to Wenatchee for six weeks of internal medicine training and teaching PS to ski at Mission Ridge.
- The birth of our only son, Robby, on a Sunday morning in February 1982 was a great highlight and having him born at exactly 8:00 a.m. with our Jewish doctor saying, "God has smiled on you today. Not only do you have a son, but he's born on Sunday. He will be spiritual."
- Doing psychiatry training in Alaska at the Alaska Psychiatric Institute and taking Jessica and Robby with us. Driving up to the Matanuska Glacier where they filmed the *Superman* movie.

CHAPTER 14

BEFORE KINGS AND RULERS AT THE NIH

After working hard and fulfilling all my graduation require-
ments early, I found that there were still six months left before
graduation from medical school. This allowed us to visit PS's
family for Christmas in the winter of 1983. While in Maryland, I felt
impressed to look up one of my clinical professors from UW who left
the university to become the head of Nuclear Medicine at the NIH
(National Institutes of Health in Bethesda Maryland).

While visiting his office, he asked, "So you're interested in ophthalmology?" Did you hear? We are just about to start a research
project looking at imaging ocular tumors with radio-labeled monoclonal antibodies? How would you like to come and join us for a few
months of research?" I couldn't believe my good fortune!

I said, "Of course, I'd love it! Can I?"

Dr. Larson told me to go to an administration office and see
a certain lady about the NIH Medical Student Fellowships. When
I arrived, she said kind of jokingly, "Oh, you do, do you?" (Think

you can get accepted to the highly competitive Medical Student Fellowship program?) Then I told her that Dr. Steven Larson had already approved it and that he said to call him if there were any questions. She immediately picked up the telephone and called Dr. Larson.

"Dr. Larson, I have a student here, a Mr. John Jarstad, who thinks he can start the medical student fellowship program and… Yes, yes, sir… Well… Well, it's highly irregular… Well, yes… Yes, sir… Okay… Of course… Okay… Yes, sir… Goodbye…

"Well, you are a very lucky, young man. Do you have any idea how competitive these fellowships are? We don't just take anyone off the street. Fill out this form, and we will need you to fax this back to your school for your dean's signature, and looks like you're in. Congratulations and welcome to the NIH."

I couldn't believe it. I was a medical student fellow at the NIH. I met with Dr. Larson weekly and attended the Nuclear Medicine and Radiology conferences. I met with the doctor from India who was working on making a miniature gamma camera to do eye scans for ocular melanomas, but the research was slow in getting off the ground.

Dr. Larson was very gracious and allowed me to attend the eye conferences and go off campus to the Wilmer Institute at Johns Hopkins in Baltimore and to the Armed Forces Institute of Pathology and take the eye pathology course from Dr. Lorenz Zimmerman and Dr. Ian McLean, who were the world's foremost experts in ocular melanomas (cancerous tumors of the eye). I worked with an eye resident from Howard University Robert "Bobby" Copeland, who would later become the chief of ophthalmology at Howard University and a well-known cornea specialist. We ate lunch together every day and did the pathology course together, often talking about religion and politics. It was surprising how well we got along, considering our diverse backgrounds.

One day, I was told about a weekly conference at the National Eye Institute, shortly after beginning my fellowship at NIH. It seems they had weekly grand rounds over at the eye building 31 on the NIH campus. I was excited to hear about that, and Dr. Larson said,

"I realize eyes are your thing, so if you hear of any conferences, go for it."

I had my NIH map, and as I was getting off the elevator, a kindly older scientist asked me, "You look a little lost, son. Can I help you?"

"Yes, thank you. I'm looking for the eye institute and building 31?"

"That's right where I'm going. I'm Dave, Dave Cogan. Nice to meet you."

I couldn't believe it! Dr. David Cogan? Probably, the most famous ophthalmologist in the world? Cogan's syndrome. Cogan's map-dot-fingerprint-dystrophy? WOW! I was speechless.

"How long are you here for, and what are you doing here at the NIH?" he asked.

I told him my story. How I was here until the end of April and that I'd received word I was accepted at Mayo Clinic for my internship and eye residency which would begin on July 1.

"Well, why don't you spend the next four months with me?" he offered.

"We have a pathology conference at the AFIP (Armed Forces Institute of Pathology) with Zimmerman and McLean, and our weekly grand rounds are here, and then, of course, I do a little neuroophthalmology with the residents from the Washington, DC, area residencies, which you are welcome to attend as my guest. We'd be delighted to have you."

I couldn't believe my good fortune. I felt a little guilty of such luck and wrote in my journal that I felt a lot like Robert Redford in the movie *Hot Rock*, which I had just recently seen, where he gets the diamonds at the end of the movie and walks out of the bank or wherever and has this huge grin on his face. I was walking on air and very, very grateful to my Heavenly Father for opening an effectual door to me for some wonderful experiences with the world's greatest scientists.

One additional experience that I must share is of a missionary experience I had with Dr. Jones, the section head in the radiology department who worked closely with Dr. Larson. He called me into his office one day and said, "I've noticed something different about you. I don't know what it is, but I'd like to talk to you for a few minutes in my office." When we sat down, he asked, "Are you LDS?" I was surprised. "We have some good neighbors who are Latter-day Saints, and I've wanted to ask them about their beliefs for quite a while. I see your temple off the Beltway every day and wondered what you all believe in."

WOW! Where do I start? I was excited. I felt like here I was before "kings and rulers" of the NIH given a golden chance to teach the gospel. I thanked Dr. Jones for the opportunity to be at the NIH and proceeded to tell him about the restoration of the gospel and felt impressed by the Spirit to explain the plan of salvation.

"Have you ever wondered where we came from, why we are here, and where we are going after this life is over?"

I then explained to this noted scientist about the temple and how families could be sealed together for eternity. He had lost a daughter at a young age and was excited to hear that doctrine. It gave him hope, he said. We discussed gospel concepts freely, and the Spirit was there in great abundance.

Then as we were finishing with what turned into ninety minutes of gospel discussion with questions and answers, a thin veil of darkness crept in as he said, "I'd like to have hope in that. But..."

I didn't know what else to say except to bear my testimony and invite him to ask his neighbors to share more with him and have the missionaries meet with him. He said he'd think about it seriously and talk to his wife about it.

He also told Dr. Larson about our conversation, and now Dr. Larson was quite interested to meet with me as his mother had just died about a week or two before. He invited me into his office where we had a similar but shorter conversation. He was still grieving and said he "would like to believe" what I had explained but could not discuss it so soon after his loss."

Dr. Larson thanked me for taking the time to explain things and also mentioned what an impression I had made on Dr. Jones. I told him how much I appreciated his help in mentoring me in my very first clinical medicine class (physical diagnosis) at University of Washington in Seattle during the entire second year of medical school, and I apologized for knowing so little as a second-year student.

He laughed a little knowing that we were pretty green, and he did show tremendous patience listening to Scott Rice and I ramble on about our history and physical findings on patients we worked up at the Veteran's Hospital in South Seattle in 1981–1982. It must have been rewarding for him to see the before-and-after progress of one of his assigned medical students, who would be going on to the Mayo Clinic.

Other memories from medical school included the following:

The death of my first patient. I cried. He was from Wenatchee and had leukemia. I got to know him very well, taking daily blood samples to monitor his white blood counts.

"Catching babies on my OB-GYN rotation." It was there I learned of the faith of a Samoan woman who was scolded by her MD who told her never to get pregnant again since her uterus nearly ruptured for the second time. (She had great faith and another healthy baby.)

Receiving academic honors in reproductive medicine, ophthalmology, ophthalmic pathology, emergency room, hematology, radiology, and a few other elective clerkships as well as my research fellowship at the NIH was the icing on the cake of my medical school experience.

The birth of our third child, Allison, occurred at the end of the final year of medical school. Three days before finals and a month before graduation, PS decided to be induced so that she wouldn't miss my medical school graduation.

I was doing a cardiology subinternship at Pacific Medical Center trying to learn everything I could about heart patients before leaving for Mayo Clinic. PS called and told me she was going to the hospital and to come as soon as I could. I met her at Northwest Hospital. They wouldn't let her be admitted until I took care of the financial arrangements. Even though I would be an MD in three days, they wouldn't budge and said without insurance I would either have to pay $800 as a down payment or file for DSHS (welfare). I was at the end of eight years of school and down to my last $300. I told them I didn't have $800. So they had me meet with a financial person and fill out a form listing my assets.

Nothing of value, except our eight-year-old Chevy Malibu station wagon. They said we qualified for welfare, and PS was admitted in labor. An hour and forty-five minutes later, we were in the delivery room. Allison R. Jarstad was born on May 30, 1984. She had the intense brightest-blue eyes. She frantically searched the room and, once she locked eyes with her dad, settled into a relaxed state of sleep. We were now the parents of three healthy children, all under age five!

CHAPTER 15

INTERN AT THE MAYO CLINIC

There wasn't much time to relax since we were due in Rochester, Minnesota, by July 1 to begin internship at the Mayo Clinic. We said our goodbyes to all the family and friends in Seattle and packed up a U-Haul van and our station wagon, and my mom and dad drove their white Chevy Malibu along with our family of five to Minnesota. We stopped along the way at Mt. Rushmore, South Dakota, and saw the four presidents and lots of buffalo. We arrived in Rochester in time to close on our home and move in just a couple of days before orientation. I loved Rochester!

My maternal grandfather, Marcus Stokes, was born just an hour's drive away in Read's Landing, Minnesota, near Wabasha on the Mississippi River. Many of my ancestors were buried in Cannon Falls Cemetery, and even my dad's Jarstad side of the family had local Minnesota and Iowa roots. We settled into our three-bedroom rambler house with a full basement and backyard with a small four-hundred-square-foot garden where we planted corn, pumpkins, and tomatoes. There was a play fort and sandbox for the kids and a school just a block away. The ward was two blocks away, and the church members and neighbors were very kind and friendly. We made a canoe trip down the Zumbro River from Cannon Falls to town and also visited Decorah, Iowa, where my Jarstad relatives had ties for the Annual Nordic Fest, soon after we arrived.

Orientation consisted of a group welcome meeting at the Ballroom of the Kahler Hotel with all nine hundred or so new doctors and fellows at Mayo. A friendly doctor from Arkansas who reminded me of Jim Nabors's "Gomer Pyle" character in the way he talked befriended me immediately, and I would meet him again about three months later in the hospital cafeteria.

"Hey, John Jarstad! It's me, Wallis. Okay if I sit here?"

"Sure," I said.

"So are you married?"

"Yes," I said.

"Any kids?"

"Yeah, I have three."

"Whoa! You must be either Catholic or Mormon."

"Yeah, I'm LDS or Mormon."

"I think you are the tenth Mormon doctor I've met since I've been here. Are all the doctors at Mayo Clinic LDS?" he asked.

"Maybe, most of them," I exaggerated.

"So what do y'all believe in, anyhow?" Wallis asked.

I proceeded to explain the history of the Church of Jesus Christ of Latter-day Saints and some of the basic differences (living prophets today, eternal families). Then I began to explain the story of the *Book of Mormon*. At this point with breakfast over, Wallis got up and began to leave the cafeteria.

"I'm heading over to the science library. Are you headed that way?"

"Sure, Wallis, I'll go there with you." (So I could finish my story and testimony.)

"So I know that the *Book of Mormon* is the Word of God, another testament of Jesus Christ. How would you like me to get you a copy?" I asked.

"I appreciate the offer, John, but I'm sure they would have a copy at the local library, so I'll just check one out. But it was good talking to you." And I didn't see Wallis for about two months.

I next saw Wallis as I began my internal medicine portion of my intern year on the nephrology service. He was a transplant surgery fellow. Because I loved surgery, I asked him to page me anytime I was in the hospital when he had an interesting case or emergency surgery, and I would come down to the OR and scrub in and help. We got to become close friends that year, and Wallis began taking the missionary lessons at our home. Pagers went off; sometimes in stereo, kids cried. But somehow we made it through all the lessons, and Wallis was challenged for baptism.

Wallis was engaged to Billy Graham's secretary and was very close to a Baptist minister back home. His fiancée was not as understanding as his boyhood Baptist minister, who told Wallis that if he felt in his heart that this was the right thing to do, he should go ahead with it. After investigating the church for over nine months, he had reached a decision.

One night in early spring, I received an emergency page to report to the doctor's lounge of the Rochester Methodist Hospital. I went as quickly as I could and was surprised to find Wallis and two missionaries waiting for me.

"I've decided to be baptized into the Church of Jesus Christ of Latter-day Saints, John, and since you are the ward mission leader, I'd like you to interview me."

I was shocked but excited. We went directly over to Wallis's apartment, where I filled out the baptismal interview form and proceeded with the interview.

"What changed your mind? What was it that convinced you to join the church?" I was so curious.

"John, I read the *Book of Mormon*, and I know that it is true."

"Some of the members will probably think it's because of their friendship or fellowship, and that's okay if they think that, but to be totally honest with you, it was the *Book of Mormon* and Joseph Smith being a prophet that are the reasons I know this church is true."

Just prior to leaving Rochester, Minnesota, and Mayo Clinic for Pittsburgh Children's Hospital to work on a transplant team, Wallis was baptized into the Rochester Church of Jesus Christ of Latter-day Saints Ward. It was a wonderful spiritual experience. Wallis loved our son Robby and said several times that "John, that boy is special. He is so pure and loving."

We said later that Robby was as big an influence on Wallis joining the church as anyone and that he was Robby's first convert as a boy missionary.

We were blessed in Rochester with many missionary opportunities since the Church of Jesus Christ of Latter-day Saints was not very well-known. After my first year of teaching fifteen-year-olds in Sunday school, I was called as Rochester Ward Mission Leader. Within a few months, I was ordained a seventy and then called to serve as Rochester Stake Mission President and seventies president for the same stake that my ancestors found the church in, nearly a hundred years before.

We gradually got the program going full speed. Whereas there had been very few convert baptisms in several years in Rochester, we were blessed with several the first year and then about fourteen the second year, and the next year the ward was divided.

I understand that as of 2021, there are several wards and a new stake center in Rochester. It was gratifying to see the missionary program take root and bear fruit. There was a great feeling of brotherhood in the Rochester ward with events such as Vladimir Kochansky, the noted LDS concert pianist visiting and giving a free piano fireside concert. Football Heisman Trophy candidate Robbie Bosco, the BYU quarterback and nephew of our stake president, gave a youth fireside and television interview. There was also a very successful ward pizza project where each month the ward members would meet to assemble pizzas to sell to the community for about three dollars each to cover our ward budget.

One of the funniest experiences at Mayo Clinic was when a patient I had operated on for cataract returned the next morning, going from only able to see the biggest *E* on the eye chart to nearly perfect 20/20 vision as we removed her eye patch.

"You're Dr. Jarstad?" she asked.

"Why, yes, I did your eye surgery yesterday."

"Oh, dear! I'm afraid I told my husband a terrible lie."

"A lie? What do you mean?"

"Well, I told him you were tall, dark, and handsome."

With that, she covered her mouth in embarrassment.

"That's okay, ma'am. I'm just happy you can really see."

It's fun and interesting to see the patient's reactions when their eyesight is restored.

It was a very emotional day on July 1, 1988, as we loaded up our car and U-Haul truck to leave Rochester, Minnesota. I remember being overcome with gratitude to my Heavenly Father for the miraculous opportunity given to me to learn from the best doctors, nurses, and scientists in the world for the past four years. This would be something that would shape my life and also provide well for my family the rest of my life.

Despite the overwhelming feeling of gratitude, I couldn't help but feel a major letdown. After being chief resident and spending four incredible years at the Mayo Clinic, along with being named one of the "outstanding teachers in ophthalmology" by Mayo Medical School, it seemed to me that life and my medical career could only go downhill from here.

Little did I know at the time what fate and God's hand had in store for me, and—as we shall soon see—what incredible experiences awaited me.

Jarstad children in Rochester, Minnesota, 1988
Clockwise: Robby, Jessica, Stephanie, and Allison

CHAPTER 16

FIRST MISSION TO AFRICA (ZIMBABWE)

"Dr. Livingstone, I Presume" statue with John O. W. Jarstad (Dad) and our "escorts" who followed us everywhere we went at Victoria Falls, Zimbabwe.

There was always a mixture of fascination, fear, and odd respect in my time growing up near the "hilltop" area of Tacoma for Black African Americans. My dad, who as a sports announcer and evening news sports anchor, observed and commented frequently on the outstanding genetic heritage and drive of the Black athlete. "Poetry in motion," he often exclaimed as we watched a Black running back in the NFL or acrobatic guard in the NBA or shortstop in Major League Baseball. He taught me to be color blind. However, growing up in an inner city junior high school where Black students were bussed in and a few with difficult home circumstances would "roll" us for quarters before lunch for their food money gave me some fear as a slightly small for age seventh grader. We were confronted daily by a classmate who was over six feet tall and could punch us in the chest so hard as to take the wind right out. My distrust was also deepened by my harrowing experience in junior high school mentioned in an earlier chapter, where I was nearly killed by a Black neighbor kid, who pushed me in front of a speeding bus.

Balancing these negative impressions was a remarkable experience that took place soon after my older sister Kristin had just started driving. We were in the family station wagon and visiting the "day old" Wonder Bread bakery near Martin Luther King Way (at that time K Street) in Tacoma's hilltop area. After we stopped at a light, the car suddenly flooded as my sister tried to move forward in heavy traffic. Cars were honking, and not a fellow White person was anywhere in sight.

It was during the race riots of the late '60s and racial tensions were high. Suddenly, out of nowhere, a young Black man in his late teens or early twenties ripped open the driver's side door and pulled my sister out of the car. I thought, *We're dead!*

To my surprise, he said, "You flooded it, sister!" And with that, he put the gear shifter in neutral, put the gas pedal to the metal, and turned the key.

VROOOM! The Ford station wagon started right up.

"Don't ever say those Black nig—rs never done nothin' fo' ya." He smiled and laughed as he strutted away in a colorful, bright outfit.

"Thanks!" We both gasped. And home we went.

"Do you know just how lucky we were?" my sister asked. "We could have been killed."

I've never forgot the kindness of that stranger and his good-natured sense of humor at a time of flammable racial tension. Truly, he was a good Samaritan, and I hope he was or will someday be rewarded.

With this limited cultural background, I was attending the American Academy of Ophthalmology annual meeting in Dallas, Texas, in November 1992 when I made an appearance at what was to be my last Liahona Ophthalmology Society meeting. This was a group of ophthalmologists who were members of the Church of Jesus Christ of Latter-day Saints who met each year on a Monday night during the annual eye meeting and had a social hour and dinner together while they were away from their families.

Most of the doctors were from Utah, and the group was much smaller than it is today with about twelve to eighteen ophthalmologists in attendance each year. Typically, the meeting began with greeting each other and then sitting down for dinner where each member of the group stood and described themselves and their city, their specialty, their church calling, and then how many children and grandchildren they had and what they had accomplished since last year's meeting.

Typically, the conversation went something like this: "I'm John Smith from Bountiful, Utah. I'm a glaucoma specialist in a three-man group. I'm in the Stake Presidency of the Little Cottonwood East Stake, and my wife here is the Stake Primary President. We have a son on a mission in Finland and a daughter who is the starting point guard on the University of Utah women's basketball team. I'm looking forward to adding an associate and retiring in the next three to five years."

Well, maybe it was because I was from Washington State and not Utah that I felt a little left out. Or maybe it was because I remember thinking, *Wow, with all this talent and potential in this room, why isn't anyone doing more to serve the third world or medical humanitarian work?*

I vowed this would be my last meeting listening to Dr. So and So talk about his change from stake executive secretary to second counselor in the Young Men's Presidency. It just seemed like with such talent in the room like this, much more good could be accomplished (at future meetings, I would learn of the tremendous volunteer humanitarian missions performed by the Church of Jesus Christ of Latter-day Saints members of the group from Utah).

On the positive side of the meetings, it was always great to see classmates and famous Church of Jesus Christ of Latter-day Saints EyeMDs like Johns Hopkins's Professor Ron Michaels (who pioneered intricate retina surgery) and Dr. George Hilton, who was Chairman of the Eye Department at University of California San Francisco Medical School and invented pneumatic retinopexy (a revolutionary technique to repair a detached retina without surgery using a gas bubble injected into the eye).

It was at this meeting I was introduced to Dr. Roger Hiatt, a pediatric ophthalmologist at University of Tennessee who wrote what I still consider one of the finest works on coming to know the Savior Jesus Christ, called *Life in the Time of Christ and His Physical Attributes* (J. Collegium Asculapium 1984—see appendix).

In any case, as the introductions were proceeding in their usual fashion (I was the newly called ward mission leader and my wife the "Basket of Joy" coordinator in Relief Society, my attention was turned to one very dark-skinned African surgeon who introduced himself as Solomon Guramatunhu, from Zimbabwe, Africa.

Dr. Guramatunhu spoke in a very familiar Queen's English and had a brilliant ivory smile and was grateful to have been invited. He had an unusual request: "Does anyone here have any experience teaching the latest phacoemulsification technology for cataract surgery? I'm looking for someone to come to Zimbabwe and teach me phaco."

As an "outsider," I waited for one of the Utah EyeMDs to volunteer. No one did. The meeting proceeded, and after things wrapped up, I went over to talk to Dr. Guramatunhu.

"Well, did you enjoy the meeting?" I asked.

"Oh yes." He smiled.

"Any success in finding someone to come teach?" I inquired. His eyes sought out the flooring.

"No, not yet," Dr. Guramatunhu replied.

"Well, I'm teaching the residents at the University of Washington right now. Do you still need someone to come—"

"So when will you come?" He cut me off in midsentence. I didn't even know where Zimbabwe was.

"Uh, right after Christmas is usually the slowest time for my clinic."

"So will you come?"

"Uhh, okay," I said without thinking.

"Oh, and can you bring over some donated supplies too like IOLs and viscoelastics?" he asked, like an afterthought.

"I guess so. Where would I find them?"

"The drug companies are pretty good about it," someone said.

And so a trip was born. I remember thinking, *What did I just get myself into?*

I promised I would come; and after living in Minnesota (where a man's word was as good as a signed contract), I always kept my word. Now the work began. I began contacting all the major suppliers of ophthalmic goods and asked for donations. Initially, it was hard to ask (beg in a way), but the response was tremendous. Each company I contacted went out of their way to provide me with supplies.

The next two and a half months went by like lightning. Passports, letters to the drug companies, IOL companies, and equipment vendors. I stopped by the next day at the Mentor Company (now Paradigm) to try out a tiny compact phaco (cataract removal) machine that was on display as a new product that looked like it would fit in a small camera bag. I introduced myself and explained that I had been invited to teach phacoemulsification cataract surgery in Zimbabwe to introduce the technology for the first time ever and would they ever consider loaning or leasing their machine for those kinds of trips. I was grateful for their enthusiastic response.

Hardly anyone in the USA was using their company's Mentor Odyssey cataract machine at the time, and for a US surgeon to try it out was a huge coup for them. They graciously outfitted me with all the equipment and tubing and hand pieces with plenty of spares. It was a relief to be able to take their small compact machine rather than another large bulky device promised by a competitor.

I was grateful to both companies, indeed; so many were willing to help that when I asked for fifty of something, I was usually sent two hundred. In all, I received enough supplies on that first trip to Zimbabwe to fill twenty-three cartons measuring airline dimensions of about eighteen by twenty-four by forty-eight inches and several wheeled duffle bags all weighing in just under the airline's seventy-pound weight limit. I had made contact with Deseret International Foundation and a Dr. William Jackson from Ojai, California.

"Any relation to Bill Jackson who attended BYU and was accepted at UCSF medical school in about 1979?" I asked.

"That's my son," the older Dr. Jackson replied.

I couldn't believe it. It was Dr. Bill Jackson's son who was my study partner from BYU and Friday Harbor Marine Biology. Small world!

Alcon of Ft. Worth, Texas, particularly came through with intraocular lenses, surgical knives, sutures, viscoelastics, and eye drops. Allergan sent bottles of Balanced Salt Solution, lens implants, suture, needles, and cystotomes, and helped to arrange additional state-of-the-art foldable silicone intraocular lenses (a rare donation). Mentor of Boston (now Paradigm of Salt Lake City) loaned me a brand-new phaco machine the "Odyssey," which they allowed me to demonstrate first in my own OR and which performed superbly. The Odyssey was inexpensive to operate, and they offered to sell it to the Africans at a substantial 27 percent discount below their lowest permitted US cost, if I would donate (my) sales commission.

The nurses at St. Francis were especially helpful in collecting and sorting leftover surgical supplies and eye drops from our eye cases, and these were saved along with used surgical gloves over the next two months. I had a record number of cases in December doing forty-nine cataract operations and seventy-one total surgical procedures. The Lord truly blessed me even before I went.

I estimated altogether I was taking about $150,000 worth of donated supplies to Zimbabwe, or in 1993 terms about the average net income of an ophthalmologist in the USA for an entire year's work!

Other items included used eyeglasses, sunglasses, dilation drops, a teaching head for their operating microscope, a model eye, videotapes of my surgery for the students and residents to learn from, an entire tray of surgical instruments for cataract and strabismus (cross-eye) surgery, and a diamond knife keratome.

I called the Church of Jesus Christ of Latter-day Saints Mission Home in Harare and spoke to President Vern Marble and asked if there were any items he could use; and I included eight cassette tape recorders and two cases (ninety-six) Snicker's bars, and my wife arranged for each donated tape recorder to also have a copy of "Hymns of Faith" included, for the missionaries. The final two days before leaving Seattle, all four of my children helped box up and label the supplies. I felt that we prepared "every needful thing" and was very grateful that everything was accomplished in a timely fashion.

With about a week to go before the trip, I realized after an all-day session Saturday packing cases of eye drops, intraocular lens implants, and surgical supplies that I needed help. I summoned my kids—Jessica, Robby, and Allison—to help. Their little fingers were well suited to unwrapping cartons of eye drops and putting them sans package inserts into Ziploc baggies and consolidating space for the journey. About this same time with a week to go, my dad, John O. W. Jarstad, arrived at our home and asked if I thought I'd need any help getting all those boxes to the airport next week. Then a stroke of inspiration hit me.

"Dad, why don't you come along?"

"Oh, I don't know. I can't do anything medically. I suppose I could carry your suitcases though and maybe film a little?"

"And that way we could get more baggage on the planes too."

With twenty-three cartons plus all the bags, it was way too much for one person to handle. It was a great idea. Dad was excited to go too. It would be the trip of a lifetime.

A couple of days prior to departure, several of the supplies had still not arrived, and fortunately, I called; and two large boxes of Occucoat, an essential substance for doing modern cataract surgery with ultrasound, had been shipped to Provo, Utah, by mistake. They had arrived at the headquarters of Deseret International which was helping me to coordinate the trip. I called Dr. Jackson, president of Deseret International (now Charity Vision), and fortunately got the number from his answering machine to the office in Provo where I was able to reach a Dr. Brown who said he'd received the box of supplies and didn't know what to do with it and was going to either wait till Dr. Jackson got back or send it to Uganda with some dental supplies.

I told him it was imperative that I have those supplies right away and instructed him to send them Federal Express overnight. He said that was too expensive and not real possible, because Utah had just experienced the largest snowfall in history (forty-four inches in two weeks) and he didn't think they could get the boxes to us in time (three days from leaving).

When I promised to pay the shipping cost and asked him to try UPS 2nd Day Air guaranteed delivery, he did, and they arrived just in time, one day before our departure.

Then a lady named Vi Brown, from the Storz (now Bausch & Lomb) company in St. Louis, called and felt so bad she had not sent more supplies that she said she had shipped an additional box of one hundred units of Occucoat to arrive overnight FedEx at Sea Tac Airport the day of departure. These were picked up by my dad and Rick Boudreau on the way to the plane and added to our cache of supplies.

At the last minute the night before leaving, the Lion's Eye Bank (whom I'd contacted about cornea transplant donor tissue) dropped off six preserved corneas which I added to the near frozen viscoelastics supplies I had been keeping in our unheated garage on top of my 1987 Blue Pontiac Fiero to keep between thirty-six and forty-six degrees Fahrenheit.

The job was almost done! *ALMOST.* We completely repackaged all the supplies doubling up or eliminating excess wrappers, packages, and stuffing, and wrapped each box in a baby blue plastic Mayo stand cover. All our boxes matched, and I was pleased at how organized it all looked. This would help us track the boxes at the airports, and Rick and I taped and roped the boxes to ensure they'd be water tight and secure. Also easy to spot if anyone tried to make off with them.

The *Federal Way City Herald* interviewed me about two weeks before the trip; and Emilie Forte, the reporter, wanted a photo of the family packing up the boxes helping to send me off. So we got all the kids out of school early and assembled them together, and the photographer was fifteen minutes late and then said they'd discussed the story and decided not to photograph the kids (I was concerned about them being identified by the newspaper with some of the crazy people around nowadays, so I asked Emilie if she would not mention exactly when I was leaving to protect my family).

Her article was excellent and made the front page. The photographer ran a color photo of me at the slit lamp, and the title read, "Eye Doctor Plans Trip to Africa." I was pleased that the name of the church was mentioned and that the facts were accurate, exactly as I had quoted them to her.

PS and the kids worked really hard to help sort and box the supplies, and I was very appreciative of their support. We spent the last night packing my personal suitcase and tying up loose ends. We finally finished everything about 10:00 p.m.; and Rick, Dad, PS, Jessica, Robby, Allison, Stephanie, and I had a family prayer.

In our family prayer circle, I prayed and thanked the Lord for His mercy and help in getting so much accomplished in so short a time frame. I prayed for everyone's protection and that the Holy Ghost would guide and protect us on our "mission." The Spirit was so strong. I had not felt that strong a spirit in our home before as we knelt, and I poured out my heart to my Heavenly Father for His providence and help.

It was nearly impossible to sleep as the excitement of the trip began to dawn. I awoke early about 6:00 a.m. after six good hours of sleep. I was able to walk Jessica to school at 7:00 a.m. (our daily morning ritual to the junior high school four blocks away) and ran home the one-fourth-mile route through the neighborhood at a good speed. I showered, dressed, and shaved. I asked PS if she would like a priesthood blessing. I blessed her as a wife and mother and that others would help her while I was gone, that the trip would go smoothly and that we would return safely. I felt appreciation for her and the children for helping with preparations for the mission trip.

Earlier that night, I stopped by the Stake President Richard Mitchell's office to pick up a letter verifying my "good standing" and "sound moral character" required by the government of Zimbabwe.

I asked if he would mind giving me a priesthood blessing. I was just a little nervous with the unknown and the possibility of a dangerous environment. He quickly agreed and gave me a wonderful blessing, promising me that I would be safe and that I would be successful in sharing my talents and also that I would have many missionary opportunities to share the gospel with people of many nations. Also, that the Lord was pleased that I was going to serve in some cases "the least of these thy brethren" (Matthew 25:40).

So on January 17, 1993, my father and I boarded a Northwest Airlines flight to London by way of Minneapolis. All was not smooth at the airport. They didn't want us to put twenty-three extra cartons on and said it would cost an additional $3,000 or so. I called Bill Jackson.

"Talk to a supervisor," he advised.

So back in line I went, and sure enough, the supervisor took my letter of invitation from Dr. Guramatunhu and a letter from Bill Jackson, stating that I was a volunteer medical doctor for Deseret International; and they let all the packages on free of charge. I later learned that the president of Northwest Airlines, Mr. John Dasburg, had personally approved the excess baggage which was about two hundred pounds over the limit. Once we cleared Seattle, the boxes would go all the way through to Zimbabwe without any trouble.

The flight to Minneapolis was very pleasant, and I felt inspired to talk to a young mother who sat next to me. I felt she needed the gospel or would make a great member of the Lord's church. As we talked, I was organizing my briefcase and left out a letter written by President Mitchell with the Church of Jesus Christ of Latter-day Saints letterhead. She was already a member! Very pleasant lady with a nine-month-old baby. She had a master's degree in technical writing, and her husband had been the swim coach at a college in New Mexico. They had joined the Church of Jesus Christ of Latter-day Saints shortly after they began dating and now lived in Wilkes-Barre, Pennsylvania, where they both taught at Murray State University.

When we reached Minneapolis, I had feelings of homesickness for Minnesota but not as strong as when I lived there. The Minnesota children, seen bundled up and trudging along the airport causeways, especially brought back the memories of some happy times in Rochester years before.

I called home and spoke to Jessica, my oldest daughter. Bless her heart, she had used her only quarter to call me from school and was told I'd already left for the airport, so she was feeling bad she hadn't had a chance to say goodbye, so it was good now to have a chance to talk with her. I love her and all my kids so much. I said an emotional goodbye, and tears filled my eyes. I called Rick and asked if he'd fax a couple of "testimonial" letters from Dr. Shields, a noted retina specialist in Tacoma, and Dr. Kramar, stating that I was fully trained and an "expert" eye surgeon, which the Zimbabwe Health Ministry required.

The flight to London was not very crowded, and Dad and I exchanged a center section of seats to sleep halfway each. I couldn't help but think of my time in England as a missionary for the Church of Jesus Christ of Latter-day Saints nearly twenty years earlier. I promised myself when I left Stoke-on-Trent and had a very strong spiritual witness that I would one day return to that city. Not as a discouraged, beaten missionary (I didn't baptize or teach a soul hardly) but as a "somebody." That I would one day "return with honor." And my mind was filled with the excitement of the possibility after eighteen years almost to the month that I would have a chance to fulfill that promise to myself and my Heavenly Father.

In London, we had instructions on how to reach Eaton Place bed-and-breakfast in an older section of town that Bill had recommended just a block from Victoria Street Station. It was cheap, and Dad immediately went to sleep and began snoring.

I was too excited to sleep. I was back in England after being away since 1977 on my church mission. Sixteen years and I was finally home! I walked the streets and visited a bakery shop and a newsstand and just enjoyed listening to the voices that had a familiar sound. I skipped back to the flat and checked on the cornea transplants that we had brought along from the eye bank at the University of Washington. Still cool. I had about two hours' sleep when the alarm clock went off, and it was time to pack up and head back to the airport. When we finally cleared all the obstacles and boarded our

JOHN S. JARSTAD, MD

Air Zimbabwe flight as two of the only White people on board, we were relieved to embark on the final fourteen-hour leg of our odyssey.

We were soon happy to learn that our plane was a brand-new Boeing 767 aircraft. The stewards and stewardesses were so professional and very highly educated. I remember how impressed I was with them.

"This is one of the highest-paying jobs a Zimbabwean can have," one of my fellow passengers commented.

The other thing I noted was the heavenly music coming from the headsets of several local bands—"Usatambe" by the Zhimozhi Jazz Band, "Zii Zii" by Leonard Dembo, and "Mambakwedza" by the Four Brothers Makorokoto. (I would later find their album on eBay, and it became one of my all-time favorites). Incredible beat and heavenly guitar solos unsurpassed to this day by anything I have ever heard. (Unfortunately, the band members died of AIDS within about five years of my trip, I am told.)

As it was an all-night flight leaving London at 6:00 p.m. and arriving in Harare Zimbabwe about 8:00 a.m. local time, I remember getting little sleep and seeing an edited version of the *Last of the Mohicans* movie about three times. A good movie from what I could tell, or was I just so sleepy?

The Air Zimbabwe cuisine was superb. Roasted Lamb and potatoes for dinner and, eight hours later, breakfast of sausage and eggs.

We arrived at the Harare Airport and immediately were directed to passport control. Here, a little booth was set up with one-way mirrored sides so one entering could not see who was interrogating them. The encounter went something like this:

"Sttttyrrrrrr Prrrrpppssss!"

"Excuse me?"

"SSTTTTYYYRRRR PUURRRRRRRRPPSSSSS!"

"I'm sorry I don't understand."

"State yourrrr prrrrrposee!"

"Oh, I'm here on a medical mission to help the people of Zimbabwe. I'm with Deseret International."

"Parrrrsssprrrrt plleeeeze?"

"Excuse me?"

"Passssssprrrt plessse!"

"Oh, passport. Okay, here you are."

"Whhhhrrrrrr urrrrr styyyyynnnngg?"

"Excuse me?"

"Urrrr stttayyyynngggg?"

"I'm really sorry."

"Wuhhrrrr yyyoooooorrrrrrrrr sttayyyyynnnnggg?"

"Oh, I'm staying with a local doctor, Dr. Solomon Guramatunhu."

"Nnntkkkktttt plleeezz."

"Excuse me?"

"Urrrrrr rrrrrtttuurrrrrrn nnnttkkkktttt pleezz."

"Oh, sure, here is my return ticket."

"Urrrr meyyyy mggghhho."

And I just couldn't resist—I had to see who this person was, in what reminded me of a confessional box with a one-way mirror. I expected to see a tall tough person and felt, after leaning up close and looking in, like catching the Wizard of Oz behind the curtain. Here was this little African man about five feet tall in the booth making life difficult for the international travelers.

Dad was next, and with his hearing situation damaged by years of running a fishing boat, I knew his situation was hopeless.

"Stttaattttt urrrr prrrrpzzzzz!"

"He's with me," I interjected.

"Move along. Urrrrr finnnizzzed," he told me. I stood just out of striking distance.

Dad's interview went quicker, and basically, they just stamped his passport after taking a look to see that he had a return ticket out of Oz.

Once we were on the other side of the passport control officers, we were at baggage claim. There we met Reginald Neald, a local church member who had been District President of the Church of Jesus Christ of Latter-day Saints in Zimbabwe until just recently. Reggie was a giant of a man and the former captain of the Zimbabwe national rugby team. We soon had all our cartons packed in powder-blue plastic Mayo covers with bright-hot-pink tags and tied with rope. Now things got interesting.

One of the young custom agents wanted to open the bags and inspect everything. Something about narcotic or drug smuggling concerns. We allowed them to open a couple of cartons, and then he asked us to open each individual sterile intraocular lens implant box.

"Absolutely not!" I complained. "Reg, if he does that, I may as well not have even come. They will be ruined."

But now it was an ego thing. The customs officer was obviously new and very young and doing everything by the book. We had reached an impasse. Reg quickly took control, shouting something in Shona, the tribal language.

Something about a supervisor, I had remembered, worked at Sea Tac Airport. Reg agreed, and soon an older native man appeared with what looked like an old war wound on his face from perhaps a glancing bullet or bayonet. He was much more compassionate and listened for about three minutes to our plight in the Shona language. Then he answered Reg and waved us through. Some heated words were exchanged with the young guard, and we never looked back. We were outside and loading the twenty-three cartons of medical supplies onto a couple of trucks and vans for our trip to Parirenyatwa Hospital in the center of Harare.

Parirenyatwa Hospital was built by the British just before 1980 when Zimbabwe declared and won independence from them. It had undergone no renovations or much maintenance since that time. The hospital was named for a young native Zimbabwean, Dr. Parirenyatwa, who was the first native to receive a medical education by going to Scotland for studies and returning to serve his native people. He was killed in an automobile accident shortly after returning and thus the name. Oddly enough, *Parirenyatwa*, I am told, means the "place of trouble" in the Shona dialect.

As Dad and I unloaded the supplies, we were assisted by a young intern named Ephraim. *What an interesting name*, I thought. *I wonder if he's meant to join the Church of Jesus Christ of Latter-day Saints someday.* (That would, in fact, happen later).

"Can you show me where your eye drops are kept?" was one of my first questions. I'll never forget them showing me to a beautiful wood cabinet, and as I pulled out the drawers, I finally found one bottle of generic tobramycin antibiotic solution eye drops. That was it. That's all they had. We soon had a small army unpacking and stocking the shelves to overflowing. The corneas for transplantation were put in a small refrigerator along with the viscoelastics, and we were finished with our work for now.

Dad and I were then taken to our apartment where we would spend the next two weeks. The mission home had graciously invited us to stay in the missionary couple's apartment as they were between missionaries right then and it was empty. I guess I was expecting stereotypical quarters more like what one sees on documentaries of starving African bush people than what we were ushered into in central Harare.

A gated condominium townhouse-style flat with hardwood floors that appeared gleaming and spotless. Two bedrooms were located upstairs with screened windows. The only drawback was there didn't appear to be any air-conditioning, and since it was January, we were in the middle of summer in the Southern Hemisphere. It felt good for Dad's arthritis, though, and he seemed to love the climate and the people as much as I did. The smell of fragrant flowers and local jacaranda and eucalyptus trees added a heavenly scent to what soon was becoming a sub-Saharan tropical paradise.

Dr. Guramatunhu and I spent long days in the operating theater beginning work most days at 6:00 a.m. and finishing some nights at 11:00 p.m. or later with the cornea transplants. Lectures in the Medical School of the University of Zimbabwe on cataract surgery and eye emergencies would occupy a needed respite from the heat and humidity of the surgery floor, and early morning rounds on some of the postop patients were additionally squeezed into the schedule.

One day, toward the end of my time in Harare, Zimbabwe, I asked the residents and medical students at the medical school if there were any other topics they would like me to lecture about while I was there. One of the student leaders asked if it would be possible for me to "please explain the origination of your church."

So on my final day of lecture, I gave the first Church of Jesus Christ of Latter-day Saints missionary discussion to the entire class of eye residents at the University of Zimbabwe School of Medicine. As I concluded and bore testimony of the *Book of Mormon* and the gospel of Jesus Christ, I handed out fifteen copies of the *Book of Mormon* that I had personalized with my testimony and a family photo on the front page. They presented me with a copper rhinoceros as a going-away gift of appreciation, and Dr. Guramatunhu presented me with a zebra pelt for my living room.

Dad had contracted pneumonia about halfway through the visit and was nursed back to health by a couple of older ladies in the townhouse complex next door with chicken soup and herbal teas. They then took him on a day of sightseeing. Our plan upon leaving Zimbabwe was to stop off in London for a few days and then return home on Monday to Seattle. Dad was still feeling under the weather, and the idea of three days in rainy England in January just didn't appeal, so he asked to go on to Seattle. That was okay with me, but I really wanted to visit my old mission area and see old friends.

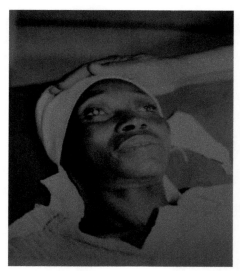

African woman with dense cataract. Note the white pupil reflex in this blind eye. Her vision was completely restored with modern cataract surgery.

CHAPTER 17

REUNION IN ENGLAND

B ack "home" in England once again, I rented a car and drove
up the M-6 motorway stopping at Cheslyn Hay just north of
Walsall, arriving Saturday at high noon. It was such a joy to
exit the M-6 motorway and see the Church of Jesus Christ of Latter-

day Saints chapel that I helped to build with my bare hands (as missionaries, we dug out the baptismal font with a pick and shovel and laid the first two rows of bricks on the north wall of the entrance hallway). What a beautiful chapel site and grounds. The Walsall Saints had added on to the church since I was there seventeen years before and now have a cultural hall and primary room with classrooms and a stage.

The Sacrament meeting talks were on service. Toward the end of the meeting, Bishop Degville, who recognized me in the congregation, called upon me to speak for two minutes. After telling the saints that I had just been to Africa on a short medical mission and feeling grateful for the opportunity I had to help many blind people to see again, I mentioned that I had also been given an opportunity to share the gospel by placing fifteen copies of the *Book of Mormon*. I then related my history of "growing up" in Walsall Ward and how really fun it was going to the Walsall Public Market the previous day and looking into the faces of the good people there, concluding with my testimony of the Savior and the restoration of His gospel.

Later that day, I was asked to help set apart Bishop Stanley Woods, the bishop during my years as a missionary in Walsall, as the new stake public communications director. This was quite an honor; and he was given a wonderful blessing by the young high councilor that he'd "be able to open his mouth at the right times and influence the right people—that there were many people who wanted to destroy the church and he would be able to contact people to help bring the Church good publicity."

After being invited to the Woods home for afternoon tea (dinner) and enjoying talking to them about their experiences in the church, I wanted to ask Bishop Woods, "What made him successful as a bishop?"

Bishop Woods said, "Positive attitude, wonderful positive attitude, always have good to say about others, always in interviews say things like 'fantastic' 'never better,' build up others, and delegate with total trust in the very best people in the key callings."

One of Bishop Wood's favorite examples of this was Brother Richard "Ken" Burton ("I can trust him with my life"). More about him in a moment.

Bishop Woods's children, Stephen and Ruth, have turned out so well since I knew them as seventeen- and thirteen-year-old kids. Ruth is beautiful, bright and articulate. She teaches elementary school. Stephen is a transportation engineer for a city in Southwest England and a city planner who has invented a board game sold in English department stores, now married and served as a bishop himself following in his father's footsteps.

After dinner, we spoke by telephone with Walsall Ward members Dennis Degville and his wife, Elizabeth; Barbie Richards, who is now married; and the Burton family.

The Woods Family and I drove up to Telford to see the Burtons. Brother Burton had been hospitalized for a heart condition and was under strict doctor's orders to stay home after recently suffering two heart attacks and two strokes. His wife, Sandra, works nights in a software disc-making plant. She served as the Telford Ward Relief Society president for nine years and comes home from her shift to teach early morning seminary (Bible study) to the high school students. Brother Burton cooks the students' breakfast and pays for it by doing a paper route to the shops at the local mall despite his failing heart.

This noble ward mission leader had done everything for us as missionaries, and now his final days were near. We had a spiritual and wonderful visit. Brother Burton brought out the triple-combination scriptures Elder Rex Johnson and I had given to him when we were missionaries in Walsall twenty-five years earlier in appreciation for all his help. Our dedicated tributes were still legible on the front page. The scripture in Doctrine and Covenants 130:2, which states, "That same sociality which exists among us here will exist among us there only it will be coupled with eternal glory," came to mind. This was that sociality.

I was given a rare glimpse into the next life and the feelings of complete and profound joy that we will one day experience in the *celestial kingdom* of our God. I was grateful to my Heavenly Father for allowing me to experience this feeling as a mortal. The Holy Ghost confirmed to my mind and heart that this would be the last time I would ever see Brother Burton in this mortal life. As this feeling came over me, I looked to Brother Burton, who had been laughing along with Bishop Woods; and when our eyes met, I could see in his eyes that he, too, realized this meeting would be our last. He asked me to give him a blessing before leaving.

We all knelt in prayer. I blessed his home with peace, safety, and the strong faith to overcome any trials or tribulations that would come along. That they were so deserving of the Lord's blessings and pleaded that we would all be faithful and be able to meet again that our relationships could continue on in the eternities. As we finished, neither one of us wanted this to be goodbye, and as the evening finally came to an end about 11:00 p.m., we embraced for the last time.

"Goodbye, Brother Burton." I nearly choked, sobbing on the words.

"Goodbye, Elder Jarstad," he said with an equal number of tears flooding his eyes.

"I will never forget you."

"Nor I you."

Someone suggested we sing a hymn. God be with you till we meet again. More tears and it was time to go.

I awoke the next morning overcome with the emotion of what I had witnessed in this faithful family and faithful patriarch who moved his family to Telford for the cleaner air and healthier atmosphere and had sacrificed so much for the gospel's sake. I feel that the Burton family truly exemplifies "Latter-day Saint." I felt so unworthy to be so blessed by my association with them. When I have so much and do comparatively so little. I sobbed like a baby, but I'm not embarrassed by it at all. I love these people with all my heart, and it pains me to the soul to see their suffering, but I'm also strengthened by the same assurance that I know they are saints who will be in the celestial kingdom of God. To think that I was given a glimpse of the literal fulfillment of the scripture from the Doctrine and Covenants was a remarkable blessing. The Woods, the Burtons, and I enjoyed that level of spirituality for about three hours. Something I hope I never forget until we can all meet again.

It wasn't long after I'd returned home that Bishop Woods called to tell me the news. Brother Burton had passed away. The funeral would be held on Saturday. How I wanted to come. And almost did. I did send a memorial by fax to be read at the service. What joy to think of a reunion someday with Brother Richard "Ken" Burton, Walsall Ward mission leader and a faithful servant of the Lord.

CHAPTER 18

SECOND MISSION TO AFRICA (ZIMBABWE)

L eaving Zimbabwe after my first medical mission, I felt like there was unfinished business. First of all, I had operated on several patients including corneal transplant cases that I was very interested in seeing for follow-up. There was also a very strong impression that came to my mind that my work in Zimbabwe was not yet finished. Third, I had been well treated and invited back by Dr. Guramatunhu and several of the resident doctors; and last and most importantly, I had given my word that I would return, and one thing living in the Midwest taught me was to always keep my word.

After returning to Federal Way and relating the stories of our first trip, my wife and children were excited at the prospect of a family vacation to Africa. We began to plan the time and supplies for the second mission trip.

This time, we would plan to visit Dr. Roy D'Souza in Bulawayo as well. He was quite keen on learning phaco, too, and was concerned about keeping up with the advances that Dr. Guramatunhu was pioneering in Harare. Both doctors were also very interested in my experience with radial keratotomy (RK) to correct nearsightedness and wanted to learn this procedure.

With the experience of my first trip behind me, I knew better what was of value to the African doctors and what was not. For example, on the first trip, I had brought over sterile gloves and sterile paper throwaway drapes which were not useful in Zimbabwe, as they usually reused both the gloves and cloth surgical drapes. IOLs of 19.0 diopter prescription power were much more highly preferred over powers from 16.0 to 30.0 as the 19.0 lenses were more or less the average prescription used in about 80 percent of eyes. A-scans (sonar of the eye) to calculate the exact lens power were available but also very time-consuming and with such a backlog of legally blind patients, improving their vision to 20/40 or 20/50 without glasses compared to perfect 20/20 vision was not so critical or objectionable as it would be in the USA. Patients were literally taken from blindness to sight in a matter of minutes. They were so grateful to see again that there was jumping and clapping and singing and crying for joy after their bandages came off.

One of the problems of such success was the inability to impress upon the African patients how important the use of their eye drops was following surgery. Typically, an antibiotic eye drop is used for one week following surgery to prevent catastrophic infection called endophthalmitis, which is an infection that gets inside the eye and quickly ruins the entire ocular contents. Without treatment, the eye must be removed to save a patient's life in a matter of hours or days. Many patients who were completely blinded by cataract and now could suddenly see did not understand the reason for taking eye drops once their vision was restored. They often stated, "I could now see so well I did not wish to do anything to upset my new vision."

This lack of understanding caused them to omit the sight-saving drops that would prevent infection or inflammation and blindness.

With the introduction of small-incision phaco cataract surgery in 1993, the cataract incision was now 4 mm or less as opposed to the old extracapsular cataract operative wound of 12 mm. This smaller incision, by itself, was a major advance in technique for Zimbabwe and led to a significant decrease in the infection rate following cataract surgery.

I spoke to Dr. Guramatunhu shortly after I returned to the USA and was appalled at the rate of infection when I inquired how our patients were doing.

"We had only two cases of infection out of our one hundred or so patients," Dr. Guramatunhu explained. I was sick.

Endophthalmitis in two patients. What had I done? I was quickly regretting ever having gone to Africa and bringing technology that maybe they weren't prepared for. Two cases of infection! I had never had a case of endophthalmitis in eight years of doing cataract operations or any since, and now two of our patients were infected and might lose their sight.

"Oh, I'm so sorry, I'm just sick," I mentioned to Dr. Guramatunhu.

"No, John, it's okay. Our average rate is about 10 percent, so this is a big improvement. Thank you, it is a huge contribution to ophthalmology in Zimbabwe."

I was amazed. "Why was the infection rate so high?" I asked the good African doctor. Sure the weather was hotter and more humid in areas.

"I think it is because of the personal hygiene situation here," Dr. Guramatunhu explained. "Most of these patients come in from the bush and the villages and are farmers and often rub their eye with dirty hands. It is a continuous problem for us."

Yes, that made sense. Efforts were made to keep the patients in the hospital for the first week after cataract surgery to keep the risk of infection down before allowing them back home. That did not make sense with my Western orientation, because we had just made the transition from inpatient to all-outpatient cataract surgery in the USA, just seven years before.

But here in Zimbabwe, it made perfect sense. The cataract patients stayed in the hospital for a week where all the eye drops were given by the nursing staff, and they were fed and kept clean during the critical first week. This might even be something to take back home to remember when taking care of farmers or loggers or fishermen in the Northwest.

Returning to Zimbabwe the second time was sandwiched around a family summer vacation. After serving my Church of Jesus Christ of Latter-day Saints mission to Central England in 1975–1977, I was excited for the opportunity to introduce my family to the sights and people I had come to love fifteen years earlier.

We worked as a family to pack medical supplies and load them tightly into rolling duffle bags and cardboard cartons secured by baby blue plastic Mayo stand covers and heavy white twine. In all, we had our luggage and about seventeen cartons of various eye drops, IOLs, a second phaco machine for Dr. D'Souza to try out, and all the equipment to perform radial keratotomy for both Dr. Guramatunhu and Dr. D'Souza.

We planned to store our supplies in London whilst we toured England for four days and then resume our journey to Zimbabwe. Unfortunately, I was clueless about customs and was soon presented a bill by Her Majesty's customs for about $30,000 on the medical supplies if I was going to bring them into the UK for any reason including storage. At this point, I was in total shock. I didn't have $30,000, and I couldn't send the supplies back home or on to Zimbabwe for another four days. Finally, I asked to speak to a supervisor. At this point, I was introduced to an angelic man, Mr. Haydn Chappell, an administrator at Heathrow Airport. After explaining my situation, Mr. Chappell smiled and kindly said, "I'll take care of everything.

Don't worry about a thing. The boxes will stay right here in my office under lock and key until you board your flight in four days."

We were off to see the sights of England. After touring the castles and visiting the chapels where I served, we took in a Shakespeare play at the Royal Shakespeare Theatre in Stratford upon Avon, which was just a few miles south of the town of Redditch where I had served with Elder Potter and Elder Jones, two of my greenies. The play was the *Tempest*. PS and I had difficulty keeping the children awake, but what they did see, they enjoyed. We stayed at a nice hotel about twenty miles from the airport with an indoor pool and slept in since our Air Zimbabwe flight was for 6:00 p.m. the next night. I also wanted to give the family one last taste of civilization before heading into the unknowns of Africa.

The next day, about 1:00 p.m., we checked out of the hotel and returned our rental van and checked with the gate about confirming our flight to Harare. I had received a nice note from the people of Deseret International Zimbabwe and instructions to contact a certain agent for Air Zimbabwe once we arrived in London to make arrangements for the flight.

There was some confusion. It appeared that they did not know what I was talking about. However, the agents in the airport finally reached the gentleman in the downtown London office for Air Zimbabwe, and he agreed to come out to the airport to meet us and arrange the tickets to and from Harare. We waited from about 4:00 p.m. until after 6:00 p.m., and finally, he arrived, and we received our tickets for the cost of fuel and taxes to Harare and returning to Frankfurt Germany on Air Zimbabwe, the national airline for this socialist African nation.

The flight was far more crowded than the January flight my dad and I had been on. It seemed smokier and longer with four children too. Fourteen hours in an airplane seemed an eternity, but we at last arrived in Harare as the sun was rising, and the Four Brothers' "Makorokoto" was sounding in my headset. We seemed to clear customs much more easily this time and were soon whisked away to our hotel. The Bronte Hotel was an English colonial built during the Rhodesian period and elegant for its time in the early 1900s. We spent a couple of days in Harare as I taught in the medical school and in the operating theater, and the family enjoyed the hotel pool and did a little sightseeing. Then it was on to Bulawayo about three hundred miles to the south.

Because we had left Seattle in August, this was now winter in the Southern Hemisphere. By the time we arrived in Bulawayo, it was cold at night in the forty degrees Fahrenheit range. Almost immediately, we were met by the Church of Jesus Christ of Latter-day Saints members at our hotel. We had a wonderful visit from the district president and several of the local leaders. They had seen very little contact with the Church of Jesus Christ of Latter-day Saints and appeared starved for any information about the church, its leaders, and any policy news from Salt Lake. Even though I told them I was there on medical assignment, not on official Church of Jesus Christ of Latter-day Saints business, they still treated us like visiting general authorities.

We took a tour of the Bulawayo handicapped branch and met with its branch president, Jairos Jiri, who showed us the communal kitchen with its huge pots. "I don't want to get too close to that one," I said. "It looks big enough to cook a missionary in." Brother Jiri laughed and said, "Who knows if we're hungry enough?" I almost thought he was serious. All joking aside, I then asked what they did cook in this huge seventy-five-gallon stainless steel pot. Mealy meal (a maize or corn) porridge and we mix with it any protein we can find, sometimes goat's blood or milk.

We followed him around the compound with a missionary couple and were impressed that the youth had made a little soccer ball of rags with duct tape, and this was the only form of entertainment for the boys in the village compound. I made a mental note to send or bring donated soccer balls on a future visit.

We ended the tour and returned to our hosts, having seen perhaps the poorest of the poor in a poor section of Zimbabwe on the poorest continent.

When we returned for dinner with our host family, Dr. D'Souza's wife, Egina, welcomed us to their home and then proceeded with an Ndebele ceremony of washing our hands before dinner. There in the living room, Egina arrived with a porcelain bowl filled with warm water and linens and kneeling proceeded to wash our hands and arms. This custom reminded me of the biblical ceremony of the washing of the disciple's feet, and I received a spiritual confirmation that this was a descendant of that ancient rite perhaps modified over time but a wonderful spiritual experience.

During the remaining days in Bulawayo, whilst Dr. D'Souza and I worked in the government hospital in the morning and staffed his private clinic and surgery center in the afternoon, my wife and the children were entertained by Egina and her daughters, Sharmane and Sherilee. Two particular favorite haunts for the children were the Creamy Inn and the Chicken Inn (on opposite street corners)—fast-food American style but with a native twist. It seems there was an AK-47 armed guard to ensure taxes were paid by the store owners after each sale.

Our time was spent doing cataract surgery with the new mentor phacoemulsification machine and teaching the nuances of small-incision microsurgery with the newest technology. Roy had excellent hands and was a quick study as was Dr. Solomon Guramatunhu in Harare. Both doctors had used innovation in constructing efficient and clean clinics which had the highest reputations in their locales. It was fun for me to rub shoulders with the best and the brightest Zimbabwe had to offer. I also learned a few things that would help me in areas of efficiency, time management, and cost saving that I would immediately transfer back to the USA on my return.

One of the most startling revelations was how much we Americans waste, not only in our consumption of natural resources but also in medical supplies. Our "throwaway generation" would do well to emulate the Africans in so many ways.

One specific example was in preoperative supplies. In 1993, the standard of practice in the USA was to use an individual bottle of three different eye drops which were instilled into a prospective cataract patient's eye with two or three doses about five minutes apart and then throw away these nearly full bottles of eye drops believing they were "contaminated" after a single use. The cost to the pharmacy for each patient's preop eye drops was over $100 for the three or four bottles and an additional $100 for the postoperative eye drops and ointments placed into the eye before placing the eye patch and shield over the eye at the conclusion of the cataract operation.

In Africa, eye drops were handled and treated like gold, and bottles of drops were reused! So long as sterile technique was employed and the dropper tips were not touched to the patient's eyelids, they could be safely used on more than one patient. Many more than one patient. Indeed, one set of eye drops could be used for an entire day's surgical patients, bringing the cost down to a tenth or less of our wasteful US technique.

Returning home, I soon presented this proposal to the nursing staff of St. Francis Community Hospital where I was chief of ophthalmology at that time. They were reluctant to change the proven routine but finally agreed to try on one condition, that if we found even one case of infection, the experiment would be terminated. The pharmacy was more enthusiastic. "Do you realize how much money this will save the hospital?" was their response. Fortunately, there were no infections, and Dr. Weingeist and I reported our findings at the American Society of Cataract and Refractive Surgeons' 1999 Annual Meeting using multidosing and reusable supplies. The hospital saved over $200,000 per year by instituting the African practices and awarded me the "Sister Dora"* Award for contributions to conserving hospital resources (*Sister Dora was a famous British nurse during WWII, who sterilized ends of sutures for reuse, conserving medical resources).

The final experience (and one of the most gratifying) was in sharing the gospel with Roy's wife, Egina. As we were leaving for the airport to fly home, Egina came to me and said how much she enjoyed visiting with PS and that she noted a special spirit about her that she could not describe. She wondered if I knew what she was referring to.

"Egina, in our faith, we believe in the Holy Ghost or Holy Spirit. A member of our church who is living their religion has this spirit with them constantly. What you were feeling with PS was the Spirit of the Holy Ghost.

"I wish I had more time to explain more about our beliefs, but I would like you to accept this gift before we leave. You have been so kind to us and so hospitable. We hope you will accept this *Book of Mormon*, which tells more about the Spirit you felt and also explains what we believe. It is another testament of Jesus Christ and tells of a visit He made to the Americas after He was resurrected in the Holy Land. I would be honored if you would accept it because it, along with the Bible, is the most important thing in our lives."

With that introduction and a little about the Prophet Joseph Smith, Egina promised to read it, and we departed for home.

On my next visit to Africa, I would learn that Egina had kept her promise, had read the entire *Book of Mormon*, and stated, "Thank you for sharing the *Book of Mormon* with me. I read it, and I know that it is truly the Word of God. I know for myself that Joseph Smith was a prophet of God. Unfortunately, I cannot be baptized at this time, because Roy and I have not had a formal wedding. But I hope you don't mind I shared the book with my brother who lives in Harare, the capital, and he read it and was able to be baptized and is now what you call the Elders' Quorum President in your church."

"Everyone knows men are not suited for hard labor," these Shona women said when asked why they were carrying these loads of heavy firewood on their heads near Harare, Zimbabwe.

CHAPTER 19

BOWLING WITH THE AFRICANS

With our new African friends, we mentioned if they ever came to the USA, we would be most happy to host them. They took us up on the offer right before the American Academy of Ophthalmology annual meeting in San Francisco, California, about a year after our visit to Zimbabwe.

The D'Souza family arrived about two days before flying to California for the conference, and we gave them the usual tour of the Seattle sights including Pike Place Market, the Ballard Salmon Locks, Jarstad Park in Gorst, and a sunset ferry boat ride from Bremerton to Seattle, watching the city rise up out of the water of Puget Sound just as the city lights were coming on.

But I sensed that something was missing. "Is there anything you girls really wanted to see or experience here in America that you've not done yet?" I asked Sharilee.

"We were hoping to do something very American before we go. Something we can't do at home in Zimbabwe."

We all thought and thought, and then inspiration hit. *Bowling! We'll take them Bowling!*

"Have you ever been bowling?" we asked.

"No, what is that?" they replied.

"We'll show you!"

This would be good, we thought. Nothing quite like an American bowling alley and game of ten pin bowling. We arrived at Secoma Lanes south of downtown Federal Way and rented shoes and helped them pick out their bowling balls.

It didn't take long before they were avoiding the gutter and knocking down pins with the best of them. Roy actually got two strikes and several spares on his first game, and the girls had a ball. They were so enthusiastic about knocking down the pins with such controlled destruction. It was truly a night to remember "bowling with the Africans."

Eastern "Cataract" Victoria Falls, Zimbabwe
"The largest cataract in the world" at 101 meters.

CHAPTER 20

THIRD MISSION TO AFRICA (ZIMBABWE)

T
he third mission to Zimbabwe came about in a rather unusual way. While I was on the teaching faculty of the University of Washington and working at Pacific Medical Center teaching the new residents in ophthalmology cataract surgery, Dr. Piro

Kramar, the ophthalmology department head, would frequently question me about my experiences in Africa. Seems it was a place she had always wanted to visit. She had been to Tibet and to K-2 and Everest and lived alone on Vashon Island with about ten cats and a friend. She was from Hungary and had come to the USA shortly after WWII and attended medical college at University of Oregon as one of the very first women in medicine at the school to choose ophthalmology. Dr. Kramar was an accomplished and gifted surgeon, a very compassionate physician, and a great teacher.

As Dr. Kramar was about ready to retire, she asked if I had any connections or recommendations for her to link up with the doctors in Zimbabwe. Because of my good relations with both Dr. Guramatunhu and Dr. D'Souza, I offered to help her put together a mission trip to teach over there and for them to help host her.

As she was preparing to make the trip, she felt a little uneasy with the idea of traveling alone to a part of the world she had never been to before. She asked if there was some way others could come along, and it seemed no big deal to me after going twice before. So we agreed to go along.

Dr. Kramar was about twenty-five years older and my boss. We all met for breakfast and lectures, but afterward, she would teach plastic surgery of the eyelids, and I taught cataract and refractive surgery. About day three, we left Dr. Kramar and traveled to Bulawayo to meet with Dr. D'Souza, and she left a day or two later for a tour of Victoria Falls and the Hwange Game Park, along with a whitewater rafting trip down the Zambezi River. I think she really enjoyed her trip and thanked me for helping with the arrangements. I gave her a *Book of Mormon* with my testimony in it on the plane ride home.

While on this third trip to Zimbabwe, I contracted cholera and nearly died of dehydration when I momentarily forgot about not drinking the water and added ice cubes from the hotel ice machine to my soda pop. I became sick the next morning whilst assisting Dr. D'Souza in his operating room, alternating vomiting with severe diarrhea, at one point sitting on the toilet with a basin in my lap and spewing from both ends at once. At last, I cleaned up and staggered to the postop area where a saintly anesthetist gave me a World Health

Organization cholera cocktail to drink and started an IV which literally saved my life. A few days later, in grateful appreciation, I performed successful radial keratotomy surgery to cure this angelic anesthetist's 8.00 diopters of myopia.

One of the more striking examples of faith and spirituality was noted in the example of a sixteen-year-old Zimbabwean girl who was born with severely crossed eyes. She was an outcast in her village (in African culture, if someone is thought to be possessed of the devil, the tribal chief takes a large stone and throws or casts the stone as far as he can from the outer most village hut, and that is where the "outcasts" need to set up their hut) because of her condition; and when she heard an American eye surgeon would be visiting, she convinced her mother to walk with her for sixty kilometers (about twenty-five miles), completely confident that she could be helped. Her eyes were successfully straightened, and she returned to her village where she was examined by the tribal chief, who danced around her chanting and sprinkling goat's blood and pronounced her healed by his actions. She was so happy to return with a new self-esteem and to a normal life. She later sent me the nicest note, telling me she "even had a boyfriend now."

Another interesting patient was a blind older gentleman with cataracts from an outlying village who had a large family to take care of him. I asked him the obvious question: "Why do you want to have surgery on your eyes?"

"Because of the animals," was his reply.

"Oh, so you can see all the beautiful African animals, like the giraffes, the lions, the elephants, and rhinos?" I could understand that.

"No, so they do not eat me," he corrected me.

Now that's a reason for cataract surgery I'd never heard of in the USA!

It was on this trip that I also had difficulty with logistics. I had promised a *Book of Mormon* with my family picture and testimony for each patient I operated on. There were going to be 124 books needed. I only brought twenty with me, and I needed to buy over 100 more. Unfortunately, my last day in country had arrived on a

Sunday, and the local Saints were willing to follow up and place the family photos and testimonies inside and distribute the books if I could get more of them.

We called the mission office and were told there was nothing that could be done since the office was closed on Sunday.

Then I remembered the scripture from Mark 3:4 about whether it was better to do good or evil on the Sabbath and asked one of the Neald girls to beg the mission president again if we could buy the books and also if they might mention that scripture and remind him that my flight home left Sunday night. He immediately opened the mission home, and we got the books. Mission accomplished! Next time, I'll be better prepared.

Remember Ephraim in chapter 16? Six months after this mission to Zimbabwe, I received a letter notifying me that Ephraim and his wife had been baptized, all because I had kept my word and returned to Zimbabwe. I felt immense gratitude to my Heavenly Father that Ephraim had the integrity and faith to follow through with the missionary lessons and join the church. The Deans (both missionary dentists from San Diego) sent me a picture of Brother and Sister Ephraim and their daughter Pridemore on their baptism day.

CHAPTER 21

FOURTH MISSION TO AFRICA (NIGERIA)

The Church of Jesus Christ of Latter-day Saints Dr. Kunle Hassan with two "bodyguards" in Lagos, Nigeria

n 1996, after two years and three trips to Indonesia, I was asked to return to Africa to help perform and teach the very first refractive (radial keratotomy) eye surgery in that nation. I didn't really

127

think too much about it, but I was cognizant that medical history was about to be made as it was in Zimbabwe in 1993 with my introduction of the first phaco and no-stitch cataract operations in that nation.

Dr. Kunle Hassan, also a member of the Church of Jesus Christ of Latter-day Saints living in Lagos, would be my contact. He had learned of me from Dr. Bill Jackson at Deseret International (now Charity Vision International) and asked if I would be willing to come and teach RK and no-stitch cataract surgery at his Eye Foundation Hospital in Ikeja, Lagos, Nigeria.

There would also be an opportunity to staff the resident eye cases and participate as a major guest speaker in the Annual Lagos Review Course sponsored by the University of Nigeria School of Medicine-Lagos and the Eye Foundation Hospital. I was asked to give lectures on cataract surgery, oculoplastic surgery, and radial keratotomy. The press had been informed that a new eye surgery would be performed for the very first time in Nigeria and the equivalent of a *60 Minutes* documentary film crew and reporter like Nigeria's answer to Peter Jennings or Dan Rather would interview Dr. Hassan and me after the operation.

Kunle faxed me ahead of time and asked what criteria would be best in selecting the first patient for RK in Nigeria.

I told him, "If you can find a young woman in her midtwenties with about a minus 5.00 diopter nearsighted prescription and minimal astigmatism and realistic expectations, that would be great."

That's exactly what he found—the perfect patient! She also had a very happy positive personality and outlook.

Dr. Hassan asked me to perform the surgery on her first eye and in the "see one, do one, teach one" fashion, he did her second eye. Both eyes were immediately clear, and she could see. The next day, she and the office were floating off the earth when her vision measured 20/20 in both eyes without glasses. She was so happy, and Dr. Hassan was excited to see the new technology and a successful result.

Happy first RK surgery patient in Nigeria (above).
Nigeria's *60 Minutes* news team (below) with Dr. Hassan.

As a fellow member of the Church of Jesus Christ of Latter-day Saints, I felt honored to be invited to Dr. Hassan's home to stay rather than a hotel. Dr. Hassan lived a short ten-minute drive from his clinic and had two bodyguards. When we arrived at his home, the most striking thing was the twelve-foot brick wall surrounding his entire compound with razor wire in a three-foot roll on top.

"For the burglars," he commented.

"We have a real problem with thieves here," he lamented.

As we entered Dr. Hassan's home, I could feel the concern. His family had been moved to the USA and was living in St. Louis whilst Dr. Hassan stayed in Nigeria for three months at a time. Then he was allowed "home" to St. Louis for six weeks with his family before commuting back to Nigeria, for another three months' work.

This arrangement allowed safety for his family. The newspaper in Lagos said in its headline, during my visit, that "the youth of Nigeria today are learning three trades or professions: murder, extortion, and kidnapping." It was a very dangerous place.

Still in the midst of this turmoil and trouble, there were civilized, educated, and refined people doing their best to help Nigerian society.

One was a psychiatry doctor who had been the past head of the World Health Organization. He invited Dr. Hassan and me over for dinner or "tea" one evening. He was a Black Nigerian man married to a White woman from, of all places, Birmingham, England, where I had served my mission twenty years before. They were quite formal but very kind and perhaps the most refined people to this day that I have ever met anywhere in the world and living in one of the most lawless places on earth.

During the time I was in Nigeria, the US secretary of state had issued a warning to travelers that Nigeria's Lagos Airport was not secure, and travelers who went to that country did so at considerable risk and without the approval of the US State Department. It was a little disconcerting to see that sign as I left home for my overseas destination. I soon found out why.

As I left the airport and walked outside to search for Dr. Hassan, my host, a young Nigerian man approached me and asked if I needed a taxi. "Oh no, thank you. I have a friend meeting me here." "No, MON, you don't understand. You DO need a taxi!" And with that, he pulled an AK-47 rifle from behind his back and pressed the barrel firmly against my forehead. He was shocked that I didn't react. "Oh, I guess I do need a taxi," I calmly replied (one of the signs of a person having a past near-death experience is that they no longer fear death).

Just then, Dr. Hassan appeared and yelled at the young man in Ibu (the tribal language), and he backed away, apologizing.

I was transported around Lagos in the back of an ambulance with a white sheet placed over my head to simulate a dead body. The guards at checkpoints wanted nothing to do with a dead body, so we were immediately waved through rather than stopped for bribes. Also on this trip, while I was in Lagos, an American obstetrician was killed when he would not relinquish his passport to muggers. The final shock occurred on the night before my flight left for home. On the same road to the airport and at the exact time I would be traveling the following night, a car was blown up, killing all the occupants.

Dr. Hassan was accustomed to the danger as evidenced by his daily prayers: "Dear Heavenly Father, we are so thankful that John and I were not killed today. That no one shot us or stabbed us or kidnapped us. We plead and beg of Thee that Thou wilt allow us to finish this day alive if it be thy will, that John may return home to his family, and that I may live to see my family again. We are thankful to be of service to thy children and hope Thou wilt bless us to be instruments in thy hands to do thy works. We plead again for our lives if it be thy will, and please bless this free-range chicken and sweet potatoes and rice that they will nourish us. We are grateful for them. And bless our families whilst we are away, in the name of Jesus Christ. Amen." How's that for a sincere prayer?

The free-range chicken was served in this manner. I was asked if I liked chicken, and then a huge platter about twenty inches around and piled nearly a foot high was brought out.

"You've got to be kidding?" I asked. "I could never eat all that."

Perplexed looks by Dr. Hassan and his bodyguards. I soon found out why. Free-range chickens are just that. They are not feed pellets or grain and fattened up like here in the USA. They have to range freely over the land and try to find whatever they can eat to stay alive. They had almost no meat on their bones, and a platter described earlier would just barely satisfy an average man.

One of the dishes I happily brought back from Nigeria and introduced to my family the day I returned was fried plantain. You can buy them in the grocery stores here, and they look like very large bananas, only pink inside.

You leave the skin on and cut them into small slices transversely and then peel off the skin before deep-frying them in olive or canola oil with a sprinkle of salt and sugar on them. Kind of tastes like banana chips, only chewy and good!

After bringing over an entire instrument set to perform radial keratotomy complete with tabletop micrometer microscope, diamond knives, and markers, along with all the teaching videos and slides I could round up, I left Nigeria very light with the few clothes I brought along that could be squeezed into my overnight bag which had transported cornea transplants and intraocular lens implants.

One heart-wrenching case was performing a cornea transplant, along with a cataract removal, on a gentleman with severe high blood pressure who developed a near-expulsive hemorrhage with vitreous pressure tenting up the lens capsule and eventually requiring me to perform a vitrectomy to relieve the high eye pressure enough so I could close his eye and fit an IOL inside. Miraculously, he saw the 20/200 "E" the day after surgery and did well. This man who was blind in both eyes from a mine explosion rapidly improved to 20/60 by the time I had to leave for home. He was so thrilled to see again. It was in Lagos, Nigeria, that I was shot at for the first and only time on a medical mission. This occurred as Dr. Hassan and I were walking from his clinic to lunch when he suddenly turned and shouted "John, get down!"

"Why?"

He shoved my shoulders down as I heard a bullet whiz past my right ear with a characteristic *whooshing* sound. We ran to the restaurant and narrowly escaped death.

The author with Dr. Kunle Hassan at the Eye
Foundation Hospital, Ikeja, Lagos, Nigeria, 1996

CHAPTER 22

NEARLY CURED OF TRAVEL

When my British Airways flight arrived safely back to London Gatwick Airport, I leaned down and kissed the Tarmac. Honest. I was so relieved to be back "in civilization."

No one was pointing any guns at my head, and no one was being shot nearby. I still had the "Nigerian Twitch" (this is a sudden and continuous one-hundred-millisecond turn of the head to the far right or left repeated every thirty seconds or so—performed to watch one's back in case thugs or kidnappers were about to strike); but after a day or two at "home" in London and the British Midlands, I relaxed and the Nigerian Twitch left as mysteriously as it appeared shortly after the taxi incident at Lagos Airport.*

Perhaps subconsciously, the trip to Nigeria affected me more than on the surface.

I was very relieved to be alive and almost euphoric to be "home" in England once again. I quickly made my way to baggage claim and then on to the rental car lot where a Sterling coupe was waiting for me.

I was soon on the M-25 motorway and then onto the familiar M-6 headed to the Midlands of England. I touched base with Bishop Woods and his family in Walsall and then went shopping at the Walsall market and town center. It was so wonderful to hear the familiar accents as I popped in to a "Wright's the Baker" shop and ordered, in my biggest Western US accent, "One of them there iced Banberry hot cross buns and a vanilla slice and also how 'bout one of them there orannnggg joooseez."

Needless to say, the entire crew came out from the back of the shop to see the Yank who had just arrived. Boy, did they have fun trying to get me to repeat everything so all the staff could hear me talk "American." I repeated the order at least three times until everyone was laughing hard, and I made my way outside to the empty bench in the middle of the mall. I soon finished my treasure and just couldn't stop smiling. Soaking up the ambiance of Walsall, England, my home for nearly eighteen months from 1975 to 1977. It was fun to be back!

A friendly Bobby (British policeman) soon appeared and started a conversation with me.

"Yer not from 'round these parts, eh, mate?"

"No, sir, I'm from the USA. I was a mission'ry here twenty years ago, and it's so good to be back after all these years," I replied.

"Oh, for the Mormons?"

"Right," I said.

"Lovely church they've built down by the M-6 motorway."

"Thank you. I helped build that chapel in 1975," I stated with a touch of heartfelt satisfaction.

"I know some Mormons." The Bobby went on: "Lovely people, just lovely. They've quite a good reputation in these parts as well. What do they believe in different from us, then?"

I went on for a little while about the plan of salvation and families are forever and the *Book of Mormon* and a living prophet today. The Bobby then realized he was on duty and excused himself with a smile and said, "Welcome back. I do hope you enjoy your stay."

The Church of Jesus Christ of Latter-day Saints had arrived (in **my** mind)! What a difference from 1975 when no one knew much about us. "Walsall" knew where the Church of Jesus Christ of Latter-day Saints chapel was, and we had a good reputation in the community. I was overcome with emotion and felt vindicated. My mission along with the work of the other Church of Jesus Christ of Latter-day Saints missionaries and members had not been in vain!

Then it was off to visit people. I looked up Peter and Kathleen Russell, near Cannock Chase (forest). They were home, and I got to meet Ian, now twenty-seven years old. He was a computer specialist working for a large national grocery store chain. Debbie was a nanny working in New York City! We had a wonderful visit and went out for dinner.

Sunday, I attended church in Walsall Ward. The building I helped construct twenty years earlier looked beautiful; and I was asked to speak in Sacrament meeting, teach a Sunday school lesson, and give a priesthood lesson in the High Priest group all on missionary work. Monday, I returned home.

CHAPTER 23

PRESIDENT OF THE EYEMDS

Returning from Nigeria and England, I found a difficult situation with a new clinic and surgery center just completed and severe financial pressures. We had chosen an architect who used "creative billing" practices according to my attorney and a builder who was consistently behind schedule by more than three months. During this time I was also serving in the mission presidency of the Federal Way Stake. I had served for the previous two years as a counselor in the mission presidency, and when the current president moved to San Diego, I was interviewed and asked to succeed him as president.

It was an overwhelming task. I quickly chose counselors, Steve Howell and Mitch Toland (retained) with Rick Schafer as counselor/secretary; and we divided the twelve units of the stake into fourths so each one of us would be responsible for three church units. Each member of the presidency would be responsible for his home ward (which we would attend anyhow and could keep an eye on things) and two neighboring units often in the same building. It was nearly a full-time job keeping up with and typing the monthly reports.

We were united as a presidency and could feel good things about to happen. We had a good cadre of ward mission leaders and stake missionaries in each unit. We spoke in meetings and had monthly stake mission training seminars. Baptisms began to happen in record numbers. The success was overwhelming. We were approaching a hundred convert baptisms for the Federal Way Stake for the year. Then Satan was unleashed. One member of our presidency lost his job, another had health problems, another had financial problems, and I had trials like I've never known, including getting a call from the children's hospital telling me to come right away because the doctors felt my anorexic daughter would not survive the night, among other family members' illnesses.

With all the turmoil at home, it looked like I had definitely served my final medical mission overseas. What point was there in serving humanity all over the world if my home and personal life had fallen apart? Again there was discouragement and much soul-searching. No medical trips were undertaken for almost five years. During this time, I busied myself with other projects.

I was a consultant for several pharmaceutical and eye surgery instrument companies. At the suggestion of one of my resident doctors at the University of Washington, I designed an eye surgery instrument the American Surgical Instrument company named the **Jarstad Refractive Cataract Surgery Incision Marker,** which was marketed worldwide with much success under an advertisement in medical journals under a banner with my picture as "the Mark of Excellence."

I spoke in several medical scientific meetings. In the fall of 1998, I felt an inspired obligation to run for office in my state ophthalmology specialty society. I called the director's office and spoke to Kory Diemert, the secretary of the organization. The only office without a candidate was president at that time, though she had heard of several doctors who were considering entering the race. "Am I qualified to do that?" I asked. She indicated that she thought I should run, so I said, "Okay, what the heck? I'll apply."

The voting was 150 to 3 for the next highest candidate, and so I was elected president of the Washington Academy of Eye Physicians and Surgeons. Fortunately for me and especially for the academy, the new president does not assume office the first year but has an apprentice year as president elect to attend all the board meetings and leadership training provided by the national ophthalmology organization—the American Academy of Ophthalmology. The first year was spent attending every eye leadership conference I could find to prepare myself for the coming year.

My tenure occurred during a pivotal time for ophthalmology in the state of Washington. A past president introduced himself to me at a Seattle Sonics professional NBA basketball game and stated, "I'm sure glad you are president this year and not me."

"Why is that?" I queried.

"Well, everyone knows the optometrists are going to get surgery privileges this year in the legislature, and you are going to be the one who will always be remembered as the president who was in charge when they did."

The gauntlet was dropped or flung. I vowed right then and there that it would NOT happen on my watch. I worked with our lobbyists and appointed an Internet specialist to communicate with the membership to establish a grassroots legislative alert hotline by e-mail. I met with the optometrist's president to size up what their plans and strategies were. I gave it my full effort and even met with our association's attorney and also helped to hire a public relations firm to educate our ophthalmology board members on media training and relations so we could be effective communicators on the airwaves if the bills in the legislature went out of committee and were winding their way to the governor's desk.

Our state senator Tracy Eide (D-Federal Way), a brilliant woman in her late thirties or early forties and a very honest and capable legislator, called me one day in July to invite me to a fundraiser at her home for Governor Gary Locke's reelection campaign. I would have an opportunity to meet with the governor briefly and perhaps ask him a question or two. I was excited to go and particularly with a mandate by my EyeMD colleagues to try to influence the governor or at least plead our cause. I had experienced political fundraisers before, "pressing flesh" with constituents for my uncle Glenn

Jarstad's mayoral campaigns over the years, and remembered how reluctant the invitees were to intrude on the time of the candidate.

The governor's "handlers" were in attendance and ensured that no one citizen monopolized Mr. Locke's time. I was introduced by Senator Eide in this fashion: "Governor Locke, I'd like to introduce you to one of our outstanding citizens of Federal Way, Dr. John Jarstad. Dr. Jarstad is a huge supporter of our schools and has done many charitable projects for the school district with the clothing bank and eyeglass donations."

"Honor to meet you, Dr. Jarstad."

"Very pleased to meet you, Governor Locke. I'm very involved in scouting and understand you are an eagle scout. I'm sure this is a busy time of year for you, but I did have just a couple of questions."

I proceeded to get him on the record to say that he opposed giving surgery privileges to the optometrists. The full text of our conversation I reported in the fall issue of the state ophthalmology newspaper where it was the headline of the front page.

After a long, hard-fought, tough battle, the optometry bills passed overwhelmingly in the House but never made it to the floor of the Senate for a vote (thanks to Senator Eide and also Senator Sid Morrison from Aberdeen and Westport whom I called and left a message that a former Westport charter boat skipper and deckhand (now eye surgeon) thought the bill (giving surgery and all drug-prescribing privileges to the inadequately trained optometrists) was a bad idea.

My watch was secure. As my year concluded, I was given the president's gavel and the Humanitarian of the Year Award at the annual EyeMD meeting by the Washington Academy of Eye Physicians and Surgeons for my medical mission trips and for initiating, along with Kiwanis, the eyeglass and hearing aid drive, which, at that point, had collected over thirty thousand pairs of eyeglasses to be distributed to third world countries through Deseret International Foundation.

In my final speech, I thanked those who had helped me get through the difficult year as president—my wife; Kory Diemert (promoted to be our new executive secretary now that I had streamlined the office and accepted Mr. Steven Hanson's resignation—another difficult decision and tough accomplishment in a time of budget tightening); my cardiologist (I had suffered a cardiac episode and required angiography on December 26, 2000, immediately after performing the last of thirty-nine patients' LASIK operations. The test found no blockage, only coronary artery spasm with the additional finding I had no left heart circulation—amazing considering I had been a state finalist in the two-mile run [9:47] in high school and a state champion and school record holder in cross-country distance running); and the doctors and staff at my clinic who filled in for me when state eye issues intruded. I apologized for anyone I had offended particularly with my MBA semester thesis on "price elasticity in LASIK eye surgery" that I had implemented to compete with the cut price Canadian laser eye surgeons who were taking all our business to Canada.

I told the group I had learned firsthand that $499 per eye for LASIK eye surgery was predatory pricing and lost money. I also bemoaned the fact that due to the critical optometry political wars, I was not able to carry out my desired agenda of working on charitable projects in the inner cities and educating the public more on eye diseases and screening through the media.

At the conclusion of my term, I felt humbled by the fact that I had been able to complete my year as president in a dignified and competent manner and that some good things had been accomplished. It was somewhat disappointing that I did not succeed in accomplishing what I had hoped for in the way of charity work and public education (even though I was able to use new associations to switch the society's public education advertising from an infrequently viewed cable TV network to KOMO TV 4—my dad's old station and the highest-rated Seattle station at the time—and its Eastern Washington affiliates for less money and greater successful coverage). My wild ride in politics was over.

CHAPTER 24

DISTRICT CHAIRMAN – BSA

The years from 1997 to 2001 brought amazing growth of the clinic business and total devotion to family. A few weeks after being released from stake mission duties in 1997, my stake president asked if I would serve the community and the Church of Jesus Christ of Latter-day Saints as district chairman of the North Pierce South King County (NoPiSoKi) District of the Boy Scouts of America. I was excited to serve, and while I felt totally inadequate in this high-profile community position (I had never made it past second class in scouting due to my being beat up at scout camp one summer and then leaving scouts to work in Dad's ski and motorcycle shop about age twelve), I accepted.

My chief concern was fundraising and coordinating activities between the Church of Jesus Christ of Latter-day Saints and non-church units and volunteers. There had been some very negative feelings between the two groups, and I don't think anyone realized I was LDS on the board for many months. I proposed a change in meeting venue from the Church of Jesus Christ of Latter-day Saints building and then the Episcopal Church to my medical office (a neutral site), and several great things were accomplished during our service together.

CJ Gaddis, Bill Richards, and I made up the district executives; and the volunteer board members were some of the finest men and women of Federal Way. We achieved our fundraising goals each year and our membership drive goals thanks to Mr. Steven Smith, a local meat cutter for Safeway. We were named quality district all three years of my service, but more importantly, I felt we were all able to help the district get back on track and achieve unity and cooperation between the Church of Jesus Christ of Latter-day Saints and non-church units (though there were some trying times as some board members resigned after my appointment when they learned I was LDS).

Shortly after my cardiac episode in 2001, I asked for a release as district chairman for health reasons (I was also taking an online MBA program; and the combination of full-time medical practice, scouts, family, and church took its toll). I enjoyed being a dad and made it a point to attend all possible track and cross-country meets, speech and debate tournaments, and ska band concerts that my children were involved in. My few weeks off were relaxing (I even took a last-minute three-day weekend trip to Hawaii alone and visited Robby at BYU Hawaii after my heart surgery); but that would be short-lived.

CHAPTER 25
FIRST MISSION TO INDONESIA

Island of Karimun at sunrise (above). Indonesian Navy PT boat (below). Note fifty-caliber machine gun on bow to deter "pirates."

While I had felt uneasy making additional trips to Africa due to the political instability, my attention now turned to Indonesia. After working with Deseret International (Charity Vision International) and my college friend Bill Jackson's father Dr. Bill Jackson Sr., I received a call from the older Dr. Jackson asking me if I would be interested in visiting Indonesia and participating in a humanitarian project there.

A Cataract Safari had been organized by the foundation of Suharto, the president of Indonesia. His charity foundation, Dharmais Perdami, invited me as the first non-Indonesian ophthalmologist to participate and arranged for us to visit outlying islands where no ophthalmology care was available and provide a week's worth of charity eye operations. There was an opportunity to teach the latest eye surgery at the University of Indonesia Medical School and work with the best doctors in that Southeast Asian country. It did sound intriguing. That was a part of the world I had never seen, and my yearly conference trips to Hawaii over the years for the Royal Hawaiian Eye Meetings made me curious to see what lay beyond the last Hawaiian island.

Soon after accepting the assignment, I began a fax machine correspondence with a Dr. Istiantoro of Jakarta Indonesia (the Internet was not yet widely available).

Dr. Istiantoro was the chairman of the Department of Ophthalmology at the University of Indonesia in Jakarta, is a Christian, and had a founding interest in the Jakarta Eye Centre, the premier private eye clinic in all of Indonesia. Jakarta Eye Centre was a world-class facility which I would later pattern my more modest Evergreen Eye Center in Federal Way after. Istiantoro sounded very competent and hospitable in his faxes and assured me that I was welcome to participate in the Katarak Safari to Pulau Karimun (Karimun Islands) just across the Strait of Malacca from Singapore in Northwest Indonesia.

Istiantoro provided me a list of items I could bring but assured me all the required equipment was available locally.

He asked if I could lecture to the medical school and faculty in the eye department on the latest developments in cataract surgery. I selected a talk on no-stitch cataract surgery, which I had helped pioneer, along with the foldable Allergan Medical Optics lens, which I, along with the other original sixty EyeMD researchers, started studying in 1987.

My wife, PS, accompanied me on the trip; and we arrived in Jakarta just in time to meet up with the other MDs and catch our flight to Batam where we transferred to a military PT boat complete with a working fifty-caliber machine gun placement on the bow and headed on to Pulau Karimun.

We were fairly tired after twenty-five hours of flying; however the excitement kept us both going. After about three hours in the boat, we arrived to a hero's welcome on the tiny island of Karimun about thirty square miles in size.

I was not prepared for the welcome reception we received on the island of Karimun. The Islamic village elders dressed in their finest robes and hats met us at the pier and welcomed our party formally to the island. Dr. Istiantoro selected me to accompany him first off the boat, and we were met with pomp and ceremony. We were dressed by the village elders in a batik hat and lavalava and then given a betel nut, which Istiantoro told me to chew a couple of times and then remove from my mouth with my hand discretely and throw in the water. It was very bitter.

We were then led by two young Muslim boys holding palm fronds in a parade up the pier, through the main street of town, and into the village square where a martial arts display was given on our behalf. We then proceeded to the district governor's mansion where we were served fruit juice, sweet pineapple cakes, and Jell-O. We were introduced to the local dignitaries and given more juices and food. We could hear a band rehearsing in the back of the mansion but thought nothing more of it. At last, after being awake for perhaps thirty hours straight, we were taken to our hotel to get settled before dinner.

We showered and soon fell asleep. We woke up and found it to be about 7:00 p.m. and checked in at the hotel desk. A message invited us back to the governor's mansion for a party, and we were quickly transported there by a bicycle rickshaw device.

We learned that the best ten bands and singing groups from the neighboring islands had been rehearsing for several days in preparation of our arrival and had prepared a rock concert of American songs in our honor. How embarrassing it would have been to have slept and missed it.

These bands were outstanding! They could cover any band or group in the USA and, in many cases, sounded better. Unbelievable singers, particularly, the women. About thirty minutes after we arrived, the MC took the stage and invited "our American guests" to come forward.

"Now we would be honored if Dr. John and Mrs. John would entertain us with your native song from your tribe." We were on the spot!

PS was completely tone-deaf, and I hadn't sung a song in years. Even in my high school garage band, I was the bass player and didn't ever sing. I motioned to the MC.

"Please, my wife doesn't sing."

"Okay, even better yet, how about performing your native tribal dance?"

For the life of me, I couldn't think of anything that I would classify as our native Washington tribal dance.

"Wait a minute," I said as inspiration hit. "We could do the West Coast Swing!"

PS and I had taken a Latin dance class at BYU when we were engaged and still remembered how to do it. We told the MC we would try to do our native dance but that we would request a swing or jazz number.

The band quickly obliged, and we were soon spinning and dancing the West Coast Swing. I don't think anyone on that Indonesian Island had ever seen an American, much less American dancing.

The Indonesians usually do not move their upper body at all when they dance, so seeing those crazy Americans flinging each other around and pointing to the floor and sky alternatively must have been quite a sight. We soon had a crowd of mimics surrounding us laughing at our strange dance and trying feverishly to imitate our every move.

When the song ended, we were given a standing ovation by the crowd of perhaps four hundred invited quests. We pulled it off! Whew! What a relief! We listened to the next three bands and then excused ourselves to go catch up on some much-needed rest. It was an incredible trip, and we hadn't even been in Indonesia for twenty-four hours!

The next morning, we awoke at 7:00 a.m., dressed, and went down to the hotel lobby and out on to the bamboo deck overlooking the brown sea surrounding Karimun Island.

The unusual thing I noted right away was that there was virtually no tide at the equator. So no waves either. The water lapped easily at the piers, and dead fish and other flotsam and jetsam stagnated around the sleepy island, which depended on the rare tropical storm to cleanse its surrounding waters.

After a nearly raw soft-boiled egg and a piece of toast and freshly squeezed local orange juice, we were transported to the community health center on the island and began preparing for surgery. I had been able to borrow a Mentor phaco unit again and was anxious to begin teaching the resident doctors my latest technique for cataract removal.

We set up the Katarak Safari in a local health unit on the island and began working out of two rooms equipped with a microscope that reminded me of one of those dissection scopes they use in a high school biology class which was mounted with a C-clamp on a large table that the patient would lie down on.

Probably very uncomfortable. The eye surgical instruments were sterilized by placing them inside a ten-quart pressure cooker which was placed on a hot plate (at least an improvement over cold alcohol sterilization we witnessed in Africa). The instruments were shared between two tables and were sterilized at the beginning of the day and at the end of the day after all the operations were over. I guess one just hoped that the patient before you did not have AIDS or any communicable infection.

As I began to set up for surgery, I placed the Mentor camera-bag-sized phaco machine on an adjoining small table and plugged it in to go to work. Immediately, I heard a *pop*, and we all smelled burning plastic. The machine was 110 V, and Indonesia was 220 V wired. The plug fit, and I was told before I left the USA that there was an automatic conversion from 110 to 220 V, but apparently, this particular machine did not have that device installed yet. The phaco unit was ruined and unusable. Here I had such great hopes of introducing the latest cataract surgery in Indonesia, but from here on, I would be limited to doing cataract surgery the old-fashioned way with a large 11 mm incision and seven stitches as opposed to a 3 to 4 mm incision and no stitches. The surgery time would also be affected by the loss of the machine. Instead of taking ten minutes, each case would be twenty to forty minutes. Still there was no turning back. Some of these patients had sailed from outlying islands in small open boats to have their sight restored, and we owed them our best efforts.

Our team began operating, and the first couple of operations went fine. Then as I was beginning the capsulotomy analogous to removing the skin of a peach with the nucleus of the cataract similar to the pit of a peach, suddenly, with only touching the capsule to begin, the entire capsular bag and lens went south, deep into the vitreous of the eye. Try as I might, it was not retrievable. I had heard of eye surgeons positioning a patient on their side or facedown for a few minutes to move the cataract back near the front of the eye (this was tried), but nothing worked.

Dr. Istiantoro, sensing my frustration and delay, came over to take a look.

"Oh, you've couched that one. Good. You are all finished."

I had couched the lens (pushed the cataract lens back into the vitreous gel and out of the way); and since it had been held by at most two or three zonules (the lens zonules are like springs holding a trampoline to a frame in holding the lens capsule taut against the surrounding sclera), it was now floating freely in the vitreous cavity out of the line of sight.

"Are you going to put in a lens?" Istiantoro inquired.

"Do we have any anterior chamber lenses?" I asked.

Someone found one, and I was able to implant an artificial lens and help restore vision. Hopefully there would be no inflammation from the cataract lying in the back of the eye. Otherwise, it would be a long trip to see a retina specialist for this poor man.

Another memorable patient was a middle-aged woman who sailed for twenty-four hours in a small open boat to have vision restored from pterygia (a winglike fleshy growth) that had grown from the conjunctiva overlying her sclera to completely cover her cornea in both eyes. She was completely blind from these sunlight-induced growths. It took over an hour to scrape these growths off her corneas without the aid of a mechanical polishing burr available at home, but the surgery was successful, and her faith and courage were rewarded with the return of her eyesight after three days of painful healing.

We completed over four hundred successful cataract surgeries during our four days on Karimun. We worked hard from about 8:00 a.m. until 5:00 p.m. or 6:00 p.m., usually without a break except during Islamic call to prayer.

At these times, the Muslims in our group (nearly everyone except Istiantoro, who was Catholic) would quickly change into their prayer robes and find a closet or adjacent room next to the operating room and bow to the floor in the direction of the holy city for prayer. I remember how impressed I was that this was done without apology and with fervent dedication (and sometimes we are embarrassed to bow our heads and say a silent prayer at a restaurant).

In the evenings, we would go out for dinner to one of the local restaurants and try the local delicacies. Rambutan (a fruit that looked like a ten times larger than normal strawberry that one cut into, and inside was a shiny cream-colored fruit that looked like a hardboiled egg), star fruit, stink fruit, (of course) pineapple, guava, and mango. Rice and fish were plentiful along with chicken and beef satay (no pork because of the Muslim restrictions, which we respected).

After dinner, we went on two occasions to a karaoke bar and rented a private booth to enjoy soft drinks and sing. The machine had a good variety of both English and Indonesian songs. The Indonesian eye docs would sing the English and American rock songs, and I would try to sing the Indonesian ones. It was hilarious!

One of the Beatles songs lost a little in translation coming across as "I want to hold your hand. Oh yes, I want to hold it."

One can only imagine how I must have sounded trying to sing in Bahasa Indonesian. We all laughed so hard that we could hardly stand it, so we returned to the hotel.

The nights were hot and muggy, especially as we were right under the equator. As in Africa, we were soaked in sweat by the end of the day. A shower was a welcome way to end the day before retiring.

As we reached our final morning before catching a ride in several white minivans to the Karimun pier, we began to unload all the food; drink; and emergency supplies like gum, juice packs, and jerky that we would no longer need as we headed for home.

A couple of young boys, about ten and twelve, were the main beneficiaries of our elaborate preparation in packing enough to sustain our lives before we left home just in case there was no edible food or drink on the trip. I think they may have sold most of the stuff, but we threw in a couple of soccer balls for good measure.

We left a personalized autographed copy of the *Book of Mormon* with the customs agent who was one of the few people on the island to speak decent English, and he seemed appreciative to have a souvenir of the American doctor's visit.

At the pier, we were met by a smaller crowd than at our arrival, but there were handmade signs thanking the team for coming and volunteering for the Katarak Safari. The last image we had was the group of local doctors and nurses and a few grateful patients waving and holding up a bright-pink ten-foot-by-three-foot sign saying, "*Selemat jalan and terima kasih*" ("Goodbye until we meet again, and thank you").

We were all fairly exhausted and slept part of the way on the boat back to Batam. Istiantoro and the other team members (except TD, PS, and I) went on an overnight trip to Singapore. We stayed put and met them in Batam.

We shopped in Batam and found some pretty good bargains on clothes and souvenirs. The shop girls had fun asking us questions and trying out their English. Kids stopped us in the street and wanted to just touch us or my strawberry-blond hair or take our picture. Some asked if we were movie stars or from Hollywood. Probably the first Americans many had ever seen.

We arrived back in Jakarta where we stayed in a Wisma (a bed-and-breakfast type arrangement), and I prepared to give a lecture at the University of Indonesia the next morning.

I remember debating with myself what I should wear after spending the previous week wearing batik shirts and shorts or khaki pants and sandals. Then I thought, *Okay, I'm an American, so I should dress as an American.* I put on my white shirt and conservative tie and navy blue suit.

Good thing too. I was expecting a third world medical facility with maybe an airplane hangar-type medical school lecture hall. When we arrived at the University of Indonesia School of Medicine, we were led to the lecture hall, and as I walked in, it was impressive! Mahogany and teak wood panels, theater-like seating, and all the best audio-video electronics Asia could offer.

My slide presentation worked fine, but when I attempted to show video of my small-incision cataract technique, the tape player didn't work! Asia ran on PAL, and unfortunately, I brought VHS tapes. Eventually, someone rounded up a VHS player, and I was able to show my videos.

As I finished, I made a presentation to Dr. Istiantoro, who was chairman of the Department of Ophthalmology at the time. He was presented with a giant official University of Washington husky football team umbrella.

In return, I was awarded a really neat carved, wooden blowgun from Iryan Jaya and the Lecturer's Medal from the University of Indonesia. I was overwhelmed. Such a very formal setting, and I was so thankful I made the right choice that day on what to wear.

As we prepared to return home, we made a short shopping trip to Pasaraya Big and Beautiful department store and bought a few souvenirs, and then we were off for home.

Looking back, I will never forget the welcome we received on Pulau Karimun. It has stayed with me to this day. Whenever I get discouraged, I think of the welcome waiting for us on that tiny island. I felt impressed that maybe that is what heaven or paradise will be like. A big welcome with everyone whom we may have helped in our lives, along with all our loved ones, ancestors, and relatives cheering us, "Welcome home." I felt a deep spiritual impression that this was a message to give me hope and courage. I hope it's like that.

The Arrival Ceremony at Pulau Karimun (above)
Reception in the town square (below).

CHAPTER 26

SECOND MISSION
TO INDONESIA

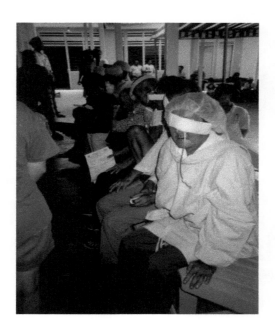

'll have to quit attending medical conventions. It seems that whenever I go, I'm invited to give another lecture. Before we left Jakarta, the Indonesian doctors were already discussing plans for me to attend the Asia Pacific Ophthalmology Meeting in Bali, Indonesia, about eight months later. It sounded like a heavenly venue for a medical meeting, so I tentatively told them I would come, and they invited me to speak and participate on a speaker's panel with some of the noted ophthalmologists in the world who would be attending.

Dr. Bill Jackson put me in touch with a gentleman on a neighboring island, Brother Ben Copley, who was the only member of the Church of Jesus Christ of Latter-day Saints on the island of Lombok. We arrived in Denpassar, Bali, and checked into our hotel on the beach. We planned to arrive two days early so we could do a little sightseeing and shopping before the conference began. We also went parasailing at the resort, and I remember looking at the harness with these worn-out leather straps that were hanging by threads and could snap off any moment and thinking:

"Do I really want to do this?"

The meeting began, and I enjoyed presenting my slides and video and participating on the international distinguished panel of experts for cataract surgery. I also spoke about my experiences as a patient after having had PRK (LASIK) laser surgery on both eyes two years earlier in a talk entitled "The Excimer's New Clothes." It was a novelty to have Americans there, and wherever we went, we attracted attention.

One of the greatest things about the Indonesian ophthalmology meetings is their "social program." Each night after the meetings, a traditional music program or rock concert and dance was planned. The Bali meeting featured an opening night gala with traditional Balinese dancers in full costume and traditional Balinese music.

Later in the week, we were invited to a dinner for all the speakers and dignitaries held at the resort restaurant. They had a great band, and about halfway through the evening, Istiantoro announced that "Dr. John Jarstad would be going up on stage to play with the band."

They handed me a bass guitar and plugged me in to the amp, and I selected "Funk 49" by the James Gang and played the bass line after telling the lead guitarist the chords. It was fun. Afterward, I gave each band member $5 (about 7,500 rupiahs) and a copy of the *Book of Mormon* in English with our family picture and testimony with a note of thanks telling them how great they were as musicians.

During the days on Bali's white sandy beaches, PS became quite the negotiator with the local salespeople. As we walked along the beach from the hotel, young men and a few older ones would come up and ask if we wanted to buy a watch, cigarette lighters, etc. They had faux Rolex watches that looked just like the $21,000 presidential models, selling them for $50.

I thought they looked great and bought one. Then they asked if we wanted more. PS began negotiating; and finally after several pleas of "C'mon, lady, you killing me," she bought ten more watches for a total of about $40 more. Four dollars apiece for ladies and men's "diamond" "Rolex" watches? Unbelievable (back in 1994, we were not aware of any restrictions of bringing "faux" merchandise home; today, there would likely be large fines for such action)!

As the convention drew to a close, it was time for school to begin for the four Jarstad children back in Federal Way, and PS flew home early so she could be there in time for the first day of school. I had made a commitment to visit Brother Ben Copley and meet with Dr. Farida Santiybowo, a highly educated lady ophthalmologist on the island of Lombok, just next door to Bali; so I said goodbye to PS and boarded a twin-prop cigar coffin plane for the twenty-minute flight from Bali to Lombok.

Dr. Farida and her husband, an ENT surgeon, met me at the airport; and I was impressed that there were so few cars on Lombok. I was taken to meet the district governor where I was introduced as a visiting eye professor from Seattle and treated royally once more. Then it was on to check in at the hotel.

The Sangiggi Beach Hotel was right on the water and consisted of some of the most beautiful scenery I had ever seen. Mentor Corporation had loaned me another phaco machine aptly named the "Odyssey," and this time, it did have the automatic conversion from 110 to 220 volts. I would teach Dr. Farida phaco and small-incision cataract surgery. Things went well. Mentor also sent over about a dozen of the first acrylic foldable lens implants to ever be implanted by an American surgeon (me) to try out. They worked perfectly.

Near the end of my trip, I remember giving a lecture to the hospital staff at Lombok General Hospital, and at the conclusion of the lecture, one of the internists asked me point-blank if they had a cataract patient who needed referral where in all of Indonesia would I recommend they be sent.

My answer was diplomatic and true: "I've spent the last two days with Dr. Farida, and she is one of the most gifted eye surgeon's I have ever worked with. You are very fortunate to have an ophthalmologist right here in Lombok with her skills and abilities, and I can recommend her highly."

That brought a palpable level of new esteem for Dr. Farida among her colleagues. Not that she didn't deserve it, but to have "one of the premier ophthalmologists in the world" (their words not mine) visit from the USA and pronounce her as one of the finest— well, it made her day, I'm sure, and went a long way to granting her the recognition and acclaim she deserved.

During this time, teaching in Lombok, my back, which had sustained a T-10 compression fracture in a motor vehicle accident three years before (I was rear-ended at a stoplight), began to act up. All the sitting on the plane plus sitting in an operating theater caused excruciating pain in my low back with additional sciatica radiating down my right leg. I cried out in pain at night and then the next day didn't see how I could go on. I turned to prayer, and the next day around the pool, I noticed they were offering massage. I thought it would be worth a try since that is how I recovered following the car accident in 1992. But could I afford it? When I found out it was only five dollars for a one-hour massage, I booked one the last two days I was there.

I met with Brother Copley, and he introduced me to a couple of young people who were investigating the Church of Jesus Christ of Latter-day Saints on the island. Because I was from the USA and a church member, he immediately assumed I knew all the general authorities and the twelve apostles personally. Even though I had met several of them as a missionary and Elder Neal A. Maxwell once babysat our children together with his grandchildren when we lived in Rochester Minnesota, I did not know them all personally as Brother Copley had thought.

He also spoke of an ancient language kept by the people on the north side of the island and wanted me to be sure and tell the general authorities about that when I "got back to Salt Lake."

On Sunday, the two of us met, and I administered the sacrament at his request. Since there was no organized Church of Jesus Christ of Latter-day Saints branch anywhere on the island, I assumed it was okay to do so (I should have contacted the mission president first, I later learned). It was a spiritual event, and the surrounds were beautiful beyond description. Outside my room were various trees and plants labeled with the name of the plant in Indonesian and English—for example, *guava* and *mango* trees, and there on the tree was the fruit. Amazing!

I returned to Jakarta and spent my last night at the Church of Jesus Christ of Latter-day Saints mission home before flying home, celebrating my fortieth birthday in Indonesia and having Subandriyo (at this time, the counselor to mission president, Dr. Vern Tueller) and his family sing "Happy Birthday" to me in Bahasa Indonesia. They also presented me with gifts including a carved blowgun and a beautiful batik quilt Steffi Subandriyo had made for us.

We assisted with a vision screening at the Jakarta Church of Jesus Christ of Latter-day Saints branch and gave away about 150 pairs of eyeglasses. We started the screening in the cultural hall where three copies of the *Book of Mormon* were set on a table with three increasing powers of reading glasses +1.25, +2.00, and +3.00.

We tested distance vision using the large print cover of the Church of Jesus Christ of Latter-day Saints *Ensign* magazine at about twenty feet, and if they could see that, we then took their reading vision with the *Book of Mormon*. Once the vision screening was completed, those who still could not see with glasses or who the screeners felt needed or wanted a more extensive exam were brought into the chapel where a table was set up with my examining instruments and lenses.

Dilating eye drops were instilled, and the patients were thoroughly examined. A group of people from the US and Canadian embassies also arrived telling the organizers that they'd seen a notice in the newspaper and wanted to stop by.

One had a serious retina condition and was referred by me to the Jakarta Eye Centre. Another young woman had a blind, painful, disfigured eye, and wanted to know if there was anywhere in SE Asia that she could go to have an artificial eye prosthesis (I had just finished talking to doctors from the Singapore National Eye Institute, and they had mentioned that they did offer that service). She was so appreciative of the referral and wrote later enclosing before-and-after photos telling me it had changed her life and that she (who at that time had "no hope") was soon to be married.

After the screening which also found a patient with a new vitreous hemorrhage, several with cataracts, and a cornea that needed transplanting, we headed back to the mission home. Additional Church of Jesus Christ of Latter-day Saints members arrived from outlying areas until 10:00 p.m., which we happily accommodated with exams, eyeglasses, and encouraging words.

When I returned, I called PS from the airport in Los Angeles and learned that PS's brother Scott and his stepson, David, had crashed in their small private plane in Midland, Texas, just after their first refueling stop. They had been on their way from Houston to see us and then fly on to a fishing trip in Alaska.

Tragically, both died in the crash. I was shocked and saddened and was surprised at how strong and unaffected emotionally PS seemed. She would be leaving for the funeral in Texas, and I stayed and looked after the kids. It was stressful preparing for construction of the Evergreen Eye Center building, but together, as a family, we got through it. Jessica, our oldest, was especially helpful getting the other kids ready for school and keeping tabs on everyone.

CHAPTER 27

NEW EYE SURGERY CENTER

Evergreen Eye Center with St. Francis Hospital in background.

Seeing the Jakarta Eye Centre was an epiphany. After buying land next to St. Francis Community Hospital in Federal Way in 1992, we were preparing to break ground for our new eye clinic as I returned from Indonesia. Could I borrow some of the ideas from the Jakarta Eye Centre, and would they translate here in the USA?

Just before the decision to move ahead, there was a day when over twenty patients were waiting outside my office in the hallway of the St. Francis Medical Office Building, because the original office had only twelve chairs in its waiting room. It seemed every patient that day told me, "You need a bigger waiting room, Doc," or "You need a bigger office!"

After many delays, in October 1994, we finally broke ground, and after many difficult months with a creative architect and his creative billing practices (my attorney's words), the building was near completion in December 1995.

It was an amazing place. Three floors. Over ten thousand square feet. Nearly an acre of land. After shelling out about $250,000 for drawings, permits, environmental, traffic, and feasibility studies, and another $1.75 million for construction, it would be nice to finally move in. With the extra room, it would be possible to bring in partners and hopefully see more patients. It would allow us to establish a "center of excellence" in eye surgery.

With all the efforts of planning, building, outfitting, and staffing a new eye center, I did not travel again until November of 1996 (see "Mission to Nigeria"). With teaching part-time at Pacific Medical Center for the University of Washington ophthalmology residents and running a new clinic, I did not return to Indonesia again until 2001.

CHAPTER 28

FIRST MISSION TO THE PHILIPPINES

With our only son, Robby, preparing to leave soon on a church mission, I had planned to take him along on a visit to Indonesia and the Philippines in January 2001. Philippine Airlines had a two-for-one business class special flying to Manila, and Robby was excited to come with me to get a taste of foreign mission life before he received his own mission call. Unfortunately, my little heart episode put a delay on all that, and we postponed the trip until after he finished the winter semester at BYU Hawaii.

By June of 2001, the political situation for Americans in the Philippines was dangerous with the Abu Sayyaf terrorist activities making headlines. A protestant missionary couple had been kidnapped and two Americans killed just before we were to leave. Americans were being warned not to travel to the Philippines, and family members were very concerned—even begging us not to go on our trip. They were probably right, but by June, I felt much better from my coronary vasospasm, and the trip went off as planned. It seems right before each and every medical mission trip, Satan has a hand in world events, making it seem impossible to travel and do good.

We flew first to the Philippines, where we stayed in the Mabuhay Deseret International house, in a typical missionary room with two twin beds and cold running water.

There was a water shortage in Manila at the time, and so drops from a leaky shower head were caught in a large twenty-five-gallon plastic container, and we used a ladle to lather up and rinse in the bathtub. We were scheduled to visit Fatima Medical College and were greeted by our host Dr. Vincente "Vic" Santos, the chief of ophthalmology, a brilliant and very hospitable friend who picked us up from Mabuhay Deseret House and drove us to the medical college.

Dr. Vic's father, a brilliant and pioneering obstetrician, had started the Fatima Medical Center and introduced me in the lecture hall.

"Before we begin, we would like to start with a word of prayer," Dr. Vic began.

He called a medical student forward, and the handsome young man gave a very kind and warm prayer of gratitude and also asked that "The Holy Spirit would guide the lecturer (me) and the students in their quest for truth."

I was so touched by this and felt I was among friends and at home. It reminded me very much of a Church of Jesus Christ of Latter-day Saints meeting opening prayer. Not only the ophthalmology faculty and residents attended, but it seemed the entire medical school was also invited with a lecture hall filled to standing room only and over 250 doctors in white coats.

Robby had worked diligently on transferring all of my teaching slides from 35 mm to PowerPoint, and he even edited video clips into the presentation.

One talk was titled "Top Ten Pearls of Cataract Surgery." We had an introduction video from the *David Letterman Show* of the intro to his TOP TEN LIST. It was pretty funny. Then when one of the final pearls was my Jarstad Cataract Surgery Marker, we edited a clip from the movie *BACK TO THE FUTURE*, where Doc Brown shows Marty the drawing for the flux capacitor, and ends the clip by saying, "It works. It works! I've finally invented something that really works!"

This was in the early days of PowerPoint video, and they all seemed to enjoy it.

About twenty minutes of questions, and we were off to sight see the Tagaytay Highlands and the famous lake inside a volcano inside another island inside another volcano. At least it was cool way up there in the highlands, and we ate lunch at the restaurant overlooking the volcano lakes.

Our next day was spent teaching at the University of the Philippines, with just the eye residents in attendance. My topic was "Twenty-Five Cataracts in One OR in Eight Hours." The idea of performing so many cataract surgeries in an eight-hour day was foreign to them, but they seemed energized to try to improve their surgery and room turnover times. I donated one of my Jarstad Cataract Surgery Incision Markers to the university, and they accepted it gratefully.

We also went with Grace Teh from Mabuhay Deseret to President Jose Rizal's birthplace in the Laguna province for a charity eye-screening day at the Church of Jesus Christ of Latter-day Saints chapel. (Dr. Jose Rizal was an ophthalmologist and revered as the "George Washington of the Philippines" in that country's fight for independence and many considered him the father of their country.) We were nearly mobbed at the chapel when more than a thousand local residents showed up for the free eyeglasses.

We ran out of glasses about 4:00 p.m., so we asked the staff to keep a notebook of the prescriptions and names of the patients, and I promised to purchase the needed eyeglasses in Indonesia and drop them off with Grace on my way back to the USA after our conference in Jakarta (TD was able to find an eyeglass supplier who sold us four hundred pairs of eyeglasses for a dollar per pair, and I was able to keep my word and deliver the glasses to Grace Teh on our stopover at Manila on our way home).

Our charity work finished, we were taken on a goodwill visit to the district governor's office where we were formally received and made a visit to the WWII Japanese cemetery.

A second trip into the Laguna Province yielded a large amount of goodwill when we were able to discover the cause of a two-year-old's inability to develop normally—he had cataracts. Grace Teh made arrangements for the little fellow to be seen in Manila and receive the needed surgery. Funny how that seemingly small thing of Robby and me going to the Philippines may have been the only way that child will ever be able to see and have the chance of a normal life. I guess no one suspected cataracts could be the cause of his failure to thrive. Sometimes, out of small things procedeth that which is great (1 Nephi: 16:29 *Book of Mormon*).

We returned to Manila, and I nearly died of an asthma attack in the hot, smoggy roads. Poverty like nowhere else was evident everywhere. Robby was impressed and moved by it. We said goodbye to our host family at the Mabuhay Deseret House. Robby had become quite popular entertaining the children who were waiting for surgery for cleft palate, club foot, and cross-eyes. The children all hugged him and didn't want him to go. He left them with nerf soccer balls, gum, candy, and plenty of good feelings. Our host family hired a tailor next door to make us matching traditional Philippine shirts. We left Grace with all the rest of our supplies except for about a hundred pairs of eyeglasses we were taking to Indonesia, and we were off to the airport.

CHAPTER 29

THIRD MISSION TO INDONESIA

After leaving Manila, Philippines, Robby and I arrived in Jakarta in the evening and were taken to the Jakarta Coast Hotel where the Annual Convention of the Indonesian Ophthalmology Association was ready to begin. Subandriyo picked us up at the airport and transported Robby and myself to Pasu Baru shopping area to look for a missionary suit for Robby. We found a sturdy navy blue English wool-terylene cloth and had him measured for a suit with two pairs of pants, including bicycle cuff liners and fully lined jacket and pants. With the amazingly low exchange rate, it would cost about $150 for Robby's tailor-made suit at Hariom's the tailor. We looked at shirts and ties in the mall and found some great buys. With such great prices, I bought a suit for myself too.

We returned to the convention where I spoke on efficiency in cataract surgery and also gave my TOP TEN LIST of cataract surgery pearls talk. The social program once again was excellent. They had an incredible band in the hotel, and we stopped by to listen at the end of the day. The next-to-last night of the convention, a dance contest was announced. I sat in the back with TD and doctors from the Jakarta

Eye Centre. At their insistence, I was enthusiastically entered into the dance contest. They selected one of the resident ophthalmologists, Dr. Yunia Irawati, to be my dance partner. The band announced that they would be taking requests and could play anything. They had a soprano lead singer with a golden voice. I thought the band was a little too confident, so I decided to have a little fun with them by giving them an impossible request.

"You have a request, Mr. USA?"

"Okay, you said you can play anything?"

"That right!"

"Okay, do you know 'Can't Get Enough of Your Love, Baby' by Barry White?" I could hardly contain my smile.

"Okay, we try it for you."

The nine members of the band went into a huddle and came out singing… Darned if they weren't great! It was the first time I'd heard Barry White's velvety baritone song in high soprano, but they pulled it off.

With Mr. White's inspiration, the resident doctor and I danced the West Coast Swing to first place in the contest and were awarded the grand prize of $2 million. Correct that, 2 million rupiahs or at that time about $200. Still a nice payday in a country that earns about $500 per year average salary. I was given the money in a white envelope and was shocked to see twenty 100,000 rupiah notes. I felt guilty accepting all that cash in a poor country. I thanked Yunia and offered her the winnings 2 million rupiahs.

She declined my first offer of the winnings (the custom in Indonesia is to never accept something when it is offered to you the first time—perhaps to not appear overanxious or ungrateful. The polite or politically correct thing to do is to accept on the third offering). I quickly offered twice more in succession, and she accepted half the cash and gratefully put it in her purse.

With his dad tied up at the medical conference, Robby had an opportunity to help the local missionaries for a day or two on exchanges. He wore a white shirt and tie and went contacting and teaching with the elders. A fun experience to "be a missionary" in a foreign land and a nice tune-up before he would get his own mission call to Mississippi and Louisiana three months later.

After the conference, Robby and I held a successful eyeglass screening in the Jakarta Church of Jesus Christ of Latter-day Saints chapel, with the help of President Subandriyo and the missionaries. Robby and the missionaries quickly organized the donated eyeglasses collected by the Federal Way Kiwanis Club, the many libraries, banks, and several churches into neat rows according to their power and strength of prescription. Many of the recipients were so poor that these were the first eyeglasses they had ever received. It didn't matter that the prescriptions were exact. They could see! Or they could read! The grateful patients carefully placed their new treasured spectacles in the donated cases and left the chapel with huge smiles and reverent whispers of "Terima kasih" ("thank you" in Bahasa Indonesia).

As we were returning to Manila from Jakarta with the four hundred pairs of promised eyeglasses for our patients in the Philippines, I was stopped by one of the customs agents, and my eyeglasses were nearly confiscated.

"You may have a problem, sir," the agent began.

"Are you exporting?" I was asked.

"No," I explained. I was taking these eyeglasses as donations to the Philippines for charity.

"You have choices, but I think you still may have a problem," he said. "Unless…"

"Oh, I get it," I said. I quickly leaned over and whispered in his ear, "How much?"

"That up to you," he said. "But maybe no problem."

"Okay, I get it."

I dropped my bag onto the floor and asked him to help me with my shoe and slipped a 100,000 rupiah note (at $10) into his eager hand.

"No problem now. You have nice day," he said, and we were cleared.

I had a similar experience in Nigeria where I was asked if I needed help with my carry-on bag.

"No," I replied, "it's on wheels, and I can handle it."

168

"No, sir. You don't understand. You **do** need help with your carry-on bag."

"Okay, how much?"

Five dollars or ten dollars was the answer. In the USA, I would never dream of tipping the customs people. In the third world, that appears to be the way it works. I certainly didn't want to lose all the eyeglasses at customs along with the medical equipment and teaching videos which risked confiscation. In the future, I will be bolder and just say no.

We returned to Manila and, with an eight-hour layover, exited the airport with the eyeglasses. We met Grace Teh and dropped off the donations along with all our medical supplies and extra food we would no longer need now that we were on our way home. We shopped the large mall in the center of Manila and had a great-tasting lunch at an Outback Steak House. We looked for souvenirs to take back home and then began our way back to the Manila airport.

We might have ventured around more, but at this time, an American had just been found beheaded in the southern Philippines, and we were in no mood to tempt fate. With our business-class reservations, we could hang out in the airline lounge with all the free food and soft drinks we wanted. So we bought some newspapers and books and spent several hours relaxing before catching our flight back to Los Angeles. After ten days in the tropical heat, we were both dead tired and settled into our 747 upper-deck seats with no trouble drifting off for eight hours of needed sleep on our ten-hour flight home.

CHAPTER 30

SKI ACCIDENT IN
THE BUGABOOS

*Dr. Jarstad with Dr. Brian Younge—two
"docs" at Olympic National Park*

Not long after arriving back home, Dr. Tjahjono D. Gondhowiardjo e-mailed to invite me to the next Indonesian ophthalmology conference for 2002. I have always enjoyed the meetings so much that I thought I would like to return the next summer and speak again. In the fall of 2001, I attended the American Academy of Ophthalmology meeting in San Francisco and met up with Dr. Brian Younge a renowned neuroophthalmologist and one of my favorite professors from the world-famous Mayo Clinic.

He mentioned that he had asked me, three years in a row, to go helicopter skiing in the Canadian Rockies. I always had a convenient excuse (the previous year I had been elected president of the Washington Academy of Eye Physicians and Surgeons and needed to preside at the annual convention. The year before that, I suffered a minor heart episode); and this year he wasn't going to take no for an answer.

"All right," I said, "I'll go."

We had just moved into our dream home in Federal Way on January 26, 2002. We were still in the process of getting settled and preparing to launch Robby on his Church of Jesus Christ of Latter-day Saints mission. He had to report to the Missionary Training Center in Provo, Utah, on January thirtieth. His mission farewell was on the twenty-seventh, and it snowed so heavily that our church meeting was cancelled.

In stopping by the building to warn Rex Johnson (an old missionary companion I served with in England), I ran into Bishops Brett Backman and Brent Kay. Bishop Kay overhead my conversation with Bishop Backman and offered to change his sacrament meeting so that Robby could have a farewell talk at his ward sacrament meeting. The ward choir had been preparing the song "Oh, That I Were an Angel" (a beautiful Church of Jesus Christ of Latter-day Saints hymn about missionary work) for over a month and didn't know why they were singing it that week. It all worked out beautifully. Robby had a nice farewell and open house (the last of this type since they no longer have missionary farewell sacrament meetings or missionary open houses in the Church of Jesus Christ of Latter-day Saints).

We flew with our son to Provo, Utah, and dropped him off at the Missionary Training Center (or MTC) near BYU's campus. Tears were flowing all around, and we prepared to say goodbye for the next two years. We were proud of our son and his desire to serve the Lord and felt like we had prepared him as well as possible.

Two weeks later, we would be back in Utah for the Olympics. Rob Potter, one of my missionary companions from England, was able to procure tickets to the Olympic ice dancing, hockey, and aerial skiing events. We flew to Utah and attended the 2002 Salt Lake Winter Olympics. We had a great time and enjoyed the overwhelming spirit of brotherhood and international friendship those present were fortunate enough to experience.

About March 13, 2002, I was getting ready to pack up for the three-day helicopter ski trip in Canada when I misjudged the step in the backyard hot tub and fell and landed funny on my right foot. I think I broke my toe. I couldn't decide whether to still go to Canada, but I buddy-taped the two toes together, and it felt okay enough to try.

The next morning, when I arrived at the Sea-Tac Airport, I suddenly realized that I did not have my passport with me. Since the terror attacks of September 11, 2001, even travel to and from Canada now required a passport. I called PS on my cell phone. I didn't even remember where my passport was. She quickly found it and raced to the airport. I sprinted from the curb to the ticket counter and was told I had five minutes to reach the plane. I didn't make it. Security was too thorough and the lines too long.

I was originally scheduled to fly on Delta to Salt Lake and then Salt Lake to Calgary for a cheaper fare than Seattle to Calgary direct. Now I was in big trouble because there were no more flights that would allow me to meet up with the group in Calgary on Delta.

If I missed the group rendezvous, I would be out $3,500 for the heli-skiing fees. I explained my situation to the ticket agent, and a Seattle supervisor found me a code-sharing ticket with Alaska Airlines that left in an hour and would get into Calgary about three hours sooner than my original ticket through Salt Lake City. I sat around the Calgary airport and read everything I had while waiting for Dr. Younge and the other members of the group to arrive from Rochester, Minnesota. We all met up and were soon off in a rental car for Golden, British Columbia, and helicopter skiing!

We arrived at the hotel, and I shared a room with Brian, my former professor. I brought along an insurance appraisal for our new house which had aerial shots and views of each room. Dr. Younge was impressed. It was fun to catch up on old times and hear of Mayo Clinic plans and progress. The next morning, our party of twelve doctors/skiers had breakfast together and then headed up to the helicopter lodge where we were instructed in high mountain skiing and survival.

We had an hour-long drill with our survival packs and emergency beacons on how to find a snow-covered skier and how to dig him out of an avalanche. We joked about it and headed for the chopper.

For many of the Mayo Clinic doctors, this was becoming an annual event. For me, it had been thirty-three years since I'd gone helicopter skiing as a twelve-year-old boy with my dad on a filming expedition above Icicle River in eastern Washington.

On that trip, I had nearly died when I was accidentally left by my dad on top of the mountain. I took a wrong turn and ended up with a group of skiers who were bivouacking overnight. Since I had no sleeping bag or tent, I had to climb up a hill and follow the tracks of the other groups of skiers down to the Icicle River. Near the bottom of the run, I had to make a quick decision to go right or left, and I chose left after giving it a quick prayer. Correct choice. If I had gone right or straight ahead, I would have skied right off a cliff into the Icicle River and possibly drowned.

This was quite a different experience. We drove to the heli-skiing lodge and filled out our paperwork and waited for the other members of our group to arrive. Each chopper would hold twelve skiers and a pilot. Six seats on each side of a center aisle facing each other, so half of us would be facing forward and half facing the rear of the aircraft. Quarters were so cramped that we straddled or alternated knees to make adequate room to avoid claustrophobia. One would certainly not want to be in the center if we went down suddenly and had to evacuate quickly. We alternated taking the center seats on trips up the mountain.

The runs above Golden, British Columbia, were long and powdery. It was great to ski for miles without having to ride a chairlift. I remember thinking how these military-style choppers were just like the ones being used in Iraq or Bosnia and suddenly felt patriotic, like maybe I should be going there to help sometime soon.

The chopper quickly whisked us up to the top of a peak at an altitude of over ten thousand feet. We would jump out and crawl in the snow to a landing position about twenty yards away from the rotating blades. After everyone was outside, the guide and a volunteer would toss the skis and snowboard into the snow, and everyone would kneel down and bury their heads behind the back of the skier in front of them to shield it from the whirlwind of snow from the helicopter blades as it took off to pick up and transport the second of three teams of skiers it was responsible for each day. The chopper would roar away, and only then would we rise up and find our skis and strap on our bindings.

Once everyone was outfitted, the guide, Jean Luc, from France would lead out, instructing us to follow, one at a time, leaving a gap of five seconds between skiers. We would make a couple of drops from the chopper in the morning to ski down two thousand to three thousand vertical feet. Then we stopped for lunch, and after lunch, we took a couple more runs. We were told we would ski about thirty thousand vertical feet or about six miles straight down over the three days.

At the end of day one, we were all pretty exhilarated with the mile-high Canadian Rocky Mountain air and high on life too. We went to dinner at a local French restaurant recommended by the guide who was from the Alps of France originally. I went café hopping with Brian's son and his friend from Toronto not necessarily because I wanted to but because I thought I'd keep them out of trouble as their designated driver. I felt a strange responsibility to "look after" Dr. Younge's twenty-seven-year-old son.

We went into a sports café and caught some of the basketball highlights on the big screen and then to one other place in town where we didn't stay much longer than it took to down my soft drink. I just left and headed back to the motel. Several of us hit the hotel pool and went to bed. Tomorrow was another day of great skiing.

The second day, I almost rented a snowboard. I had watched the one guy in our group who used one and thought he had a little easier time in the steep and deep stuff. The downside was that some of us had to pull him on the flat traverses. I ended up making a fateful decision and kept the wide, heavy, deep powder skis I'd rented from the helicopter company.

This second day was much like the first. One particularly fun run for me was "Top of the World." It started at the top of a huge high peak and had several long straight, steep schusses with some gently rolling bumps for variety. I kept up with Jean Luc, as I always liked to ski fast and was having a great time.

After lunch on our last run, I was starting to feel it a little in my legs and decided I would take it easy since this was to be our last run of the day. I remember thinking, *You know what they say about the last run of the day.* (That's when most people get hurt or injured if they're going to.)

So instead of my usual aggressive first position right behind and pushing the guide, I lagged back to the tail of our group of skiers, taking in the scenery and just enjoying a smooth final run.

Some of the younger guys wanted to take a few small cliffs near the bottom of the run, so the guide was leading us over that direction. It looked safe enough. It was a twelve-to-fifteen-foot drop into powder with a flatter run out below.

The other option was an icy chute to the right with several rocks sticking up. There were no other options that I could see. I started first for the chute. Then looking at a couple of guys struggling near the rocks, I quickly changed course and decided to follow the crowd over the small cliffs.

"How's the landing?" I yelled.

"Great. Not bad," were the answers.

"Oh, and take it with a little more speed, Dr. J. Show us a trick or two."

Okay, I thought. *I've still got a trick or two in me.*

So I started up a little higher than the others had taken off from and let the skis fly. I was soon airborne and immediately realized this was a mistake. The cliff was more like thirty feet high with a sharp run out to the right. *Never mind*, I thought and launched into a double daffy (a fun air-walking maneuver). Next, I did a little

175

side-to-side twisting action. I ended my aerial combination with a huge spread eagle, completing the routine by locking my knees and assuming a straight-up position with my arms out, forming a perfect human "T" on the landing.

Just before sticking my perfect landing, I noticed ahead that I'd need to make a sharp turn to the right to avoid the trees, rocks, and skiers in the gallery below; so I began to edge even before landing and leaned to the right.

CCRRRAAACCKKK! It sounded like a rifle shot went off. My left leg was numb and hurt like crazy. My right ski had come off on impact, saving that leg from injury, but the binding had not released from my left leg. My helmet had come off, along with my goggles and poles. It looked like a yard sale.

But where was my left leg? The pain was intolerable. I screamed, "AAAHHH! Help me! My binding won't come off. My binding won't come off. Help me get it off!"

The first skier on the scene, one of the younger guys, took one look at my disfigured left leg turned completely backward and promptly emptied the contents of his stomach onto the snow.

Dr. Younge arrived and was able to release the binding and help me pull my left leg out from under me and the snow.

"I think it's broken," I postulated, as the bone could be seen poking out just inside the skin.

Then I started shaking uncontrollably. I was going into shock.

"Look, buddy," Brian urgently explained, right next to my face. "You're in really bad shape. You've got a broken leg, and we're a long ways from help. We'll get you out of here, but it's going to take a while, and we don't have anything we can give you for the pain. You're just going to have to bite the bullet and hang on."

I have always trusted and respected Dr. Younge. He was not only one of the world's foremost experts in neuroophthalmology; he was also a brilliant and very resourceful former Canadian Air Force flight surgeon. He had been in tough situations before (he actually walked away from a plane crash several years before, when his small private plane had flipped over on an emergency landing attempt in a cornfield during bad weather). I immediately felt a calming influence and tried to help my rescuers. The snow was knee deep and even chest high in places.

"How are we going to get him out?" asked one of the skiers.

"We don't have a toboggan, and the snow is too deep to carry him?"

One of the skiers had a snowboard.

"How about putting me on the snowboard and pulling me out?" I asked.

"That might just work!"

The guide had some rope, so I was fastened to the snowboard.

"What about a splint?"

A small air splint was removed from the guide's pack. I suggested from my experience as a Boy Scout leader that my two legs be lashed together.

"We don't have any more rope!" one of the rescuers announced.

"We've got to find a rope to pull him with."

Everyone began to look for something that could be used to pull the improvised miniature rescue toboggan and its critically injured patient out of the woods and about four hundred yards to the waiting helicopter.

It was taking so long. I was in shock and getting colder by the minute. We were also now fighting the clock. It would be dark soon, and the pilot was not instrument rated, which meant he could not fly after sundown.

Finally in frustration, I raised both my hands and yelled, "Here! Take my hands, and use them as handles, and pull me out!"

We began sliding out of the woods toward the waiting helicopter. Every ten yards or so, the snowboard pulling me headfirst on my back would tip over, and I would be facedown in the powdery snow, still tied to the snowboard.

After the third tip over, I started to laugh. I was going to die here in the mountains because I was getting tipped over every two or three minutes. Like the *Three Stooges*, it was a comedy of errors, and I wasn't going to get out in time. Several other members of the group furiously packed down a snow track with their skis, which made the going easier and the tip overs less frequent.

The combination of everyone working together and the one skier who decided to snowboard that day, along with Brian's quick thinking and challenge to hang on, saved my life.

After about forty-five minutes, we emerged from the woods and made it to the waiting chopper. I knew at that point I was going to make it. As everyone else was being seated in the chopper, I was still strapped onto the snowboard. Rather than try to fit me in the chopper in a sitting position (because my leg had swollen so much by now that my left knee would not bend), the last four skiers simply hoisted me atop the snowboard with one end of the snowboard on the rear seat and the other end next to the pilot's head in the front of the cabin.

Away we went. I remained conscious until we landed. It was a pretty quiet ride, and I was able to see the waiting ambulance at the landing pad near the lodge as we approached Purcell Heli-Skiing in Golden, British Columbia.

I was quickly loaded onto a gurney and placed in the ambulance for my two-mile ride to the Golden Community Hospital. I was given morphine and intravenous fluids and brought into the hospital emergency department.

Soon I was met by a pleasant but concerned ER doctor who gave me the usual questions of where, when, what, why, and how, and then asked, "So I see here that you're an ophthalmologist. So, Doc, what do you think is wrong with you?"

I had a hunch. After all, I did do an orthopedics rotation in medical school.

"I'm pretty sure I've got a tibia plateau fracture," I guessed.

"Oh, you think so, huh? Well, we'll soon see about that." She chuckled.

Imagine an ophthalmologist making a bone diagnosis. She returned a few minutes later, now dead serious.

"Well, Doc, you were right. It looks like you do have a tibia plateau fracture, and it's one of the worst ones I've ever seen. We're going to have to transfer you. You can go to either Calgary or Banff."

"Do you have any final requests before we transfer you?" one of the emergency staff asked.

"Yes, could I borrow a telephone book?" I asked, half drugged on morphine.

"A phone book? No one in your situation has ever asked for that before. Who are you going to call in Golden? You don't know anyone here?"

"I'm going to call the Church of Jesus Christ of Latter-day Saints missionaries to give me a blessing," I responded. I was given more morphine and don't remember if the elders ever arrived.

Dr. Younge had now arrived, and I asked for his advice.

"What do you think I should do, Brian? What about Mayo Clinic or University of Washington?"

"I think you need this fixed right away, and I don't think there's time to go that far," he answered.

"What would you do?" I asked.

"Well, the orthopedic surgeon for the Canadian National Ski Team is in Banff. He'd be my first choice."

So with that recommendation, the ER doc attempted to remove my ski boots so they could be returned to Purcell's. I nearly passed out from the pain and audible bone-crunching sounds. More morphine, and I was transferred to Banff.

I remember being in and out of consciousness for the next few hours. Saturday evening had come and gone, and I remember thinking I was glad I wasn't going to be skiing on Sunday. I waited around Sunday receiving pain medicine and then remember finally going into the operating theater in Banff and getting a spinal anesthetic. Within minutes, for the first time since the injury, I was finally pain-free. I could hear the crunch of my left leg bones as Dr. Heard began the procedure, and then I drifted away.

The next thing I remember was waking up hearing, "I've never had one last this long."

I could hear a heart monitor in the background, but it seemed to be going awfully fast. I moaned.

"Oh, thank God you're awake."

The young ER doctor seemed very concerned and very nice.

"Dr. Jarstad, were you ever an athlete maybe in younger years?"

"Well, I was a distance runner in high school and college. I ran the mile and two-mile and was a member of a state championship team in cross-country."

"Thank goodness. You'll probably make it. Your heart rate has been running over two hundred twenty beats per minute for the last three hours. Your oxygen saturation has been really low. When we take you off O2 even for a minute, your sats (oxygen saturation levels—normal is above 95 percent) drop down to the sixties or seventies. I just ordered a chest X-ray, but it looks clear to me. You're an MD. Would you mind consulting on the X-ray and taking a look for me?"

I had to admire the doctor. It was about 2:00 a.m., and he had done everything right so far.

"Let me see. Yes, the lung fields are all clear. The heart is not enlarged. It sure looks like my right hemi diaphragm. Here is elevated. I'm wondering if I could be having a…"

"PULMONARY EMBOLUS!" the ER doc and I said in almost perfect unison.

"So that means the next step would be for me to get a V/Q (ventilation perfusion) scan, right?"

"Oh, but we don't have that test available here in Banff. We'll need to transfer you to Calgary," the good doctor said.

I was really laboring to breathe. It felt like I was breathing a hundred times faster than normal and like I had just run a two-mile race and couldn't catch my breath. (In retrospect, a heart rate of two-hundred-plus beats per minute for three hours would be like running a twenty-six-mile marathon at almost a sprinter's pace.) Being in shape was saving my life!

The arrangements were made to transfer me to the university hospital in Calgary. As I entered the ambulance for the next ride, I saw PS. She had been called by Dr. Younge shortly after the diagnosis was made of the fracture in Golden, and he explained to her how serious my injuries were. She caught an Alaska Airlines flight directly to Calgary and then drove a rental car to Banff, arriving just before my Sunday afternoon surgery. Now she would follow the ambulance to Calgary in the rental car.

As we loaded up, I began to feel my left foot getting cold. A few minutes later, it began to get numb. I asked for another blanket for my foot. It didn't help, and now it was really starting to hurt. I started to complain, and the first reaction was to offer me some morphine.

"I'm not sure, but I think I may be getting a compartment syndrome," I mentioned to the attendant in the ambulance.

"What's that?" he queried.

I explained that a compartment syndrome was where the swelling in an extremity was so extensive that it began to cut off the circulation. If it was not remedied in a matter of minutes to a few hours, there could be permanent damage, with either nerve damage or even gangrene. The foot could die without an adequate blood supply. He called the driver on the two-way radio, and suddenly the ambulance went from fifty to about eighty miles per hour. I could only imagine PS driving in her rental car on a mountain highway at night going eighty miles per hour on unfamiliar roads.

We arrived at the Foothills Hospital in Calgary, and I was immediately seen by the orthopedic resident on call (a young woman resident with straight blond hair).

"Mr. Jarstad, I understand you had a tibia plateau fracture with open reduction and internal fixation with a bone graft from your left hip, and now you think you have a compartment syndrome?"

"They tell me you are to be evaluated for pulmonary embolus as well?"

"What kind of MD are you? Oh…an ophthalmologist."

Again, a slight chuckle (as in "not a real doctor" compared to the blood, bone, and guts of orthopedic surgery).

"Well, we'll soon see about that, eh?"

After demonstrating to the other residents and interns and medical students a textbook example of a compartment syndrome (a pulseless, painful, pale foot), I was off to the radiology department to do the ventilation perfusion scan for the most life-threatening problem. The pulmonary embolus was confirmed, and I was told I had three of my five lung lobes blocked by a massive blood clot.

I needed an immediate placement of a Greenfield filter to save my life. I really didn't have much choice the radiologist said. I could have the filter, or I would die. That made it an easy decision. They numbed up the right side of my neck. A stainless steel birdcage device that would look like a small cocktail umbrella when it was unfolded was placed through my right internal jugular vein, through my heart, and into my inferior vena cava, the largest vein in the body. It opened correctly, and I noted an immediate easing of my breathing trouble.

I believe it was the next day when I was taken to the operating theater. A fasciotomy was performed on my left leg to relieve the swelling and compartment syndrome. (This operation is basically a fillet job to both sides of the leg just below the calf muscle and down to the bone extending all the way down to the ankle. The wound is left open until the swelling subsides and the circulation returns to the extremity.) I came to this time and found my leg wrapped in blood-soaked bandages. An intravenous line dripping whole blood was going into my left arm.

Over the next two days, I would receive fifteen units of blood transfusions to the point where I became concerned about the risk of DIC (disseminated intravascular coagulopathy—a condition where a patient's immune system begins to attack the new blood and chews up platelets, and this causes widespread new bleeding from every-where in the body).

Whatever blood thinner they were giving was causing me to bleed out from my leg dressing just about as fast as the transfused blood was going into my arm. They listened to my concerns, and when my hematocrit kept dropping into the twenties, my transfu-sions stopped. I was taken back to the operating room. The fasciat-omies were closed and a skin graft placed on the lateral aspect of my ankle. (The swelling and necrosis of my lower leg did not allow for a primary closure, and the gap on the lateral side of my leg was too large for healing by secondary intention.)

The Calgary doctors performed still another operation to har-vest skin from my upper-left thigh and sewed it onto my left ankle. Dead necrotic muscle tissue was also removed from my lower leg. In retrospect, they maybe could have operated sooner with the fasciot-omy, but the pulmonary embolus (a more life-threatening condition) took precedence. Hindsight is always 20/20.

I also remember fighting with an anesthetist who tried to intubate me with a general anesthetic. Because it was about my seventh operation in a week with a general anesthetic, my vocal cords were swollen, and it felt like he was trying to cram the stylet of the trach tube down into my valecula. I gripped his hand very hard and pulled the tube back out each time he tried to ram it down my throat. He was scolding me for being uncooperative, not realizing the pain he was causing me.

PS had called the mission home in Calgary on our arrival, and the office sent over two missionaries to give me a priesthood blessing. We were also fortunate to have a visit from President Keith Wood, the former Calgary Church of Jesus Christ of Latter-day Saints stake president who also gave a priesthood blessing. President and Sister Wood looked after PS and my sister, Karen Jarstad, who came up to take vigil at my bedside in alternate twelve-hour shifts so I would not be alone.

Responding to my concerns, the Canadian doctors, nurses, and paramedics had saved my life and my left leg. I certainly owe them my gratitude. Some of my highest praise would also go to the Canadian nurses. They were guardian angels (very impressive and hardworking). I don't think I ever waited more than thirty seconds after pressing my call button before someone was standing at my bedside, asking what they could do for me. I was heavily drugged and probably invited all of them to come visit our family in Seattle.

The internists, especially Dr. Alain Tremblay, were also very caring and conscientious. After two weeks and my sister's constant inquiries, the doctors agreed I was stable enough to transfer by Lear jet air ambulance to Seattle's Harborview trauma center. I was going home! I remember entering the twelve-seat Lear jet and thinking how small and low of ceiling it was. I also remember worrying if my pain control would be adequate for the one-and-a-half-hour flight to Boeing field in South Seattle. I arrived in the evening before Easter Sunday and went up to the intensive care unit for orthopedics after an evaluation in the same emergency room I had worked in as a fourth-year medical student at Harborview some twenty years before. I was relieved to be home!

I had several unexpected visitors at Harborview. One of the most surprising was Jay Durtschi, who had been my senior missionary companion in England in 1975. Jay lived in Spokane and came over frequently to scuba dive in Puget Sound and just happened to phone the same day I arrived in the hospital. Several relatives, including my cousins Gilbert and Gordon Mc Fadden and Gene Jarstad (practically brother), stopped by as well. Mardy Toepke, another missionary companion in England who now lived in my new Federal Way Ward, and Rex Johnson, one of my junior companions in England, visited too.

The hard work of rehab was about to begin. I was fitted with a full-leg brace. I began physical therapy to learn to walk on crutches and try to navigate a six-flight stairway so that I could go home. It took two more weeks, but I finally left the hospital.

It was disappointing to not be able to coach my daughter Allison with her pole vaulting now that she was in her senior year of high school. We had gone on recruiting trips together to UNLV and had hoped to visit other colleges when my accident stopped all of that. Allison still managed to break the Federal Way High School record in the pole vault at 10'0" and actually was the first pole vaulter to clear ten feet at the South Puget Sound League Championship (eventually coming in second to the future Washington State champion Stevie Marshalek). Allison held the SPSL girls' pole vault record for a total of fifteen minutes.

I spent the next ninety days at total bed rest with my sister Kristi and my mom alternating with PS at my bedside. I was heavily medicated for pain, taking up to five 10 mg oxycontin pills every three hours for the excruciating stabbing and aching of my left leg. It kept me up all night at its worst and only allowed a couple of hours' sleep here or there between pain cocktails.

Of course, rumors flew when my patients found out about my accident. We didn't get too concerned until several patients called the office requesting to have their medical records transferred because they heard that I had died in a skiing accident. Actually, a good friend, an obstetrician in Tacoma, did fall to his death at a resort east of Seattle one month after my accident. He was a close family friend and also a member of the Church of Jesus Christ of Latter-day Saints.

Something had to be done. I counseled with my office administrator and brother-in-law Rick Boudreau. We decided to call the newspaper and take out an ad to tell the community that I was going to be okay.

The newspaper found the story interesting enough to run a front-page picture and story with the headline "The Doctor Is Out." We brought in a locum tenens doctor, Linda Day, who did a great job; and I returned ninety-one days after my accident working a few hours, two days a week.

Also of note was the unselfish and heroic kindness of Dr. Dean Rockey, a former all-American caliber football player for the University of Washington who worked with us after we merged his practice into ours about eight years earlier. Dr. Rockey worked all spring and summer for Evergreen Eye Center in the Auburn office and wintered with his wife in Maui, Hawaii. As soon as he heard of my ski accident, he boarded the very next flight to Seattle and arrived Sunday evening in time to take over seeing my patients without skipping a beat first thing on Monday morning.

Twelve months of painful rehab followed with my progressing from crutches to a walker to a cane. When I began to show a valgus deformity of my left knee, I felt impressed to visit Mr. Karl Entemann, who owns Preferred Orthotics and Prosthetics. His office and workshop was next to mine when I was in my first 1,200-square-foot office space next to the hospital at 34509 Ninth Avenue South 101. He suggested a new type of knee thruster brace called a Bledsoe brace which helped immensely in getting my leg straight and pain-free. I was so grateful I cried.

During this dark, painful time, the things that kept me going were the near-daily visits of my daughters and my only grandchild, Emily Washburn. She seemed to sense how much I needed her and would give me a big hug and kiss each time she was over.

As April arrived, I was also able to wheelchair out of the house for my daughter Allison's track meets. It was inspiring to watch her soar over the bar each week at FW Memorial Stadium. She would attract quite a crowd of followers who would come out each week to see if another school record would be broken in the girls' pole vault. She began to play to the crowd a little bit, too, wearing a bright-blue body stocking under her track outfit and painting her long fingernails bright blue to match her outfit and hair attachments.

As 2002 ended, there was hope that I might journey abroad again someday. Dr. Gondhowiardjo had invited me to attend the Indonesian Ophthalmology Association's Annual Meeting in Jogykarta in June. Since Allison made the University of Utah women's track-and-field team as a pole vaulter and the dean's list as a math major, we decided to reward Allison with a trip to London and Paris in May 2003.

The London trip allowed a nice reunion with the Horton's in Brighton. We then headed north, and I made a couple of ski runs in the Snow Dome in Tamworth (two refrigeration warehouses hooked together with artificial snowmaking equipment and a conveyer belt used to transport the skier to the top of the incline before taking the run to the bottom in seven or eight turns). PS thought I was crazy, but I was back on skis!

Leaving England, we caught a flight to Paris. We toured the Louvre, visited Euro Disney, went up the Eiffel Tower, saw an interesting show in the theater district, and took the night boat trip on the Seine.

Jarstad home above Puget Sound with Mt. Rainier in the background. I would spend three months at home in a hospital bed recovering from a severely broken left leg here, looking at the beautiful sunsets over the Olympic mountains each night.

CHAPTER 31

"ROCK STARS"
(FOURTH TRIP TO INDONESIA)

Rick Boudreau with all-pro running back Shaun
Alexander of the Seattle Seahawks and Dr. Jarstad, Read
to Lead Fundraiser, Federal Way, Washington.

After winning the dance contest two years before and being so impressed by the musicians and hospitality the Indonesians displayed at their annual eye meeting, I had a strong impression that if I came to Indonesia again, I should bring along Rick Boudreau, my brother-in-law (also my business manager).

Rick had grown up in Hawaii and was an accomplished musician. He had played at several of the best Honolulu hotels and resorts as a drummer and guitarist. He was excited at the opportunity, though once again, the political turmoil with the Bali bombing by the al-Qaeda and Abu Sayyaf was a big concern to the family members, who urged us not to go. After much prayer and thought, we both felt good about going and went about collecting the needed supplies and equipment (we were able to bring about four hundred pairs of eyeglasses and an equal number of cataract lens implants and supplies).

It was an honor to be asked to give one of the keynote addresses on the topic of "Treatment of Complications of Cataract and Laser Eye Surgery" at the Annual Meeting of the Indonesian Ophthalmology Association. With Robby on his mission in Mississippi, my son-in-law Alan Washburn (a computer science/electrical engineering major at University of Washington in Seattle) was pressed into service at the very last minute when my four months of video editing crashed and wouldn't run on my laptop. After buying a new laptop with a bazillion GB of space, a faster processor, and Alan's expert help, the presentations were saved.

Our flight to Indonesia would involve passing through Taiwan on China Airlines. Taiwan was in the middle of a SARS (viral acute respiratory syndrome) epidemic, which was killing people all over Asia. There was no hope of a cure or treatment. It was tempting to stay home and allow Satan to dissuade us once again from doing good. We paid no heed, even though our families expressed their serious concerns about our sanity.

We left Seattle, and after twenty hours of flying, we arrived in Jakarta. We were hosted by several resident eye doctors in the Department of Ophthalmology. Over lunch, we had a nice political discussion with three brilliant Muslim resident eye surgeons and defended our nation's policy in attacking Iraq and standing up to terrorists. We then returned to the airport for our flight to Jogykarta. We arrived at this inland city about 8:00 p.m. and were taken to an airy outdoor restaurant for dinner where the leading eye surgeons from throughout Indonesia were waiting.

It was great to see Dr. Gondhowiardjo, Dr. Istiantoro, Dr. Purba, and so many other Indonesian colleagues again. The food was exotic with every possible combination of meat (except pork), fruits, vegetables, and desserts. Rick was immediately pressed into service with the house band for a couple of numbers on the drums.

At last, we made it to our hotel—the Sheraton at Jogykarta (pronounced *joke* Jakarta). The accommodations at the hotel were unbelievable, and the service was first rate. We arrived a day before the conference and were able to do a little sightseeing. Borobudour, the world's largest Buddhist temple, was amazing. We also toured the Sultan's Palace, where later that evening we were guests of honor at the eye convention's opening ceremony and dinner. I was even able to shake hands with the Sultan and speak to the princess for a few seconds, an honor not accorded often to Westerners. She was very gracious and thanked me in English for coming.

We had arranged with Elder Subandriyo, now mission president for Indonesia, to conduct an eyeglass and vision screening during the day, followed by a musical fireside and testimony meeting in the evening. Rick and I had practiced a few songs before we left the USA to perform at the firesides ("Brown-Eyed Girl," "Love Song," and a few others Rick would do solo on the acoustic guitar).

Rick was introduced first and bore a brief testimony of the gospel and the Savior, and then we performed two songs. I was introduced and did my best to say a few things in Bahasa Indonesian like "*Selemat malam. Nama saya Doktor Mata* John Jarstad" ("Good evening. My name is Doctor John Jarstad") and that I had *satu laki* ("one son") and *tiga parampuan* ("three daughters"). Following this, I bore my testimony. I told of how I had started out poor as a salmon fisherman and, through the gospel, was able to go on a mission, become educated, and do advanced training in ophthalmology. Now I was here as a keynote speaker at the National Indonesian Eye Conference.

I bore my testimony of the restoration of the gospel through the Prophet Joseph Smith, of a modern prophet President Gordon B. Hinckley, the *Kitab Mormon* (*Book of Mormon*), and the eternal nature of the family. They seemed to enjoy me trying to speak their language, and the music was a big hit.

We also did a fireside in Jakarta, which was equally well received. We did about two hundred eye exams in the Church of Jesus Christ of Latter-day Saints chapel in Jogykarta and a similar number in Jakarta. It was a wonderful combination of utilizing all the talents with which the Lord had blessed us. It was so very satisfying to serve the people with our talents and bear testimony. I truly felt the joy promised in my patriarchal blessing I received at age fourteen that states, "Thou shalt find joy in the Lord in testifying of Him."

The conference presentations were also well received. The Indonesian doctors were especially interested in Rick's talk on improving clinic and operating theater efficiency and my edited version of "the three-minute cataract operation."

I began my keynote talk on complications of eye surgery with a video segment from *Minority Report* with Tom Cruise chasing two eyeballs down a cobblestone street as my segue to "loss of the eye" as an extremely rare, major complication of cataract surgery. Everyone laughed.

Dr. Bobby Osher, a famous ophthalmologist from Cincinnati, Ohio, sent me several of his **"Video Journal of Ophthalmology"** vignettes of complications from cataract surgeons all over the world. I spent several weeks editing them into a tight fifteen-minute review that was enjoyed by the conference participants. I gave a total of four speeches and assisted Rick in the first Indonesian practice management seminar for administrators and eye doctors.

At the evening social program, the hottest musical acts from all over Indonesia were invited to perform on an outdoor sound stage in front of about two thousand Indonesian and foreign EyeMDs, their families, and staff. Several talented hospital groups came up and lip-synched to classic rock hits (one of the most memorable was "Bohemian Rhapsody" by Queen done by four eye residents from Bandung).

With a little inspirational thought, I went backstage and talked to the master of ceremonies in between numbers. "Did you know that a very talented musician from the USA is here and might be willing to perform?" This caught the MC's attention, and he offered Rick a chance to do one song. Rick asked if I could accompany him.

In between Indonesia's top two female vocalists, Rick and I took the stage with borrowed guitars and began "Chokolat Mata Parampuan" ("Brown-Eyed Girl" by Van Morrison).

You can imagine how it was received since all Indonesians are brown eyed. They loved us! We were joined immediately by the best drummer in Indonesia who liked what he heard and immediately recognized the tune. The crowd gave us a standing ovation, and suddenly pocket cigarette lighters brightened the night sky. The MC asked us for an encore. We played "Love Song" ("I want to sing you a love song, want to rock you in my arms all night long..." by Loggins and Messina). Unfortunately, no one had ever heard of "Love Song" in Indonesia. But we were the talk of the conference after that.

Playing bass guitar and singing backup to Rick in "Brown-Eyed Girl" in front of two thousand cheering brown-eyed Indonesians was exhilarating. Performing music in front of the Doctors Mata and their families on a professional sound stage at an outdoor rock concert in front of a giant jumbotron was as good as it will ever get for me. If I never perform music again in this lifetime, I'll be satisfied (and others will be thankful) as it was an all-time high and an experience I will never forget. It couldn't have been scripted better for Rick's inaugural trip to Indonesia.

Dr. John Jarstad—Eye Doctor World Ski Champion—Cortina Italy

CHAPTER 32

WINNING IN ITALY–
WORLD SKI CHAMPION

I n 2006, just four years after my devastating helicopter ski accident and while I was still using crutches and a cane to ambulate, I received a notice on the Internet about an inaugural Eye Doctor World Ski Competition to be held in Cortina, Italy, the year after the 2006 Winter Olympics in January of 2007. The competition was open to all eye surgeons worldwide and would use the same downhill slalom and giant slalom courses used in the Olympic winter games, along with the timekeepers and officials hired during the 2006 Italian Winter Olympic Games as a part of the annual meeting of the Society of Ophthalmology of Italy (SOI) to be held for over three days in Cortina D'Ampezzo in the Italian Alps.

As an Olympic hopeful during my teenage years, I competed each week against future Winter Olympic champions and gold medalists Phil and Steve Mahre, along with Bill Johnson, during my junior high and high school days in the mountain alpine ski racing courses all over the Pacific Northwest. When it became clear I would not be making a US Olympic team, despite my coach believing I had all the tools to make it as an Olympic ski racer, I finally gave up my young life's dream and dropped out of ski racing when high school varsity athletics and dating cute, fun girlfriends competed with my ambition to train for the Olympics.

Later as I decided to go to medical school and become an eye surgeon, this "what might have been" moment with the invitation to compete in an Olympic-caliber race in Italy captured my imagination, and I decided to enter the competition and begin training for "**my** Winter Olympics."

I was already a member of Bally's Gym in Federal Way, Washington, located about a mile from my medical office, and began training with a goal of getting into the best shape of my life in the six-month window prior to the competition. I worked out with a personal trainer for the first month, learning how best to develop my legs to withstand the grueling shock of high-speed chattering effects of skiing on an icy course at fifty-five to seventy miles per hour and making carving turns while being strong enough to stand on one leg at a time if need be. It was three hours of workouts six days a week as I devoted all my extra time and energy to this one goal of competing and hopefully coming home with a medal.

My thinking was, "If these are full-time eye surgeons, they certainly couldn't have time to train and be great ski racers, and if they were outstanding world-class skiers, they probably wouldn't be able to pass ophthalmology board exams and be good surgeons." I would soon find out I would be wrong on both counts.

Soon the day in January 2007 would arrive, and I asked family members if anyone would like to accompany me to Italy for the event. My daughter Allison, an excellent skier and snowboarder, was working as a tax and customs accountant for the Weyerhaeuser paper company and was excited to return to Italy, where she had taken study-abroad courses in college and had a good grasp of basic Italian, at least enough to translate the essentials. We flew from Seattle to Venice and, from there, drove a rental car for the two and a half hours to Cortina, arriving in a snowstorm with twelve inches of new snow overnight. We even got stuck in a snowdrift in the middle of the town roundabout, and Allison's beautiful (former high school cheerleader) good looks soon attracted two cute strong Italian young men who quickly pushed us out of the snowbank and back on our way to our hotel.

The next day, we hit the slopes together and had a perfect day of amazing powder snow skiing.

That night in the village, I sought out a ski shop and asked for their very best ski technician to wax my skis and sharpen the edges explaining that I was here for a ski race and was an experienced racer and would pay top Euro for the best job possible on tuning up my Olin Austrian Racing Skis for the competition.

The next morning, we were told another foot of snow had fallen and the roads up to Col Golina, the site of the special slalom competition, were nearly impassible by car; but after making a wrong turn, we arrived at the parking lot near the ski lift. The race was almost ready to begin by the time we arrived. I quickly picked up my racing bib and, with Allison along to take a video of me, headed up to the top of the course to quickly sideslip the special slalom gates and memorize the course before the first numbers were called.

Most ski racers memorize the course in their mind this way prior to the competition and go over any tricky issues noted by their coaches who radio up the troublesome gates prior racers have difficulty with to the coaches and racers at the top of the course. This was not possible, so I made my first run hanging as close to the gates and picking as high a line as possible to maintain speed. I sat back on the tails of my skis as I crossed the finish gate and tripped the timer beam with my ski tips (rather than my boots) picking up a tenth of a second or so on my run.

After my first run, I noticed that my time was the fastest by three-tenths of a second. If I could duplicate my time on the second run, I had a chance to medal or even win.

The second run went equally well, just a fraction of a second behind; and when the results were announced at the nightly ophthalmology dinner as part of the daily program, I was surprised to hear my name and was called up to receive the massive winning three-foot-high silver trophy as an Eye Doctor World Ski Slalom Champion!

When we learned earlier in the day that only two women skiers had entered the special slalom and that there would be three trophies awarded, one of the officials seeing Allison on her snowboard asked if she would like to enter the competition. She ran the women's course on her snowboard with a respectable time and was awarded a third-place silver trophy.

We were both surprised and excited to take our trophies home but a little nervous on how we could fit them into our baggage or in the overhead compartment. In any case, we were able to bring them home along with some choice memories of Cortina and the sweet savor of accomplishing a goal in competing against some of the better eye-surgeon skiers in the world. The Austrians skied at recess during grade school; and many of the Swiss and Italian ophthalmologists had designer skin-tight aerodynamic ski suits, especially the women skiers from Milan, the fashion capital of Italy. Several men in the competition were accomplished racers and had custom skis only used when racing that they carried up to the start of the course in a padded ski bag and changed immediately onto their travel skis at the bottom of the course, brought down by a fellow countryman. On kind of a lark, I had ordered a black-and-blue Spyder brand skin-tight ski racing suit on the Internet that arrived just prior to my trip. If I had not worn it, I would have been the only racer without one.

The final day of competition, I entered the men's giant slalom race. After having a poor first run and placing twenty-ninth out of 110 racers, I was able to pull out the second run of my life, placing third and receiving a small one-foot silver trophy for that competition.

We returned home after another day of great weather and skiing down the back side of the steep Lagazuoi Gondola run across from Col Golina, ending up at Alta Badia about twelve miles by bus from our origin. It was late in the day, so we took the first bus back to Col Golina, where our front-wheel drive Fiat was waiting.

After spending the following day shopping at the outdoor markets in Venice, we headed to the airport. The feeling was exhilarating as we returned home to Seattle with our massive silver trophies, like conquering heroes.

CHAPTER 33

HARP SOLOS—KOREAN TALENT SHOWS

From 2008 to 2015, I served as a high councilor for the Church of Jesus Christ of Latter-day Saints in the Federal Way Stake (similar to a diocese). My assignments included advisor to the missionary program for the area; physical facilities (including making small repairs of plumbing and heating in the four church building properties in town. Brother Ron Brekke, a talented heating and air man, was gracious to help me "jump-start" a furnace on a cold fifteen-degree day or two); and advisor during the final five years meeting with the Korean-speaking branch of the church.

The Korean Branch Latter-day Saints met in the oldest Church of Jesus Christ of Latter-day Saints building in Federal Way on 308th Street. I was assigned to attend their presidency meetings each Sunday and act as a liaison in bringing up any activities and problems to the attention of the stake president, Randy Nichols, who just by chance had served a Church of Jesus Christ of Latter-day Saints mission to the southern part of Korea in the 1980s.

I could not understand why on earth I was assigned to this branch of the church; but as we soon learn, I would gain a great appreciation for these brilliant, wise, calm, and remarkable people.

Korea means "Land of the Morning Calm," and the majority of the Korean American members and patients I met were very much this way. Federal Way, Washington, where my primary medical practice was located was made up of 17 percent Korean-speaking patients. My youngest daughter Stephanie Jarstad's best friend in junior high school, Kimmy Chee (yes, like *kimchee*), offered to teach me how to pronounce the words necessary for completing an entire eye exam in the Korean language. This was frustrating at first; but with Kimmy's help, along with my patient Korean patient's gently correcting my pronunciation, I gradually became proficient.

Little did I know that this talent would come in handy in two major ways later on: first, during my two eye mission trips to North Korea, in 2010 and 2011, and second (probably most important) when I met my wife Kyung Soek Suk—Kristine Marshall—a few months after my divorce was finalized.

Back to the Korean Church of Jesus Christ of Latter-day Saints branch.

I leaned that the Korean members loved karaoke and outcooking each other with the native delicacies of their former homeland and that they would rather starve than accept any welfare handouts. They couldn't fathom how local high school teens could waste so much time on video games and sports that did not prepare them for the SAT or getting good grades so they could be accepted at a great college or university and receive a university scholarship. It was an honor to have the leadership take me into their confidence and work with me on my Korean and understanding the culture.

I later travelled to Seoul four times and presented my research at a scientific meeting and published the results in the *Korean Journal of Ophthalmology*, one of Asia's best.

Alpensia, the site of the 2018 Winter Olympics, is to this date one of my favorite ski resorts of all time, rivaling the best of Utah or Colorado at about one-third the prices.

During one Christmas about this time, I visited my sister Lisa in Burbank, California, and while she was cooking dinner, I noticed a large folk harp in her living room near her piano. "These things are pretty hard to play, aren't they?" I asked. "Well, you play the guitar and the piano, so it should come pretty easy to you," was her reply. After showing me the basics and with the blue- and red-colored strings as my guide, I began to pick out a few Christmas carols from memory.

A year later, someone in the Korean branch noticed me playing a church hymn at Sacrament Meeting, and the next thing I knew, President Lee of the Korean Church of Jesus Christ of Latter-day Saints branch was asking me to play at their Christmas talent show. This soon became an annual tradition, even though I was not very accomplished at this stage of my harpist career. Because I knew I would be performing each Christmas season, so long as I was assigned to be the Korean branch high counselor, I began practicing about late October each year so I wouldn't detract too much from the accomplished Korean-speaking saints in Federal Way.

From there, I would begin performing in Sacrament Meeting at my own Church of Jesus Christ of Latter-day Saints Ward; and in addition to the hymns and Christmas songs like "O, Holy Night," which was my favorite to play on the harp, I even learned to play Guns N' Roses "Sweet Child of Mine" for some of my rock performances.

I'll always be thankful to my little sister Lisa Kingston for introducing me to the folk harp and helping me to develop a talent I never imagined I would ever have.

CHAPTER 34

OSAMA BIN LADEN AND A WOMAN "FROM THE NORTH"

Osama bin Laden with a Mujahedin "Freedom Fighter"

Sometime in the late 1990s, a very tall, soft-spoken individual appeared in my clinic accompanied by a rough-looking, shorter, stocky gentleman, both dressed in turbans and robes. The taller man spoke decent English and was about six feet, five inches tall. The shorter man was much older and much rougher looking, and spoke no English. "We are freedom fighters from Afghanistan, and this man needs cataract surgery. We will pay you the going rate in cash for the operation, but we cannot stay long as we need to return to our country as soon as possible."

Frequently, I will offer such patients who come from overseas or Canada a discounted rate of one dollar above the typical Medicare rate for their surgery in order to be compliant with the law. Money seemed to be no object for this duo, and the surgery was scheduled for the next day. All went well, and after a three-day follow-up visit, they were gone.

It was later I recognized this tall man is no other than Osama bin Laden—the same-style clothes, the same manner of soft-spoken speech and mannerisms. Something about him just didn't seem quite right, so I chalked up to memory all that I could, wondering just who this strange man was, but I was struck by how he was taking care of one of his soldiers and paying in cash for the services using fresh, new $100 bills.

A photographic memory comes in handy as an eye surgeon. We are trained for years to recognize subtle changes in a patient's retina, and because of this innate skill or developed trait, it becomes a blessing and a curse. Ophthalmologists can often remember exactly what thousands of patients' retinas look like from one year to the next but may not recall the individual patient's name. During my years in practice in the Seattle area, patients would often recognize me at the grocery store and ask, "Dr. Jarstad, remember me?" All I could offer was, "Oh yes, you're the lady with the small nevus in your retina of the left eye about five o'clock," or "Yes, you're the lady with the herpes cold sore virus that caused a scar near the center of your right cornea." Patients were frequently surprised that I could remember.

Since no record of bin Laden's protégé or forwarding address was kept on file, only a name and medical record along with a cash receipt of the surgery was kept. After bin Laden was killed by US Special Forces, I wondered if our visitor really was him. It stands to reason since who else would bring a Mujahadin fighter all the way to America for cataract surgery and pay in cash the thousands of dollars to restore his eyesight. I'm convinced to this day we met him in Federal Way at my Evergreen Eye Center clinic and surgery center.

One other unusual patient was brought to our clinic from Canada by relatives. When I determined that she spoke Korean, I completed the eye exam in my best Korean and then asked what part of Korea she was from. Her family answered, "From the North." "Oh, you mean the northern part of South Korea?" "Well, you could say that." I later learned she was actually from North Korea and flew to Canada in order to get into the USA for needed eye surgery that no one in North Korea seemed to be willing to perform for her there. She needed a combined cataract- and glaucoma-filtering operation, and they wanted to proceed right away so she could return to Canada and then fly from Vancouver back home. I didn't realize the urgency for her leaving until later. Other patient's relatives prescheduled surgery for the same or next day, and after the surgery was a success, they left immediately for home through Canada or stayed for one night in a local hotel for the one-day postop visit and then went back across the border into CANADA, at times, I later learned, with our patient in the trunk of their car. I have no idea how many patients from Communist China, North Korea, Iran, Cuba, Venezuela, or other places visited our clinic over the years; but I imagine a very few did.

After that experience, I thought best not to ask questions if patients were in need and that helping sick patients was my priority, regardless of their country of origin. Some were pretty courageous to come across the border hidden in the trunk of a car both directions, so I remember only giving a quick casual thought on reporting them after the fact, but to whom? And what would be the consequences? The patients I treated were often very advanced in their age and eye conditions and diseases, and frequently reported that no other eye surgeons were willing to risk operating on them at home. I felt the needs of a harmless elderly old woman with a very sick eye might be greater than our government's need to arrest and detain her here. I received a nice thank-you from her family and heard that her eyesight had recovered and her glaucoma was under control back at home "in the North."

CHAPTER 35

DICTATORS I HAVE KNOWN

I n 1993, at the American Academy of Ophthalmology meeting in Dallas, Texas, I was eating lunch; and there was only one remaining empty booth in the convention center cafeteria. As I sat down and began lunch, I noticed a tall gentleman accompanied by what appeared to be a bodyguard with a name tag associated with medicine or as a guest. The tall ophthalmologist had an unusually small round head, and I immediately recognized him to be Dr. Bashar al-Assad of Syria, whose father at the time was president. As both doctors looked for a place to sit, I motioned, palm down, for them to come sit at my booth. "Would you like to join me?" I asked.

"So what do you think of the Jews?" Dr. Assad inquired.

How should I answer that? I thought. *My great-grandmother Kauffman, from Switzerland, was likely Jewish.* "Well, I'm not Jewish," I replied.

"What do you think of them?"

"Oh, I do not like them," he interjected. "They are not to be trusted."

"You're not Jewish?"

"No," I answered, to his relief.

"Okay, then, we will sit here."

We proceeded to have a lively conversation, and I found Assad to be soft-spoken, very polite, and mild-mannered, almost meek. While at first I was shocked that Assad appeared bigoted, refusing to even eat lunch if I had been Jewish, I later learned from other Syrian doctor colleagues that it would have created a national and international stir if he had sat down with me if I had been a Jewish doctor and if someone had taken our photo together.

I found some common ties with Assad, in a way that we both spent time in Great Britain—me as a missionary for the Church of Jesus Christ of Latter-day Saints and Assad as an intern and resident in ophthalmology. Even more coincidental, his wife was British and from Birmingham, England, where I had spent the majority of my two-year Church of Jesus Christ of Latter-day Saints mission.

An interesting part of our meeting was when I asked Assad where he was practicing (Damascus) and what his plans were for the future. He told me that if it was up to him, he would be happy just practicing ophthalmology.

"Why couldn't you do that?" I enquired, tongue in cheek.

"Well, John, it's a bit complicated. You see we have a family business" (LIKE RUNNING THE COUNTRY OF SYRIA—I knew)."

As our lunch finished, I believe we hit it off much better than our initial introduction started things off. Assad was gracious and invited me to come to Damascus some time and teach cataract surgery and offered to host me.

Deseret International/Charity Vision did ask around that time if I would go to Damascus, Syria, and unfortunately, I was unable to go due to family, church, and office commitments. One visit I believe would have been fascinating.

Bashar al-Assad and Asma, his wife

CHAPTER 36

TWO MISSIONS TO THE HERMIT KINGDOM

E arly in 2010, I received a phone call from a colleague in Federal Way who asked if I would consider doing eye mission work in Korea. Since so many of my patients (17 percent of the population in Federal Way) were Korean speaking and were the most humble and loyal of patients, often referring me to many other Korean-speaking relatives and friends, I felt I owed it to consider going to Korea someday. A few months later, I received a phone call from a Dr. Lee, a family physician and Korean American. He asked if I would come with their group, Mana Mission, to set up the first eye surgery unit in Rajin, North Korea.

"You mean South Korea, don't you?" I asked.

"No, we are going to North Korea and have a hospital there that we have been visiting about three to four times a year for several years."

"I didn't think Americans could go there," I interjected.

"Normally, we can't, but because we are a humanitarian group, the state department and the North Korean government allow us in."

I was fascinated. I told my wife about the conversation and the opportunity. "You're crazy!" she said. "But that hasn't stopped you before." So we began to prepare to go to the "hermit kingdom." There was an extensive review of my credentials. The North Korean regime wanted copies of my passport, medical school diploma, college transcripts, internship and residency certificates, board certification diplomas, and letters attesting to my good standing in medicine and the community. It was a five-month review process, and I was approved by the North Korean government to go.

We prepared "every needful thing" because we didn't know what, if any, eye surgery supplies would be in country. It was a good thing. They had a few eye drops but no microscope or phaco machine. Those would be transported in from China with an experienced crew of two operating room Chinese eye nurses. Thank goodness for them and the machine and microscope.

As we arrived in Yanji, China, I lacerated my right wrist on a baggage cart. It has left a scar as a reminder of the small price I paid to serve humanity in North Korea, and whenever I look at it, it reminds me that a physician far greater than I will ever be also has a scar in the same place but on both wrists.

We would be staying overnight and traveling the next morning by bus on about an eight-hour drive across the border and the Hunan River separating China from "the North." As we entered our hotel, there were ladies in traditional Chinese dress lining up on each side of a red carpet we thought to welcome us. It was actually for a wedding. There were multiple Mercedes limousines and dozens of red balloons to celebrate the newlyweds arrival just after us. We did get some fun videos pretending that the lavish reception was for our humanitarian workers as we took turns walking the red carpet into the hotel lobby.

The next morning, we woke up early and began our long ride to the border.

At the Chinese border, we were informed that the North Koreans would perform a "Bible count" as we entered the country and that we would be inspected as we exited the country and that if we had a fewer number of Bibles on our exit, then when we entered, all of our team would go to prison. We counseled together, and we decided it would be safer to leave our scriptures in lockers at the Chinese border.

I was able to smuggle in an *English to Korean Lonely Planet Dictionary*. I didn't want to end up in the country against my will without a means to communicate.

We arrived at the Chinese-North Korean border crossing in the early afternoon. It was striking how old the customs house was. It had lever-type throw light switches that appeared to be fifty years old. Certainly, before my time.

The customs/immigration house was crowded with young women either returning from working in China or traveling from China to visit North Korea. There were many North Korean people living just across the border as we found in visiting a Christian church service on our return to China where the service at this Christian megachurch was held in Hangul, the Korean language, reminding me of one of my heroes of history—King Sejong the Great, who simplified the Chinese language of three thousand characters to twenty-four Korean letters.

As we waited our turn to pass through, I peeked around the luggage-screening conveyer belt, and to my surprise, there was no working TV screen. I was scolded by the customs guard to "get back." On the other side of the "X-ray" machine, the North Korean customs agent opened each bag and suitcase, and the contents were removed and gone through by the guards. Not only did this process take forever, but imagine the embarrassment to our women whose lingerie was placed on display for all the men soldiers to see. Something about that did not sit well with me, having three sisters and three daughters. "What exactly are you looking for?" I said loudly to the guard as I got right up next to his face. Maybe I was stupid, but he was shocked to be challenged and cowered and then backed away. The North Korean general in charge of the customs saw the commotion and came hurriedly around from his glass booth. "What's the problem, sir?" he inquired. "Your guards are going through the women's personal items, and it's embarrassing for them," I snarled back. "This is ridiculous. What exactly are you looking for?" I demanded. He put his arm on my shoulder and said, "Okay, now just calm down. Calm down just a little bit." My anger was more feigned than real, but it was still highly unusual and for anyone to challenge a North Korean military guard. I expressed my feelings that the customs guard's actions were very inappropriate and embarrassing. The general agreed and ordered the guards to move us along and waved us all through immediately without delay. To reward his kindness, I offered to examine him first the next day in Rajin as we began our screenings. He seemed to appreciate the VIP treatment and did need reading glasses which we were happy to provide him free of charge.

One other striking observation is that, in one of the poorest and most needy countries on earth, the guards would not allow any eye drops that were expiring the same month or recently expired to be admitted to the country. It's been my experience that eye drops and medications can safely be used for one to two years past their expiration date as I witnessed in Africa and other Southeast Asian countries.

With our team of six physicians and fifteen nurses and technicians, we reboarded the motor coach and were on our way across the corn rich countryside to the seaport city of Rajin.

Rajin is situated on the coast in the northernmost part of North Korea and about ten miles east and below a beautiful, wide mountain valley that reminds one of Park City, Utah, complete with three distinct mountain ranges above the valley. I asked one of the two "guards" or minders provided by the North Korean government to watch both us during our visit and each other and to tell us if anyone skied on what looked like perfect runs for skiing. "Oh yes," our taller guard said. "But how do you get up the hill with no ski lifts?" I asked. "We take turns driving a military jeep with chains and four-wheel drive, and everyone skis down, and then we switch." Similar to skiing the Big Island of Hawaii according to my Hawaiian brother-in-law Rick Boudreau, who was a member of the Honolulu ski club and made trips to the Big Island to ski on Mauna Kea in a similar fashion each winter.

I filed that one away for the day when Korea is unified. I predict a world-class ski resort in the valley above Rajin. I only hope to be able to ski it one day. It's really a perfect location for a resort with three distinct mountain slopes covering all three levels of skiing—expert, intermediate, and beginner.

When we finally arrived at our hotel in Rajin and as we approached, we noticed several buildings with Korean writing on the outside. In asking our Korean American team members what the translation into English was, they would read the signage, "Bakery, Restaurant, Grocery Store"; but oddly enough there was nothing inside. Likewise, two high-rise apartment structures were total shells with no windows or anything inside. They would appear from space to be high-rise buildings but inside were totally empty.

We were treated to meals of kimchi (fermented cabbage, a spicy and tasty staple of both North and South Korea); fresh fish and crab (that was similar to snow crab from Alaska); fresh corn on the cob; bread made in the bakery constructed by Mana Mission funds to provide employment for the hospital doctors and nurses when the medical team was not in town on our mission trips; and a salty seaweed soup. It was tolerable and actually tasted great after a hard day's work.

Each evening, we had a devotional immediately following dinner. I was surprised and honored to be selected by Dr. Lee, our team leader to give the first devotional. Dr. Lee, a very positive and spiritual man, while not a member of my Church of Jesus Christ of Latter-day Saints faith, asked each of us to pray for the entire team beginning several weeks prior to our mission. We felt the effects of our team members' prayers in a way that several miracles occurred as we prepared and planned to make the mission a wonderful success.

One particular incident I remember was that I could not locate the tiny portable machine I had purchased years before to take A-scan ultrasound measurements of the axial length of the eye to help calculate the correct lens power for our cataract patients. The correct artificial lens power is determined by a formula using the length of the eye along with the curvature of the cornea known as keratometry readings and put into a formula which will then give a fairly accurate estimation of the correct artificial lens power to place inside the eye after a cataract is removed. When this number is accurate and the correct power lens prescription is placed into the eye after removal of the cloudy cataract, most patients see 20/40 or better without glasses and can see well enough to pass a driver's license test and in many cases see 20/20 without any glasses.

Because I was not sure if the North Koreans would have a keratometer (I was justified in this concern when we found they did not have one), I decided to take the average of thirty of my Korean American patients' keratometry readings before I left Seattle. This average number was found to be 44.50 diopters; and this number, along with the results showing the axial length from the machine which miraculously and mysteriously appeared two weeks before we left after being missing for many months and (after asking members of the team to pray that it might be located), was used to successfully select the correct lens with astonishingly accurate results. Apparently, someone, either from our office or perhaps a technician or doctor who worked for us in the past had borrowed the device and located the handheld portable A-scan lens calculator (about the size of a cell phone) and felt impressed to return it two weeks before our trip.

One additional pearl remembered from multiple prior eye mission trips to Africa, Indonesia, and the Philippines was to bring a roll of duct tape which came in handy when we noticed there were no IV poles to hold our irrigation bottles during cataract surgery. The duct tape held the glass bottles to a level on the wall that allowed adequate irrigation for our Chinese phaco machine.

One of the first patients, a grandfatherly man of about seventy, we operated on was told that cataracts were an incurable disease and that he "must remain blind" the rest of his life. Imagine his joy when we removed his eye patch the next morning and he was nearly 20/20 for the first time in decades without glasses. As he clapped his hands and jumped up and down, he spoke excitedly in Korean while pointing to his other eye. "Can we do this one also maybe today?" he queried. "Sorry, but the hospital will only let us do one eye per patient on this visit," we answered. Another conversation out of earshot of the hospital workers. "What did he say?" I asked our interpreter. "He said he was told there was no cure and now feels his vision is perfect and back to normal. He says he can't believe anything his government tells him anymore." When I related that story to one of my Seattle patients who had worked for the CIA, he told me, "That's the best kind of back-door diplomacy we could ask for."

As we worked in the hospital, one of the other interesting nuances of working in North Korea was that the hospital was locked from 4:00 p.m. to 9:00 a.m. sharp every night. Also, the electricity was extremely unreliable. Many times, the electricity would go off during the surgery day, often in the middle of an eye operation. We had to either use a penlight to finish an operation with our microscope or stop surgery and wait for ten to fifteen minutes for the diesel generator to get going and bring the lights back on.

The head of the hospital, Dr. Kim, a general surgeon, was quite interested in watching our new technology of taking cataracts out using a surgical microscope and an ultrasound machine operating through a tiny 2.75 mm incision. After asking our team if he could watch, he talked almost constantly during our operation. "What is he saying?" I asked our Korean interpreter. "Oh, I'll tell you at dinner." "Really?" I asked. "YES! It will take too long to explain." Later at dinner, the interpreter told me Dr. Kim was criticizing everything I was doing, telling the North Korean staff that he should be operating, not me, and that he could do a much better job on the cataracts.

The next day as we finished the first operation, I asked Dr. Kim if he would like to do the next cataract operation. "Yes, of course. Thank you." He sat down, and I tried to instruct him. His hands were all over the place. After attempting to make the initial incision, he turned the instruments back over to me and left the room.

About an hour later, he returned to watch and, following our final case, asked, "May I speak with you in private?"

"Sure," I said.

"Would you be willing to operate on my mother?"

"I would be honored to. What's going on with her eyes?" I asked.

"She went to Pyongyang, the capital, for cataract surgery, and her operation was unsuccessful," Dr. Kim stated.

"Well, let's check on her and see if we can take care of her," I offered.

It would appear that the surgeons in the capital removed her cataract, along with the entire lens capsule, and then attempted to implant her artificial lens with no capsular support. The lens migrated back into the vitreous gel and was resting on the lower part of her retina.

"We will need to implant another lens type in her first eye, and then we can do the cataract surgery on her other eye," I suggested.

"Great! Just do it," he said.

The operations went very well, and she was seeing clearly by the next morning.

As we left Rajin, the local doctors and the Mana mission team asked if I would ever consider returning with them in the spring.

"I would really like to so I can see my postop patients and get some follow-up," I offered.

"Great! We'll add you to the team for next spring." Dr. Lee seemed pleased.

On the way back, we passed many fields of ripened corn. *It looks like a bumper crop harvest this year*, I remember thinking. *Doesn't look like anyone will starve to death this winter.* Boy, was I wrong. I was told on my next trip in the spring that "many people starved to death because the corn was sold to China to purchase more missiles to point at South Korea and the USA."

The operating microscope brought in from China did not have adjustable oculars. They were fixed at a forty-five-degree angle. There was no adjustable surgeon's stool anywhere to be found in the hospital or nearby clinic. So after standing all day on my formerly broken leg, I asked one of the hospital carpenters if there was any way he could build me a wooden platform at exactly the right height (about twenty-two inches) off the ground so that I didn't have to operate standing up the rest of the week. The next morning, he presented me a beautiful newly made upholstered box that was perfect. The only concern now was the stool they had was on four wheels, and it slid off the platform at times during an operation. DANGEROUS! Then I remembered we had always packed duct tape on our mission trips. Taping all four wheels so they would not move solved the problem for the rest of the mission. DUCT TAPE—NEVER LEAVE HOME WITHOUT IT (see also Madagascar mission)!

CHAPTER 37

MEETING KIM JONG-UN

One night, whilst relaxing in the Rajin Hotel lounge, playing billiards, a young Korean man who was obviously much better fed than anyone else we met appeared with a bodyguard and asked if he could join our game. I recognized him immediately as Kim Jong-un, the "dear leader" president Kim Jong-il's youngest son.

"Sure, I'll play you," I said, offering my hand to shake. "I'm John Jarstad, an eye surgeon from Seattle." He immediately stiffened, stood at attention, and said, "They call me MR. KIM. I will play you, and I will beat you, American!" Kim predicted confidently.

I was surprised at how well-spoken he was, along with his excellent command of the English language, despite his colorful profanity mixed in. "Where did you learn to speak English so well?" I asked. "I had many American and British friends when I studied in Switzerland," was his answer. He was a bit of a practical joker and teased us. I enjoyed firing right back; and he seemed affable, friendly, and able to take a joke and dish it right back at us as we played each other in a game of "eight ball" or "stars and stripes."

Since he was much younger, he reminded me of a fun-loving "typical frat boy" one might find at a major US university. He seemed really interested in what life was like in Seattle and what some of the differences in climate, working conditions, and college life.

As the game went on, I had about a two-ball lead when it came to calling my last shot. "Eight ball in the corner pocket," I predicted. As I lined up my final game winning shot, the thought of diplomacy crossed my mind. "Oh, shoot!" I just barely missed the eight ball on my last shot. "Mr. Kim" was the winner. "Nice game, American!" he teased. "I beat you just as I predicted!" "Yeah, you're lucky. I'll get you next time, Mr. Kim," I shot back, shaking my fist. And then he checked around the room and left as mysteriously as he arrived.

We did have a few minutes before, during, and after the game to talk about his role and his future.

"I noticed that your dad, 'THE DEAR LEADER,' looks like he has suffered a stroke (we could determine that by watching the black-and-white propaganda channel at night on the only station seen on North Korean TV in our hotel). "What's going to happen when he passes away? Will one of your older brothers become the next leader?"

"Well, John, my oldest brother, would not be suitable, because he has a gambling habit and lives in Macau. My father sends him two hundred and fifty thousand US dollars per month for his gambling addiction."

"What about your next oldest brother?" I asked.

"He would not be able to serve either. You see, he's what you would call...effeminate."

"Oh, you mean he's gay?"

"Yes, that's the word. So he would not be accepted by the military."

"So that leaves you?"

"Yes, I guess that leaves me."

He then exited the hotel lounge as mysteriously as he arrived. Little did I know that my new acquaintance and billiard opponent would be the next dictator of North Korea and such a future source of concern to our country and the world.

Another interesting experience in Rajin was when we visited a tuberculosis hospital where it appeared that patients came to die. They were all rail thin and seemed quite weak. As we walked from the highway along a two-foot-wide path, we passed homes or rather wooden shacks constructed of rough-hewn wood and held together with bailing wire. There was no door or windows, using only a blanket to keep out the elements, despite the brutal winters approaching.

One last experience occurred on the next to last day in Rajin. We were told by our North Korean "handlers" that they would arrange for us to go shopping one morning at the public market but they would not notify us until the very day we could go. This was exciting to me after living in England for two years and spending many days off, wandering through the English town "public markets" where interesting bargains were to be found frequently at half the price or less from department store prices.

At last, the appointed day arrived, and we were notified that we could exchange our money for North Korean won or pay with dollars.

I bought a North Korean Army hat and found a faux Izod Lacoste leather briefcase for ten dollars. I also found some hard candies and a North Korean flag lapel pin. As we were exiting the building, which was similar to long sheds one might find at an American state fair, another team member remarked, "Did you notice anything different about the shopping?" she asked. "No, what do you mean?" "Did it seem strange to you that our team members were the only ones taking any shopping bags out of the building?" She was right, we were the only ones bringing anything home. "DO YOU THINK THAT WAS ALL FOR SHOW AND NOT REAL?" I asked. "WHAT DO YOU THINK?" It was all a big show. Imitation Nike shoes, pots and pans, utensils, clothing, each booth stacked high with every conceivable item usually in short supply in one of the poorest countries on earth.

Guess that doesn't surprise me. The entire town of Rajin is a "show place" for visitors to convince them that this is a utopian society.

On the final day in North Korea, as we were on the bus ride back to China, we stopped at a gift/propaganda shop. There in a glass display case were books, pamphlets, and items of propaganda all indicating that the Korean War was caused by the imperialist Americans and attempting to rewrite history according to the dictates of Kim Jong-il. There was a beautiful stone-carved turtle out of jade or what appeared to be that precious stone for six hundred dollars. A little expensive for my tastes. So I settled for some North Korean candy. I paid with a twenty-dollar bill. When I received two five-dollar bills in return, there was something funny about them. Lincoln's head looked a little weird, and the metal strip found in most US currency notes was noticeably absent.

When I challenged the woman clerk, she stood back, folded her arms across her chest, and said, "So what you going to do about it?" Guess she was right, and I was mad. Counterfeit American currency. Since I hate getting ripped off, I demanded the return of my money, but she insisted I could either take the fake bills or buy more items. I decided to purchase two additional items adding up to seventeen dollars and received North Korean currency in exchange.

When I spoke to a low-ranking interested government official a few weeks later, who called me and had questions about my visit, he felt my information was very helpful in gaining a greater understanding of the living conditions in the north and reassured me that I was not breaking any US laws by providing humanitarian assistance.

As we crossed the border back into China, I had the strangest thought. I almost felt like kissing Chinese soil feeling like we were back in a free country once again. I guess we were, relative to North Korea. No "bodyguards" or "minders" and no sharpshooters on guard on the roof of our hotel (I captured them in video one morning by turning around suddenly once on my flip camera as we left our hotel to board our medical tour bus).

As we drove out of Rajin back to Yanji on the five-hour bus ride, we passed through field after field of corn being harvested by hand. Backbreaking work and my heart went out to these hardworking, kind, and honest people. I wished I could do more for them than operating on a few dozen cataract patients. So each time they looked up to see our bus go by, I would smile and wave in as animated fashion as I could. I think from the response, most had never seen an enthusiastic blondish Nordic American. My thought was, *I want to encourage you that someday your lives will be better and to hang on and persevere.* As they looked up and saw my smiling face and overenthusiastic wave, they would turn to each other laugh heartily and then turn back to look at me with huge smiles, likely thinking, "That's the craziest American or White person I have ever seen." It was the best I could do.

Upon returning to Yanji, China, we splurged and our fearless leader Dr. Lee booked a group massage treatment at perhaps the biggest spa I had ever seen. Every team member changed into scrubs; and fully clothed, we were beaten vigorously with canes and then massaged in unison, about twenty of us at a time, with the local Chinese girls keeping perfect harmony in their inflicting mild pain and relief from our long journey and days of operating hunched over microscopes and in other ministrations to the North Korean patients.

The following day, a Sunday, we attended the largest Korean-speaking Christian Church in Yanji and perhaps in all of China. I estimate three thousand attended, and whilst it was in Korean Hangul language, those translating confirmed that it was a sermon from the New Testament, First Corinthians.

The Korean-speaking choir was heavenly, and we could all feel the Spirit. And "where the Spirit of the Lord is, there is Liberty" (2 Corinthians 3:17).

We ate at the "American Hamburger Restaurant" in Yanji before boarding our flight that would have taken maybe forty-five minutes if it was direct to Seoul; but since we could not fly over North Korean airspace, it was closer to a three-hour flight rectangular journey home to Seoul.

We stayed overnight at the downtown Holiday Inn high-rise hotel and caught our early morning flight home to Seattle.

Little did I realize that no one I would ever meet in the future back home could remember meeting anyone who had ever visited North Korea. Definitely a twice-in-a-lifetime experience.

Chairman "Mr. Kim" Jong-un (second from left with arms folded and before weight gain and striking haircut)

CHAPTER 38

FIGHTER PILOT FOR A DAY

One of my childhood fantasies was to be a P-51 Mustang fighter pilot. Maybe it had something to do with my dad's similar dream during WWII. As he told it, he was all set to go into the US Army Air Corp when a freak accident while playing second base caused him to fracture his humerus. An operation revealed a benign tumor, and his flying career was over before it began. P-51 pilots had a terrible survival rate during the war, so maybe that's one reason I'm here today. Dad ended up "piloting" a D-6 Caterpillar bulldozer creating airfields in Alaska during the war.

In any case, my fascination with WWII planes led me to work on many models which, when completed, decorated the ceiling of my bedroom at 4812 (South Eighteenth Street).

Later, meeting several of my patients who actually flew P-51s during the war changed my outlook only slightly. One patient I operated on for cataracts told me that the P-51 with its Rolls Royce V12 engine was so overpowered that, unless pilots pushed hard rudder on takeoff, the P-51 could flip over just from the excessive torque. One veteran 51 pilot even gave me a copy of the P-51 pilot's manual he'd kept from his service in the war. It read and was illustrated like a comic book. Guess that's the level that connected best with the nineteen-to-twenty-one-year-old fighter jockeys. Interesting reading to be sure—everything from how to start up in cold weather to opening the cockpit canopy to bail out in an emergency.

There was one opportunity to partner in the purchase of a P-51 with a next-door neighbor in Federal Way for a half share of $250,000 in about 1995, but after hearing of the difficulty flying them, I declined the opportunity.

One year for Christmas, my wife bought me an experience certificate for a "Fighter Pilot for the Day" pass. I scheduled it for right after our mission trip on the USNS *Mercy*.

When we arrived at Boeing Field in Seattle, I was expecting just a ride along in the copilot seat. There were two Italian replica versions of the P-51 Mustang flown by experienced ex-Navy TOP GUN pilots who had retired and went around the country providing this experience for about $1,500 for the day's flying.

Immediately upon arrival, we were asked to change into a flight suit and attend ground school to go over the day's activities. There would be two of us, and we would fly simulated dogfights going at each other at about four hundred miles per hour over Lake Washington just east of downtown Seattle.

My opponent, I learned, was a Microsoft computer software engineer whose favorite program was "Flight Simulator." When asked what I did for a living, I replied that I was an eye surgeon and specialized in cataract and LASIK surgery. At that, the retired US Navy TOP GUN pilot mentioned that he had just had cataract surgery one week ago. "Who was your surgeon?" I inquired. "Dr. Aaron Weingeist," was his reply. "Oh, good," I said. Dr. Weingeist was one of my residents I trained at University of Washington and had some of the best hands of any resident I'd ever trained up to that point. "Small world."

We strapped on parachutes and hopped into the cockpit and taxied out onto the runway after a brief conversation about how to open the canopy and bail out should we get into real trouble.

Shortly after takeoff from Boeing field, the pilot turned to me, took his hands off the joystick, and said, "She's all yours." "You mean I'm going to be flying the plane?" "The rest of the day," he answered.

Wow! The pilot instructed me in the nuances of not only flying but also tactics in a dogfight (like getting altitude and how to pull high G-forces in a tight turn without passing out, along with not stalling the plane by going too vertical for too long).

Each plane had an aiming reticle just inside the windscreen to aim our laser at the enemy plane. Once it hit the fuselage of the other plane, orange smoke would be emitted from the tail of the plane we were aiming at, and a trail of bright-orange smoke would trail out from a canister in the plane's tail.

After about fifteen minutes of preliminary flying, we were ready to engage and dogfight. We would come at each other over the lake at about 220 to 250 miles per hour, each break hard right and then see who could "shoot the other plane down."

My opponent was younger (about thirty) and got me right away in the first engagement. That made competitive me mad. "Okay, I gotta get this guy. What do I do?" My instructor provided a few tips. "Let's get altitude and come at him from above on round 2," he suggested. "And make a tighter turn this time to come around behind him." Good advice, and it worked. I got him. With each dogfight, I learned something new and more about the capabilities and limitations of my P-51.

It was tied three to three going into the grand finale dogfight. As we broke right and both climbed for an altitude advantage, I was chasing "Microsoft Flight Simulator Guy" going vertical and upside down when my laser connected. "You got him!" "Nice work!" "Okay, guys, let's form up and head back to Boeing." We flew in formation back to the airport, having not only survived being a fighter pilot for a day but also finding out that, YES, I could possibly have done this dream job.

We snapped a few photos, and my day as a fighter pilot was over. Definitely an unforgettable experience.

CHAPTER 39

MUTINY ON THE *MERCY*

n 2011, I received a call from the Church of Jesus Christ of Latter-day Saints Headquarters in Salt Lake City from a "Sister Susan Puls," an orthopedic surgeon who worked with LDS charities and the various humanitarian divisions of the Church of Jesus Christ of Latter-day Saints. "Would you be willing to serve for one to four months on a Navy hospital ship in Southeast Asia?" she inquired.

"Tell me more about it. I've been to that area of the world and have some longtime connections. Where exactly would we be going?"

Indonesia, the Philippines, Vietnam, and Cambodia was the itinerary. "I've been to Indonesia several times and feel comfortable with the language," I volunteered. So she sent me an application to apply for the mission.

At first I was hesitant to take time off from my incredibly busy eye surgery practice, especially since we had just positioned ourselves to become the first practice west of the Mississippi River to acquire the latest femtosecond laser cataract machine. Yet the dream I often heard growing up of my older sister Kristin Jarstad (Boudreau) of the adventures of working as a physician on a hospital ship called the *Good Ship Hope* captured my imagination, and since Kristi taught me to read, I thought it only fitting to honor her by accepting this opportunity. I would try to include her vicariously by sending her copies of all my e-mails from the ship with my communications to the doctors, patients, and sponsors.

A few weeks later, it was time to fly to Salt Lake City for an interview. The interview was held at the Church of Jesus Christ of Latter-Day Saints headquarters Church Office Building near Temple Square in downtown Salt Lake City. Not only did they accept us as volunteers for Pacific Partnership 2012 (PP2012), but after a second interview, I was asked to be the team leader for the entire Latter-day Saints contingent of up to a hundred volunteer doctors, nurses, and technicians. The interviewers mentioned that normally the team leader would also be called and set apart at the ecclesiastical leader (similar to a branch president or bishop of the congregation); but since I was also to be teaching eye surgery, they would call a Church of Jesus Christ of Latter-day Saints pathologist, Navy Officer Lieutenant Commander Frank Zuehl to assume this leadership position. US Navy Commander (now Captain) Danielle Taysom, a respected radiologist, would be over the women on the ship. Together, we made a great team and handled the leadership duties by committee.

During the interview, I was told, "With your assignment, you will need to handle things on the same level of responsibility as a

Church of Jesus Christ of Latter-day Saints mission president, and your companion will be like a girls' camp counselor with all the young nurses who may get pretty home sick. Could you serve for the entire four months of the deployment?"

I spoke to my partners at Evergreen Eye Center who graciously agreed to take up the slack at my four clinics and my busy surgery center in Seattle for the four months I would be on the Navy deployment as a civilian volunteer and consultant at my own expense (the loss of income to my clinic during this time at the peak of my surgical career would amount to several hundred thousand dollars by volunteering).

Soon began a series of meetings with the US Navy and the other branches of the armed services in San Diego, California. We went over the mission objectives, the schedule, and the country customs in each country where we would sail to. Basically, the ship, USNS *Mercy*, would sail from home port in San Diego and in fourteen days arrive at Pearl Harbor, Honolulu, and in another ten to fourteen days travel to Guam and, following this, steam another seven days to Manado, at the northernmost tip of Indonesia where we would anchor offshore and for two weeks hold clinics and perform eye operations along with instructing the local surgeons in the latest techniques.

I was excited to return to Indonesia. I immediately contacted my good friend Dr. T. D. Gondhowiardjo (MD, PhD) and invited him to come to the ship and give lectures to the ophthalmology staff and residents. He was excited to come and see the ship and would bring along the current president of the IOA (Indonesian Ophthalmology Association), Dr. Nila Moelick, who was also the Minister of Health (like the surgeon general) for the country at the time. A cornea fellow, Dr. Ikhsan Revino (many Indonesians have only one name), would also come from Jakarta.

I realized early on that this would be a once-in-a-lifetime opportunity for the residents, and I encouraged the department chairwoman Dr. Josephine Saerang to invite as many residents onto the ship as possible. She came up with two teams of six residents each who would alternate one week at a time on board ship. Two of the leaders and chief residents would be Dr. Devy Mandagi and Dr. Teguh Susilo.

The US Navy selected Commander Dr. Brice Nicholson, an experienced cataract and LASIK surgeon, to lead the ophthalmology group. He and I would work together to train the local eye surgeons and also perform cataract and pterygium surgery at each stop for two weeks aboard ship.

Though the US Navy had never done this before, I was able to gain permission to teach on shore in the local university hospital for the first time in Navy history whilst there in Manado.

I brought my Mentor portable phaco (ultrasound cataract removal machine) in my checked baggage so we would have a second machine to use on the ship or on shore.

We were given quite a welcome by the university. Both Dr. Nicholson and I gave lectures in the medical school (Sam Ratulangi University Eye Department-Manado). I spoke on common eye emergencies, and Dr. Nicholson spoke on correcting astigmatism with limbal relaxing incisions along with toric (astigmatism correcting) lens implants.

After lectures, we conducted a wet lab using my newly designed Jarstad-Stone teaching head so the residents (all fifty-three of them) could practice capsulorhexis (tearing a controlled circular opening in the lens capsule—considered the most difficult part of cataract surgery to learn). The next day, we took Teguh and Devy into the operating room and were so happy to see that they could perform this technique on a live patient with a cataract without complications.

In speaking with Teguh Susilo, chief resident at Manado, prior to the visit by phone, he mentioned that this was the most difficult part of cataract surgery to learn and wondered if we had any ideas on how to teach the Indonesian Eye Surgery Residents this important step.

Upon hearing this, I contacted my neighbor from church, Boeing engineer Paul Stone, who brainstormed with me; and we came up with an artificial eye made from sprinkler pipe and cellophane from the Party City Store to create a simulated capsule that closely resembled and felt like a real one. We used a small amount of white clay sandwiched between two pieces of blue cellophane film to mimic a dense white cataract and to improve visibility. We even shot a training video and copied it onto several DVDs so the teaching could remain long after we left. It showed the Jarstad-Stone Teaching Head cataract capsule simulator along with the real thing shown with an actual cataract operation after placing vision blue dye inside a real eye that reinforced the simulator training.

The residents seemed to really enjoy the new tool, and Paul found a discarded Boeing crash test dummy head that fit the device perfectly and we used to complete our lifelike simulator.

We then proceeded to the ship where Dr. Nicholson and I took three of the residents at a time and rotated them, so they all put in an IOL (artificial intraocular lens) implant or used the phaco machine inside the eye so they could all say legitimately that they operated on cataracts while aboard the US Navy Hospital ship. It would turn out to be a lifetime bond with those who participated, and we have remained in close and regular contact since.

During the time on board ship, Dr. Nicholson and I operated on a record number of cataract and eye patients. Over four hundred eye surgeries during the four-month deployment which was a record for Navy hospital ship missions. I think by having the two machines and utilizing two operating rooms each day, we were able to double previous efforts.

In addition to our medical work and surgeries, I was assigned to communicate daily with the Church of Jesus Christ of Latter-day Saints headquarters in Salt Lake City via e-mail or satellite phone and hold a weekly Sacrament church meeting and a Monday night "Family Home Evening" get-together to provide opportunities for fellowship with our group of short-term medical humanitarians.

During these meetings, a gospel talk was assigned to two of the Church of Jesus Christ of Latter-day Saints volunteers, and on Monday night, we had a fun activity, with songs or a skit to entertain everyone. One topic that evolved was a "tender mercy" moment" referring to something inspirational or a blessing that a member felt was an answer to prayer. Several medical miracles occurred during the voyage.

One particular patient I remember was a young man named Adi. He was about seventeen years old and was microphthalmic (extremely small unformed eye) and completely blind in one eye since birth and was legally blind in the other eye from a condition called "Peter's Anomaly." This is a condition where the lens, pupil, and iris were stuck to the back side of the cornea and a cataract developed almost from birth. Adi could see light and dark and some shapes out of his one remaining eye but no more. As we screened him, I made the comment to the staff doctors and corpsmen that this was an operation best suited for a university hospital back home and not on a ship in the middle of the Pacific Ocean. Adi's dad approached me and mentioned that this might be the only opportunity that Adi would ever have to see again and that they wouldn't blame me if the operation didn't work or if Adi went blind from my surgery but asked if we would just try for his sake.

Well, as I thought things over, it hit me that this most likely would be the only opportunity this young man would ever have to see again and that perhaps God brought me there at that time (a Mayo Clinic-trained eye surgeon) just to help this one young man see.

We decided to go ahead. It was a difficult operation due to all the scar tissue surrounding his iris and pupil, which was, indeed, stuck firmly to the inside of the cornea. As I gently used the visco-elastic gel to separate the iris and cataractous lens from the cornea, it gently pulled away, and I was able to proceed with a successful cataract operation.

We patched his eye overnight as the custom was then and worried all night what his vision would be restored to the next morning. As we made our rounds the next morning, I had an idea—as we removed the patch, I held my hand out to shake his hand high above Adi's head to see if he really could see. Sure enough, instead of reaching straight ahead, he reached way up and shook my hand, which was suspended just above his head. HE COULD SEE! It was a miracle! His dad was in tears. They both had huge smiles, and I later learned that his follow-up vision was 20/60 and good enough to pass a driver's test and get a motorcycle license and a job. What's more—

he wanted to serve a mission for his church, and his father was so grateful that he could go back to work now that his son Adi could see well enough to stay out of trouble navigating around the house and neighborhood and no longer needed his dad's constant care.

Other interesting operations included a young girl with a cataract and an iris coloboma (a developmental defect where the lower third of her iris was missing). We used a new knot I invented on the spot as I was trying to help Dr. Nicholson remember the Siepser knot for iris repair. We called it the Fisherman's knot, based on the type of clinch knot I used as a commercial fisherman in Westport. It worked great, and I began years later to teach this knot to my residents and in lecturing around the globe: "The Jarstad Fisherman's knot for traumatic iris repair" became a keynote lecture at the All-India Meeting in Delhi in 2019, as well as a frequently used successful way to restore a damaged and misshaped pupil for many patients.

The ship schedule was intense. Each morning, the mess deck was only open from 6:00 a.m. to 6:30 a.m. Mustering (roll call) was at 7:00 a.m., and if you were ten seconds late, you were written up and given cleaning duties in the ship's head (restrooms) or kitchen patrol (KP). It didn't matter if I was on the satellite phone reporting to Salt Lake City or not. I had to be there on time to set an example according to the NAVY.

After muster and roll call, we would go down two or three flights of stairs to the patient preop and postop wards and round on our patients from the previous day or two and examine patients headed for surgery that day and measure their eyes for the correct lens implant power and discharge those who had recovered well enough to leave the ship and return home. They seemed to know where to sit in a long queue just outside the "eye room." When we were finished examining and discharging the postoperative patients, we then sprinted up the stairs and began work on the list of cataract patients for the day. Usually, between six and eight patients were operated on in each room. We would generally finish about 3:00 p.m. and have a debriefing for the day with all the surgeons on ship and go over any complications or equipment issues.

After this meeting, there was just enough time to grab a quick shower and or shave and get ready for evening dinner at the mess deck. There was a special area for the chief petty officers who had their own section and another officer's mess for the officers. As team leaders, we were permitted to eat with the officers but not with the petty officers. Not even the NAVY officers were permitted in there. I chose to eat with our team and the enlisted sailors so I could discuss with them any issues that arose during the day on their shifts.

We also made it a habit of going around the ship in the evening and touching base with the nursing staff and the Church of Jesus Christ of Latter-day Saints team members who were assigned night shifts and missed out on our team meetings. They seemed to appreciate our effort to keep them all in the loop as to our meetings and activity plans.

It was reassuring to find that nearly all our church members got along well, had each other's back, and were great examples of unselfish service and sacrifice. We even volunteered once a week as a team to serve in the mess deck line so that the cafeteria workers could have a break.

The ship had an intranet communication system, and I ruffled a few feathers when I sent a confidential e-mail meant only for the Navy brass complaining that our church member volunteers represented 25 percent of the volunteer medical staff and the Church of Jesus Christ of Latter-day Saints supplied a huge majority of the donated medical supplies from the church humanitarian center just west of the Salt Lake City airport; and yet we were not included in any of the fun offshore activities, public relations dinners with the local government officials, Navy band concerts, or other festive events like friendly soccer matches with the local children (one of our volunteers was a college division 1 women's soccer athlete) on shore. I pointed out this glaring discrimination and was called into a meeting with the Navy brass. Soon after I apologized, 10 percent or more of our people were included in the activities.

One team member created problems. Let's call him Hugh. Hugh Michaelson. He and his wife had been selected to be team leaders a year or two previously. Unfortunately, Hugh lost his balance while going down a stairwell on the ship that previous year and fell and was knocked out with a severe concussion and had other serious injuries which required him to be airlifted off the ship and fly home only two weeks into his assignment as team leader on the previous deployment. Apparently, he was told that he and his wife would be coleaders with us on this deployment. No one bothered to tell us of this arrangement. When everyone was told that I was the team leader, Hugh would smirk and try to undermine my leadership. He refused to participate in our team activities and stayed in his "officer's quarters" during our Monday evening "Family Nights" and made metal jewelry instead. When I would confront him and encourage him to participate with the team, he was very aloof and still wouldn't participate.

Several incidents occurred which were particularly aggravating,. When we reached the Philippines and went for a day to the Manila's Church of Jesus Christ of Latter-day Saints Missionary Training Center for lunch, Hugh introduced himself as Dr. Michaelson (he was a PA—physician's assistant, not an MD). He also introduced himself as our team leader. I was doubly surprised when the Philippines Church of Jesus Christ of Latter-day Saints mission president, who had arranged for a catered lunch, called upon "Dr. Michaelson, your team leader, to say the blessing on the food." Not that it mattered so much to me, but it certainly showed a lack of respect, in my opinion.

Another incident was when I had arranged for a team excursion to Tagaytay (a lake inside a volcano cone inside another lake inside another volcano). As we were slowly progressing through Manila's bumper-to-bumper traffic, we made a stop to regroup, and a registered nurse member of the bus Hugh was assigned to chaperone decided to bail out from our excursion and was going to take a taxi back to the hotel from one of the most dangerous parts of Manila. Hugh reportedly told her, "Fine, go ahead, I don't care." I quickly was appraised of the situation by another team member and, as the father of three girls, told the young woman, "ABSOLUTELY NOT! This is not a safe place for you to be alone as a single White woman. You get back on the bus right now. You're going with us." This prevented a potentially dangerous incident but again showed lack of judgment on Hugh's part.

The other attribute that was disconcerting was Hugh's attempt to "brownnose" every higher-ranking officer and, worse, any official leader of the Church of Jesus Christ of Latter-day Saints whom he encountered. He introduced himself as the team leader to our church leaders all along the way, including Elder Ian Adern, one of the Church of Jesus Christ of Latter-day Saints general authority area presidents in Manila, along with Elder Michael J. Teh (also in the Philippines area presidency) and his wife, Grace, who were long-term friends I had worked with during my previous medical missions to the Philippines. What was really galling was when Hugh's wife told us to "Shoo!" when Elder and Sister Teh were coming aboard for a special fireside meeting. This was just as we had gone down to the gangway, assigned by the US Navy brass to great their small boat as it arrived to dock with the massive Navy hospital ship. As team leaders we were advised to meet the Tehs so they would feel welcome and recognize us as a familiar face. This was the last straw for me. I confronted Hugh's wife and told her in no uncertain terms that I was the team leader of our group and a personal friend of the Tehs and reminded her that she had never met them before and that she was to stand down or I would see to it that I would send her home at the next opportunity. That seemed to get her attention, especially as the Tehs quickly recognized me and bypassed them and everyone else once they saw our familiar faces.

Once onboard ship, there was a special dinner and award recognition for the Tehs along with others, including local military generals from the Philippines. Elder and Sister Teh then had our group assemble for a brief fireside chat and inspirational meeting where they both thanked us for our service quoting the scripture in Matthew 25:40, which talks about when the Savior said, "When you have done it (service) unto one of the least of these... Ye have done it unto me."

As the Tehs left the ship and we said our goodbyes, they expressed their appreciation and mentioned that this was the very first time a Church of Jesus Christ of Latter-day Saints general authority had been on board the US NAVY hospital ship. We were grateful they braved the winds and waves that evening to visit, thank, encourage, and inspire us. True servants of the Lord.

Once on shore in Manila, we had a very inspirational meeting and tour of the WWII memorial cemetery in Manila. Here, Elder Ian Ardern, another of the Church of Jesus Christ of Latter-day Saints general authorities, spoke to us, again thanking us for all our service and sacrifice being so far away from home and loved ones. Again Hugh introduced himself as our team leader, and when Elder Ardern asked if our team leader would come forward, the group quickly corrected him, and all asked me to come up. He wanted us to sing a hymn, and since I had my harmonica with me, I played the notes as we sang.

Later we visited the Manila Church of Jesus Christ of Latter-day Saints temple. I think Hugh finally felt some guilt about his actions and suggested he and his wife remain outside while our group attended a temple session. As we entered the celestial room of the Manila temple assigned as the first to enter, we positioned ourselves so that we could greet each team member as they entered the celestial room. Tears of joy, as well as feelings of overwhelming relief and sacrifice, came welling up as we thanked each team member for their service with the realization that most of us would never meet again in this life but our bonds of service and sacrifice would live on forever in our hearts. Most of the team members would be departing for the USA the next morning, and a new group would board the ship for the final rotation to Sihanoukville, Cambodia. It was a spiritual moment I will never forget.

Back on the ship, we had Saturday night entertainment each weekend with a live NAVY rock band ensemble. Can you believe this is a real job in the US Navy? To go around the world playing music and getting paid for it? They practiced in the lowest level of the ship on the first deck. Since one of the band members was a member of the Church of Jesus Christ of Latter-day Saints and played bass guitar, I journeyed down one day to see if he'd let me try out his guitar.

"Do you ever let civilians jam with you?" I asked.

"Well, we haven't done that before, but do you play?" he inquired.

"I played bass guitar in Doc Rock and the Disorderlies for about ten years," I said.

"Well, let me check with the band director."

Soon the leader of the NAVY band arrived. "So I hear you can play?" he asked. "Let's head into one of the practice rooms and see what you've got," he offered.

I quickly played the bass line to "Brown-Eyed Girl" and a few other songs like "Wild Nights" by Van Morrison, with its frenetic bass line.

"I guess you **CAN** play," he said. "Hey, we haven't done this before, but I think we'll call you out on stage on maybe our last night for a number or two, so if we get in trouble, no one can complain to the brass. We'll tell you the day of."

"Can I pick the song?" I asked.

"No, we'll pick it, but we'll give you a few hours' notice."

About two weeks later, I received a message in the early after-noon that the band would call me up that night to play bass guitar for "Careless Whisper" by WHAM. Since I'd never played that number before, I went topside to the flight deck and, using the ship's satellite dial up Internet, downloaded the song from iTunes, taking forty-five minutes. But I had it. I could practice it on the autographed bass guitar the residents in Manado, Indonesia, presented to me as a gift for teaching them cataract surgery on the ship. It wasn't too difficult a bass line; and despite the nerves of playing a number in front of the entire one thousand shipmates (I'd only learned a few hours before), I managed to pull it off. The band tried to stop/start at the end pos-sibly to throw me off, but I was able to pay enough attention to stay right with them. There were several high fives from my teammates and the sailors. It was quite a night.

Our final stop was in Sihanoukville, Cambodia. It was here that I met a woman of great faith, whose five-year-old daughter had ptosis (droopiness) of the right-upper eyelid. In many countries, children (and adults for that matter) are shunned by their communities if they are noted to have this mild deformity. This faithful lady waited all day in the hot humid ninety-five-degree weather to receive help for her daughter. I had performed that operation as a chief resident at Mayo Clinic decades before and a few times since on mission trips and as I first began my medical practice, but on a five-year-old? That would be a challenge under general anesthetic without the ability to sit her up and check the eyelid height during the operation and make adjustments. It would be a "one-shot" operation to get it right.

We did the surgery, and it turned out great. They were both so happy. The mom, we noticed had a very peculiar speech impediment. So we asked her to open her mouth. To our surprise, she had almost no hard or soft palate. She would hiss her words and asked us if there was anything we could do to fix **her** problem. We presented her situation to the commanders on the ship and arranged for ENT to do a cleft palate type operation to repair her congenital defect before we left Cambodia. I was thankful we could help this faithful mom and her daughter.

As we prepared to leave Sihanoukville, Cambodia, we separated onto the buses that would take us to Phnom Penh, the capital, to catch our flight home to the USA. Near Phnom Penh, we visited the Killing Fields Memorial where despot Pol Pot exterminated all the educated and skilled members of Cambodian society using the most cruel and gruesome methods imaginable. The grounds felt like holy land because of the great sacrifices of this noble people.

As we gathered on the ship for our final night, an award ceremony was conducted by the thirteen NGO (nongovernment organizations) that assisted and helped staff the positions on the ship. Each group presented a plaque or memento to the ship's captain. In our case, it was Captain James Morgan, a brilliant and hard-nosed former destroyer and aircraft carrier commanding officer who stated he "really didn't want the hospital ship assignment and knew absolutely nothing about a hospital ship or medicine, nor did he care to learn anything." To our captain, this was just a "stepping-stone" to reach his career objective of being a US Navy destroyer captain. By the end of the deployment, he had earned everyone's respect, and he opened up finally as he and I rode a launch ferry back to the ship after a long hard day of work in Vinh, North Vietnam. As I related to him the story of a young ten-year-old boy named Guon, he thanked me for our service and expressed his appreciation for us and our support in his role as commander of our deployment.

Guon was a ten-year-old Vietnamese boy, who I noticed was the class clown at a school building we used for screening patients. We

JOHN S. JARSTAD, MD

noticed him running into the other kids and being bullied because of his clumsiness. When I caught a glimpse out of the corner of my eye that he had a little squint and crossed his eyes ever so slightly for a split second, it dawned on me that he might have accommodative esotropia and might need glasses. I asked around if anyone knew who he was and could bring him to the makeshift clinic we had set up in his school classroom.

Guon soon appeared, practically dragged in by the local volunteers; and as I performed retinoscopy, sure enough, my suspicions were confirmed. He was a +6.00 diopter hyperope. He was so farsighted that he was legally blind without eyeglasses. We quickly located the strongest two pairs of glasses (just in case one pair broke) and fitted him up. He lit up like Christmas with a huge smile on his face—seeing the world clearly for the very first time. We wondered as he ran home what his parents would say now that he had glasses that corrected his blindness and what change in his life would occur now that he could see and no longer serve as the butt of his classmates jokes as Guon no longer ran into them due to his newfound sight. Perhaps we will never know.

The final incident of mutiny on the USNS *Mercy* that almost led to a fistfight our last night onboard occurred during the presentation of plaques and mementos to the captain and COOs of the ship. Here again, Hugh insisted that he represent our group and present the Church of Jesus Christ of Latter-day Saints plaque to the captain. I was tired of fighting Hugh's mutinous behavior, so I relented and reminded him to keep it brief and make sure he was ready to go up right after Project Hope presented their captain's award. For some reason, Hugh hesitated; and Scotty, the Australian Special Forces sergeant master of ceremonies, abruptly concluded the meeting and awards ceremony before Hugh had an opportunity to go up and present our award. We had been encouraging Hugh to go forward early and be prepared as Project Hope was in the middle of their presentation so he would be ready; but whether he had sudden stage fright or just wasn't to be told what to do—he muffed it. As the meeting abruptly ended, Hugh was on to Scotty like a pit bull on a steak and no match at his six feet and 135 pounds to

Scotty's fireplug middle NFL linebacker-sized physique. As Hugh began to whine about Scotty ignoring him for the final presentation and Scotty apologizing once and as curtly as an Australian military police/Special Forces sergeant could, Hugh persisted. Scotty told him to back off and was about to take Hugh down when I stepped in. "It's okay, Scotty. We are okay. We can take care of this tomorrow as we disembark." "Hugh, you need to get back. I'll handle this." With that, Hugh retreated, and I spoke to Scotty. "I was about ready to tear his head off," said the Australian MP. "I know, Scotty. He's been a pain." We're okay. And with that, Scotty retreated to his many fans on the ship who loved his Saturday night monologue and jokes to accept their goodbyes.

The leaders for LDS Charities who arrived for our final few days on ship from the Church of Jesus Christ of Latter-day Saints headquarters in Salt Lake City were shocked as they witnessed the entire exchange. "What was that all about?" one asked. "I've been putting up with him these last four months. He has undermined my authority and leadership the entire way, and tonight was a prime example of the way he has behaved. "We had no idea! We are so sorry you had to put up with that, Dr. Jarstad." "Well, I'm pretty easygoing. I thought we could handle it and get by, but he's certainly made things unpleasant," I unloaded.

As we met the next morning to bid farewell to Captain Morgan and the leaders, someone suggested we sing the "Star-Spangled Banner." Afterward, we presented musical instruments autographed by each team member, as fitting reminders for the position and calling each of the four USNS *Mercy* leaders fulfilled and compared them to a successful rock band.

For the ship's merchant marine captain, we presented an ornate Cambodian drum, symbolic of a band's drummer who typically owned the van that transported the band from venue to venue symbolic of his navigating and transporting us on time to each port. To the chief medical officer, a beautiful red rhythm guitar to symbolize keeping the doctors and nurses and staff on cue and setting the tempo. To the COO, a lead guitar, signifying his ability to improvise and lead our mission and to the commandant—Captain Morgan, a bass guitar representing the heart and soul of the team, creating a soulful beat. They seemed to enjoy the analogies. Later, we learned that officers and any government employees are not allowed to accept gifts over twenty-five dollars in value. Our thought was that all one hundred of our volunteers could each give them a five-dollar thank-you card or pool our money for the guitars. Captain Morgan called us a week after we returned home to Federal Way and informed us that he really enjoyed meeting us and appreciated our service and that our guitars would be donated to the ship for future missions.

Despite the mutiny on the *Mercy*, I was grateful for the experience of a lifetime—serving with my fellow servicemen and women, having my country and church need me, and providing leadership to our team and sight to the blind for four months in the faraway lands of Southeast Asia.

CHAPTER 40

INTERESTING PATIENT CONSULTATIONS

President Abdurrahman Wahid of Indonesia

In 1999, I received a call from my good friend and colleague Dr. Tjahjono D. Gondhowiardjo, MD, PhD., Jakarta Eye Center and University of Indonesia. TD mentioned that the president of Indonesia Abdurarahman Wahid was in need of glaucoma surgery and asked if I would perform the operation. While I was extremely flattered and honored that he would think of me, I felt inspired to have him consider taking the president to Salt Lake City, Utah, where he could have Dr. Randall Olson, the department chairman of the Moran Eye Institute or their glaucoma specialist, Dr. Alan Crandall, perform this risky operation.

They seemed excited to see him and also agreed it would be a great PR opportunity for the leaders of the Church of Jesus Christ of Latter-day Saints at church headquarters to meet the president and perhaps discuss some joint humanitarian projects.

TD was one of Indonesia's foremost specialists; and his wife, Tati, was head of radiation oncology at the University of Indonesia. TD was being considered for a time as vice president of the country; and I would joke that if he ever became president of Indonesia, could we come and stay at the Indonesian White House?

While in Salt Lake, President Wahid met with Gordon B. Hinckley, who at the time was the president and prophet of the Church of Jesus Christ of Latter-day Saints. Apparently, they had a good meeting, and some mutual humanitarian projects were arranged. The glaucoma surgery was a success I learned years later, but unfortunately, President Wahid's glaucoma was so far advanced that his vision did not return to normal. Most will never know what arrangements I made to make the visit possible, and others have claimed that they set it up through Charity Vision or other organizations, but that's okay. I was happy to have a small part in the visit of two world leaders quietly, behind the scenes.

The Dutch Ambassador to Indonesia

Following my arrangement for the president of Indonesia's visit to the USA, TD referred me another VIP patient, the Dutch ambassador to Indonesia from the Dutch embassy in Jakarta. He was interested in a multifocal lens implant for his cataract surgery, and no Indonesian eye surgeons were implanting them at the time. I was happy to accommodate this gentleman, and we made all the arrangements for him and his wife by picking them up at the Seattle-Tacoma International Airport, providing them with a hotel for the week they would be in town and arranging his surgery, a dinner, and his stay.

The surgery went well, and he was able to see without glasses for the first time following the successful operation for both distance and reading. His wife was so appreciative and gave us a gift box of delicious chocolate truffles as they returned home. It was an honor to take care of them, and they have kept in touch over the years.

Major League Baseball Star

A first baseman in the San Francisco farm system from our town—one who had been a classmate of my daughter who also was a 4.0 student and helped my daughter with her Calculus homework—arrived one day for a LASIK surgery evaluation. He was having trouble with the dust from the infield getting on his contact lenses and making it difficult to see the baseball. I found that he was nearsighted with astigmatism and that LASIK or PRK would be of benefit. For professional and college athletes, I came up with the idea of fine-tuning their LASIK surgery by position. SO that in other words, instead of 20/20, which means they are focused perfectly at a distance of twenty feet in our exam rooms, I calculated their distance vision by position. For basketball players, I aimed for best focus at the top of the key about thirty feet away; for baseball pitchers and catcher, sixty feet and six inches; for infielders, ninety feet; and for outfielders, three hundred feet. This meant the refraction power I aimed for was +0.25 for basketball players and baseball pitchers, catchers, and infielders; and +0 .50 for baseball outfielders. This seemed to work as several high school, college, and professional athletes succeeded with their new "perfect for position" vision.

Travis Ishikawa not only made the starting 9 for the San Francisco Giants baseball team on opening day in 2009 but also led the National League as the best pinch hitter with the highest batting average soon after we performed his LASIK, Travis hit the "walk off" home run to defeat the St. Louis Cardinals, end the National league championship series and send the Giants to the World Series in 2014. Travis garnered two World Series championship rings after his successful LASIK surgery.

One of the greatest thrills as a surgeon was to attend opening day in San Francisco in April 2009 when Travis went three for three on his first at bats, and I photographed him at the plate batting with his face and batting average of one thousand showing on the big-screen jumbotron in the outfield. I blew up the photo, framed it, and presented it to his mom as a keepsake of his successful major league career.

The other moment that will always live forever in my memory was as above and occurred as I was watching the playoffs at my daughter's home, and Travis was up to bat and hit the walk off home run to eliminate the St. Louis Cardinals (I was living in Missouri at the time). We were all just praying he'd get a hit, and how elated we were when he shot the ball over the right field fence into the water in San Francisco Bay. "The Second Shot Heard Round the WORLD" is what it was called and will always be remembered in San Francisco Giants baseball lore as one of the most remembered plays in the history of San Francisco sports.

See YouTube Travis Ishikawa 2014 walk off home run: https://youtu.be/uogT8X26-ko.

CHAPTER 41

SELLING THE BUSINESS AND RETURN TO ACADEMIA

S hortly following my three and a half months at sea on the USNS *Mercy* hospital ship, I noticed a distinct difference in my two partners' attitude. While I was gone serving the US NAVY and our country, they were reaping the benefits of having all the eye surgery to themselves and made a record amount of money. Not that they didn't deserve to, because they had to do what I had done a few years earlier and taken on more work than ever with each taking on an extra 50 percent of one of the highest-volume cataract and LASIK practices in the Seattle-Tacoma area.

That year, both of my partners took home close to $1 million each.

Obviously, with me out of the picture, they could each boost their income considerably.

As we met in our monthly doctor/shareholder meetings, it became obvious that the partnership which consultants said was one of the strongest in the USA, putting us in the top 1 percent of eye surgery practices, was not going to stand the test of time.

With this and other revelations I won't go into, I decided that it might be a good time to break up the partnership and return to academia for the final ten to fifteen years of my working life, which provided me—a one-time uneducated, poverty-stricken, commercial fisherman—more financial success than I could have ever dreamed of.

In our next shareholders' meeting, I stated that since I had accomplished about everything I wanted to with the building of the practice; that a colleague, about my same age with a highly successful Seattle clinic, had recently suffered a stroke and looked like he was going to lose his practice; and that I was approaching sixty, I needed to begin working on an exit strategy, when the value of my practice had reached its peak.

"When you guys are ready to buy me out, I'm about ready to leave and go back into academics," I mentioned in our meeting. Big smiles by them, and as the dollar signs twinkled in their eyes, we all agreed to hire the most reputable firm in ophthalmology practice evaluations, BSM Consultants out of Incline Village, Nevada. Bruce Maller had been instrumental in our success over the years and had an impeccable reputation as being honest and fair. Neither side would get everything they wanted, but Bruce got deals done, and we knew of his reputation for successfully brokering the deals.

After several months of negotiating, we reached a deal. Rick Boudreau, my brother-in-law and practice administrator and an award-winning speaker at all the ophthalmology administrator meetings, was instrumental in the negotiations as well including getting me a "founders bonus" as the founding partner and setting up Evergreen from scratch twenty-five years before.

Both partners had an option to buy the real estate for the difference between what I paid for the surgery center and clinic and its current appraised value. They had been offered that opportunity four times and each time rejected it. But their attorney felt that option was still worth something. Because they did not want it, they agreed to be paid $62,500 each to relinquish any rights to my building.

They could have paid one-third of $2.75 million and each owned one-third. After the practice sale, an investor group paid me a multiple of that amount, which allowed me to pay off my loan on the building and have investment money for retirement.

I was suddenly nearly debt-free and would have steady high income until I hit sixty-five.

As soon as the final details of the deal were agreed upon, I began to shop for an academic position. Almost that night after the deal was decided, I submitted my résumé on line to the American Academy of Ophthalmology web site Job center. There was a job available for a glaucoma specialist at University of Missouri, the flagship university for the state of Missouri higher education system. *Why not?* I thought. Jessica, our eldest daughter, had moved there with Alan and her children from New York about three years before, and that would make visiting the grandchildren much easier than a four-hour flight to Kansas City. I applied there and also was contacted by a search firm about the department chairman's job at University of South Carolina.

The same night my résumé was into the system, I received a call from the department chairman at Missouri. It was Rick Fraunfelder, who I remembered was an ophthalmology resident in Seattle a few years before and whose father was a noted ophthalmologist and was chairman of the University of Oregon's program for a number of years.

"I know who you are. Why would you want to come to Missouri?" Dr. Fraunfelder queried. After explaining the situation, my love for teaching, my ties to Missouri; hearing about their need; and admitting that I wasn't a pure glaucoma specialist but had about 30 percent of my practice devoted to glaucoma patients and that I had spent about my first ten years of practice doing all the glaucoma surgery south of downtown Seattle and felt very comfortable doing all the procedures available at that time except tube shunts, Dr. Fraunfelder asked, "When can you interview?"

I had one other visit to South Carolina, so it would be in February, and I could start as soon as July.

The Carolina visit went well, but the program was small and on academic probation. It needed a lot of work. It would be a challenge.

The acting chairman was a retina specialist in private practice, who was a good ol' boy from the south, and when I wouldn't drink alcohol with the faculty at dinner, I got the impression that I wouldn't fit in. When I returned home, the school asked me to list what I would change or suggestions I would make if I was offered the chairman's job.

I had a concise summary including that the faculty would need to see more than twenty-four patients per day each (three patients per hour) and contribute to the financial success of the practice and department. Also, the department would need a complete overhaul with new equipment to bring it up to date. It was losing money, and one thing I knew how to do was to turn a practice around and generate income.

A few days after my interview, I was offered the position of Ophthalmology Department chairman at University of South Carolina. They wanted to fly us out to meet the dean of the medical school and president of the university and hold a press conference. I had spent an afternoon looking at homes and found the perfect place about ten minutes from campus on Lake Murray with a boat lift and an outdoor pool. I had attended the Church of Jesus Christ of Latter-day Saints temple in Columbia, South Carolina, just southeast of town; and it was exciting to see the area my brother-in-law John Kingston had worked as a missionary several decades before. I felt good about the town and the job.

About two days before I was supposed to fly out for the meetings, I received a call after work at home. It was the head of the search committee, a very nice, articulate African American professor who informed me that the reason they hadn't contacted me until late was that "it was an extremely difficult decision, but a few of the faculty felt that I just wasn't the right fit" for their department (wouldn't drink with them and wanted everyone to work harder). She also stated that my number of publications wasn't as high as they'd like it to be for the chairman's job. So after being offered the job—now it was gone!

That left Missouri as my next stop.

We arrived and were treated royally—Tiger Hotel, a gift package on arrival, dined with several faculty, and asked to present a lecture on my experience in femtosecond bladeless laser cataract surgery as one of the early world experts, having performed close to a thousand surgeries by that time.

The department had big plans for the future, and Dr. Fraunfelder was an outstanding recruiter. Perhaps the best I'd ever met. I could teach residents, have my own clinic, do research, and travel. It seemed like the dream job.

I had just advanced in rank to full adjunct professor of surgery at Pacific Northwest University College of Osteopathic Medicine after starting as an assistant and associate professor, so I was taken aback by the offer for me to start as an assistant professor at Missouri. I didn't care too much, but then I thought, "I'm willing to take one step back but not two." They petitioned the medical school dean, and it was agreed based on my experience that I would start at the associate professor level, and university policy was that in five years, I could advance to full professor at MIZZOU.

After returning home to Seattle, I visited the temple and was meditating in the celestial room when the thought hit me to look in one of the scriptures on a nearby stand. I opened to a passage that stated essentially "get to Missouri with all due haste." That was good enough for me.

CHAPTER 42

MIGHTY MIRACLES IN MADAGASCAR (LOAVES, FISHES, EYEGLASSES, AND DUCT TAPE)

n 2015, shortly before selling my ophthalmology practice, I was asked by LDS Charities to visit Madagascar and determine what equipment and supplies the twenty-four ophthalmologists (in a country of twenty-four million) and the medical school in Antananarivo might find useful.

I'd never been to the island nation before and the closest I'd been being Zimbabwe quite a few years earlier.

The flight would go through Paris from Seattle, and French and Malagasy were the recognized languages (I spoke neither). We would need an interpreter, and the Church of Jesus Christ of Latter-day Saints Humanitarian missionaries would be there, along with a local member to assist us.

We arrived and stayed in a very nice hotel right downtown. We toured the medical facilities and set up with our donated eyeglasses to stage an eyeglass day. The queue around the local meetinghouse

248

stretched outside and around the chapel as we arrived. We had only brought about two hundred pairs of reading and other prescription glasses, and as we were about to begin, I suggested we have a prayer. This was the gist of it: "Heavenly Father, we thank Thee that we have arrived here in Madagascar safely with all of our supplies. We are grateful to Thee for our talents, and all that we have been blessed with we owe to Thee. We are grateful that so many needy children of Thine have arrived, and it appears that we will not have enough eyeglasses, so with faith we pray for a miracle, just like the loaves and fishes in times of old, that we may have enough eyeglasses to care for all of Thy children who truly need them. We thank Thee. In the name of Jesus Christ. Amen."

Then we went to work. We found many people did not need glasses and had normal vision. Those who did need glasses, we seemed to have just enough for and in the correct power prescription. At the end of the day, we had two pairs of reading glasses left. Just as we were leaving, two rather tall, well-dressed men arrived and asked if they were too late. Both were on the high council of the Antananarivo Madagascar Stake. We tested their eyes and found they exactly fit the two remaining pairs of reading glasses, and our work was finished at the eye screening.

The next day, we attended church in the local ward. It was the first Sunday of the month—fast and testimony Sunday. One of the local young missionaries translated for us. A lady in a colorful dress stood and thanked God for answering her prayer. She had broken her glasses about a month before and, in a country where the average YEARLY income is about US $300, did not know how she would afford a new pair. She thanked God that she not only got new reading glasses in her exact prescription but was also allowed a spare pair toward the end of the eye screening.

As I was unloading the duffle bag filled with eyeglasses earlier in the day, I felt something give around my stomach. *Maybe a muscle strain*, I thought. The bags were heavy. Later that evening, I felt a sharper pain in my mid epigastrium. *Indigestion*, I thought. The next morning on our way to inspect a possible donation site in the country, the pain worsened, and I could feel a tiny bulge just above my belly button. *Oh no*, I thought. *I'm getting a sports hernia.*

I tried to relax and push the tiny knuckle of intestine back inside my abdominal wall, but it wouldn't budge. The thought of having emergency surgery in a developing country was not very appealing and could be dangerous.

Returning to the hotel, I lay flat on my back for fifteen minutes to relax and was finally able to reduce the thumb-sized hernia and immediately felt better. *But how do I keep it in?* I thought. *DUCT TAPE!* That was the first thing I learned about medical missions is always pack a roll of duct tape. With that, I was able to duct-tape the skin together and keep the hernia from reappearing until I returned to Seattle. Our God is a god of miracles. Miracles still happen today.

CHAPTER 43

SIXTH AFRICAN
MISSION: ANGOLA

I n 2015, just prior to my relocation to University of Missouri in Columbia, I was contacted by the Church of Jesus Christ of Latter-day Saints Charities Vision Committee and asked if I would be interested in visiting the Ophthalmology Department at Instituto Ophthamologie d'Angola, in Luanda, the capital.

They mentioned that there was a keen interest in the university professors and residents learning the latest techniques in cataract surgery and the department had modern equipment but little experience in its use. With a little persuading, and just a month or less to prepare, I began the process of getting a visa to visit.

This was far more complicated than I had imagined. I would need to present my credentials and visit the Angolan embassy in Houston, Texas, or Washington, DC, in person to obtain it.

The visit was up in the air until during the middle of a family vacation to Branson and Table Rock Lake in Southern Missouri, when the church called and asked if I could travel to the Angolan embassy

251

in Washington, DC, the next day so that I could visit and teach that next week in the medical school in Luanda. Returned immediately to Columbia, quickly packed up the supplies and equipment I felt would be needed, and caught a flight to Paris and then on to Angola.

Dr. Scott Sykes, an experienced general ophthalmologist and very good cataract surgeon from Odgen, Utah, had expressed interest in a mission trip and applied at the Church of Jesus Christ of Latter-day Saints headquarters and was assigned to go with me. Since he had served a church mission to Brazil and spoke Portuguese, he was asked to meet me in Luanda and, because of the diamond, oil, and gold rush going on at the time, possibly share a hotel room. Soon after my arrival, I realized why. An inexpensive hotel in the capital (like a Holiday Inn) was over $500 per night.

Dinner at a hole-in-the-wall off Street Café was $60 per person for a modest stir-fry dinner of rice, chicken, and kizaca (boiled cassava leaves).

Arriving at the university, we introduced ourselves to the ophthalmology program's chairwoman and discussed the needs of her training program. Soon after, as we began our presentations in the lecture hall, we noticed something a little strange. The entire department of faculty and residents (except for one young man from Spain) were all women! Since I grew up with three sisters and had three daughters (including one as an ophthalmologist), this was of no concern to me; but later after my lecture the chairwoman mentioned, "You may be wondering why our department is all women. You see, Angola had a prolonged civil war, and all the men in the department were killed."

We went on to lecture on eye emergencies, small-incision cataract surgery, and the correction of astigmatism during cataract surgery.

Each day following our lectures, we staffed the resident and attending's cataract operations. I realized that many directions for the patients were very similar in Portuguese and Spanish. By using my best Spanish and with the help of Dr. Sykes, who spoke fluent Portuguese, we were successful in teaching several of the trainees without any complications.

One resident in particular, a lady from Cuba, seemed to have a knack for the surgery and was a quick study. After staffing several of the young doctors the first few days, we decided to concentrate on Dr. Rivera, the chief resident, and help her so that she in turn could teach the others after we left.

I was impressed with the wealth of the department in that they had all the latest equipment—in many cases better than anything we had at the university or my private practice in Seattle.

As we prepared to leave, the department chairwoman asked to meet with me in private at her office to personally thank me for coming and teaching them. She also floated the idea of hiring me for an entire year to train them further. I was extremely flattered, and despite an offer of seven figures to stay and teach, I had to turn down the honor. I was grateful for the invitation to visit this up and coming program and inspired that there were such talented and brilliant women ophthalmologists in a country struggling to rebuild after devastating wars.

On the return, I was able to visit my old home of England and visit Brighton and Hove, where the Rayner IOL (intraocular lens) factory was located. I had arranged a tour of the lens-manufacturing plant through my local Rayner lens representative in the USA. I was met by the director, Mr. Jennings, who provided me a VIP tour of the sterile facility; and afterward, I had the opportunity to learn of a museum to be built in Dr. Harold Ridley's honor on the grounds of the factory. I was shown the plans, and it seemed impressive and a fitting honor for the man who persevered through all the thoughtless criticism by a few of his jealous peers and provided this sight-restoring technology to the world and was knighted by the queen of England a couple of years before he passed away. I was so happy to meet him personally in Seattle in 1999 and thank him for the (at that time) "ten thousand grateful cataract surgery patients whose lives he changed for the better" by not giving up on his invention. With teary eyes, he thanked me for my kindness in thanking him.

AUTHOR'S NOTE: Meeting so many famous world figures would seem to me to be like a modern *Forrest Gump* in my travels around the world. It would make for an incredible movie someday but if not, perhaps in the next life a short documentary on the story. I can exhibit the story of my life and the experiences Heavenly Father has blessed my life with that have added to the joy and amazement of a fortunate life indeed.

CHAPTER 44

A TEMPLE MARRIAGE WITH BRITISH ORIGINS

On the Fourth of July 2015, as I was preparing to move to Missouri, we held our annual Independence Day BBQ and rock concert at the mansion at 832 SW 295th Street (one of the largest homes in Federal Way at ten thousand square feet with three acres on the waterfront of Puget Sound). We began the morning by setting up the BBQ grills, the ice coolers, the soft drinks, the Fourth-themed paper plates, decorations, extra chairs, and tables from the local church, and prepared for the annual event by printing up a flyer and hand-delivering the invitation to all of the neighbors within a half mile or earshot of our band speakers.

We typically hired a local rock band to play for three hours in the afternoon on the condition that they would invite me up on stage for a couple of numbers toward the end of their gig. Usually, it was "Takin' Care of Business" by Bachman Turner or "Brown-Eyed Girl" and "Wild Nights" by Van Morrison or "Proud Mary" by CCR—something with a punchy bass line to it.

As the afternoon went on, I was excited and happy to see that Adrian Beech's son Matthew and his fiancée, Maddie, arrived. Matthew informed me that they would be getting married in the Portland temple in the fall and asked if I might be interested in joining them for the ceremony in Portland. I had baptized his father, Adrian, into the Church of Jesus Christ of Latter-day Saints when I was a missionary in Walsall, England, in 1975; and Adrian and his wife, Jaime, lived in Oregon City just south of the Portland temple, where Adrian was an insurance adjuster for Farmers Insurance and had served five years as the bishop of the Oregon City Church of Jesus Christ of Latter-day Saints Ward congregation. We decided that I would fly back to Portland for the day of the wedding from Missouri just after I moved and surprise his mom and dad.

The day of the wedding arrived, and I arrived about an hour before the ceremony and took a seat in the back of the room in a corner and when Adrian and Jaime arrived, there was a look of *happy shock* when they turned around for the first time and our eyes met. It was a heavenly wedding, and afterward, I was asked to stand in with some amazing photos that included the sunbeams streaking down through the perpetual clouds of dreary October Portland skies and illuminating the wedding party with a heavenly glow.

That was another joyous experience of a lifetime, and I was so thrilled to be asked to be included. I always said as a missionary that it was the greatest joy to teach the gospel to people who were more righteous than I. The Beech family definitely fits that description.

CHAPTER 45

THIRD KOREAN MISSION

L ate in fall of 2016, I learned about a conference in Seoul Korea on "Controversies in Ophthalmology." It seemed to be a perfect venue for my latest research into immediate adjustment of the eye pressure after completion of cataract surgery. The fact that one of our new faculty members and glaucoma expert, was originally from there and contributed to the data on the paper made it interesting to apply. The paper was accepted, and we were both authorized to attend the conference in Seoul, South Korea. She was planning to visit her parents in their home that same time of year, and after discussing the possibility of skiing at Alpensia and Yongpyong, the site of the upcoming Winter Olympic Games, we made plans to attend and present our research.

It also happened at this time that the Church of Jesus Christ of Latter-day Saints and LDS Charities were honoring my good friend and Indonesian ophthalmologist Dr. T. D. Gondhowiardjo, MD, PhD, for his unselfish charitable service and asked me if I could possibly attend a tribute dinner for TD and say a few words. I was delighted to accept the invitation. I would fly to Seoul and make a twenty-four-hour round trip to Jakarta and back to Seoul to go skiing with my young colleague and her mom at Alpensia.

I decided to honor TD by basing my talk on the five pillars of Islam. Under courage, I had a photo of a snowboarder getting massive air to remember TD's fearless courage in snowboarding from the top of Crystal Mountain. I was also able to find several slides showing him in action on the USNS *Mercy* hospital ship and carrying a woman through floodwaters during a storm. He was very surprised and appreciative of my visit. We kept it a secret that I would attend until the last minute. Boy, was he surprised. It was the least I could do after twenty-four years of friendship and volunteering together from the first Katarak Safari to the day on the hospital ship. His family and many friends and colleagues attended the dinner. The Church of Jesus Christ of Latter-day Saints area president and other church leaders attended. Afterward, I met with Dr. Budi Setiyo to find out what needs they might have in equipment that the Church of Jesus Christ of Latter-day Saints Charities could help them with. Another teaching microscope was about all they needed, and Bogor was happy to receive it for teaching the residents.

Catching the red-eye flight back to Seoul, I made contact with my colleague and her mom, and we boarded the bus for Alpensia. We had booked two rooms at the Holiday Inn, and I was very impressed with the facilities at the ski resort. I skied pretty much nonstop for three days, bringing my own good fitting ski boots but renting the skis to save baggage costs. I attempted to teach my colleague and her mom, but her mom was not very interested in learning to ski, so I escorted my young colleague up the beginner hill, and once she got the hang of skiing, that next morning she was ready to try the intermediate runs—after staying up all night watching how-to ski videos. By the end of the second day, she was able to try the longest run from the top without assistance.

After three days of skiing, it was time to check out around noon and head back to Seoul for the medical eye conference. I debated whether to ski that last morning, but the runs were groomed and so smooth that I said to myself, "Go for it." And so I got up early and rented skis and had four hours of nonstop skiing down the upcoming

Winter Olympic runs, and I quit just in time to join my colleague and her mom for the bus ride back to Seoul.

Back in Seoul, our poster was displayed, and we met with several top ophthalmologists from all over Asia.

What a great way to be introduced to skiing in Asia. Can hardly wait for my own kids and grandkids to try Alpensia and Yongpyong and the Winter Olympic ski runs someday.

CHAPTER 46

THE "NOT GOOD ENOUGH" MICROSCOPE

Shortly after my four-month sabbatical US Navy *Mercy* mission to Southeast Asia, I was contacted by the Church of Jesus Christ of Latter-day Saints to see if I would be willing to serve on the Vision Committee for the church's Humanitarian Department. It would require attending board meetings at the Church Administration Building at church headquarters one Wednesday each month and helping to determine where the resources from the humanitarian fund donations would be distributed worldwide from weekly donations members of the church's sixteen million members would go to.

Each month, members of the Church of Jesus Christ of Latter-day Saints fast by going without food or drink for two meals or twenty-four hours and donate what they would have spent on food to a fund the church uses to feed the hungry (both members of the church and nonmembers). We eat too much as it is, and as a medical doctor, I've seen proof that there are proven health benefits to a monthly fast.

In addition, church president Thomas S. Monson added "assisting the poor and needy" to the threefold mission of the church as he became president (the other missions are (1) proclaim the Gospel of Jesus Christ, (2) perfect the saints, and (3) redeem the dead through family history and temple work). President Monson, who served in the US Navy during WWII, was instrumental and took a personal interest in missions such as the Operation Pacific Partnership with the NAVY and in our work on the Vision Committee.

As part of my assignment, I traveled to the Philippines and visited several clinics and university eye programs to see what their needs were and reported back during our monthly meetings on what equipment the local programs wanted and what they really could use.

Some programs asked for $100,000 high-tech retina cameras when they didn't even have the basic eye examination equipment like slit lamp biomicroscopes or examination chairs, stands, or phoropters (the machine eye doctors use to check which looks better—one or two).

One program in Bacolod City (where I had served a Lion's Club mission, with Mayo Clinic residency classmate Dr. Robert Rivera and later Mayo Clinic department chairman Dharmendra "Dave" R. Patel) was a teaching institution training eye residents in cataract surgery. During our visit, I met Dr. Miguel Sarabia, an expert in manual small-incision cataract surgery or "M-6" for short. Observing him in clinic and in the operating room, I was highly impressed with his surgical skills and abilities. I noticed that he did not have a teaching microscope for instructing the residents in surgery. Instead, he would pause every so often during a procedure and have the resident in training look over his shoulder for a few seconds and then resume his operation.

A teaching microscope allows a second surgeon to view the entire operation, assist in irrigating the cornea to improve the surgeon's view, cut sutures, and help with other steps.

When I reported back after returning from visiting Bacolod City, Mindanao, Baler Aurora, Cebu, Bataan, and Leyte, I felt impressed that we should help Dr. Sarabia and the residents in Bacolod City's eye surgery program. Dr. Sarabia was already doing cataract outreach to serve the poor, and while there, we visited one of the outlying barrios and screened several patients and fit about a hundred pair of donated reading glasses. The fact that I had visited Bacolod City before with the Philippine-American Lions Club of Phoenix, Arizona, and had a good experience there previously confirmed in my mind that this was the place the Lord and the Church would want us to assist.

When I returned, I met with our Vision Committee and gave a summary of my findings. Bacolod City needed a teaching microscope, and other sites could use basic exam tools until their programs were more mature in adding additional equipment. I expressed my concern that a $100,000 retina camera could wait and that the item that would do the greatest good right now in the Philippines was a teaching microscope for Bacolod City. I mentioned that I had purchased several good serviceable used Zeiss portable microscopes from Prescott's Surgical Microscopes in Monument, Colorado, that were manually operated, had few moving parts, and were very durable. The price for one with a teaching head and beam splitter would be around $25,000. This item was agreed upon by the committee and sent up the chain of command to the First Presidency of the Church of Jesus Christ of Latter-day Saints. The prophet and president of the Church, President Thomas S. Monson, preferred to approve requests personally, perhaps because he was instrumental in adding "assisting the poor and needy" to the church priorities.

When the request came back after his review, President Monson's comment was, "NOT GOOD ENOUGH," and "Can we do any better than that?" I said, "Well, the church has substantial donations now, and the tithing slips have been modified to include fast offerings (seventeen million members of the church are asked to fast in going without food or drink for two meals and twenty-four hours on the first Sunday of every month and donate what they would have spent on food to the poor and needy) in addition to tithing and missionary options for donation, and the only other category added in streamlining the donation slips members can fill out each Sunday or donate online was "humanitarian" fund."

In response to President Monson's request, I said, "Well, maybe we should go all in and recommend a new Zeiss German Teaching

Eye Microscope that included all the capabilities for all types of eye surgery with a state-of-the-art teaching assistant scope head, a video input to record the trainees and professor's operations, and a large plasma-screen TV so more than one trainee could view each operation in real time or broadcast to a remote location."

When word came back from the prophet, saying, "Now that's more like it!" I was amazed and very happy. A few weeks later, I was asked to travel to the Philippines to represent the Vision Committee and Humanitarian Department of the Church for the presentation of the state-of-the-art teaching microscope. Little did I know what impact this donation and the inspiration of the prophet would have on the community and the city of Bacolod.

At the presentation, the three Church of Jesus Christ of Latter-day Saints stake presidents and other dignitaries arrived, and a press conference was held at the hospital. Each church leader spoke and thanked the government and Dr. Sarabia for their partnership. When it was my turn to speak, I had the opportunity to discuss briefly the fourfold mission of the Church of Jesus Christ of Latter-day Saints, along with my testimony of President Monson being an inspired prophet of God and my appreciation for his adding the fourth mission for the church in assisting the poor and needy. How this donation would help many of our church members and all other Philippine patients on the island of Negros Occidental to have vision restored with the best equipment.

Dr. Sarabia then graciously thanked the Church, President Monson, and the Church of Jesus Christ of Latter-day Saints Vision Committee for their generous donation of the teaching microscope. In his words, this was the finest operating and teaching microscope available in the world and that even the best clinics in Manila usually did not have anything as state of the art as this machine. We shook hands and high-fived in front of the TV cameras and took questions from the reporters. Then it was time to set up and try out the new microscope.

I asked Dr. Sarabia to do the honors of being the first to operate, and he quickly and efficiently performed an manual small-incision cataract surgery (M-SICS for short) and then talked me through a second case using his technique. Both surgeries were very successful with the patients reporting excellent vision immediately postop.

As I left for home, I marveled at the inspiration of the leader of our church and shuddered to think of what reaction might have occurred if the older secondhand microscope that I had suggested was presented at a press conference and Philippine National Television audience.

Dr. Sarabia could now teach his residents and fellows the latest eye surgery techniques with the very latest equipment to rival any clinic in the world. Heavens, it was nicer than the microscope I was using in my own Seattle clinic or at University of Missouri.

It was gratifying to represent the Church and the Vision Committee and most importantly provide the latest equipment to a man and program that could truly benefit from its donation and use it on a daily basis to assist the poor and needy to see again.

Just recently, a new Latter-day Saint temple for Bacolod City was announced and a groundbreaking was held. It was exciting to think that our volunteer work in that friendly city may have helped the church grow.

CHAPTER 47

HIDDEN TREASURES
OF KNOWLEDGE

I n the canon of scriptures for the Church of Jesus Christ of Latter-
day Saints, Section 89:18–21 of the Doctrine and Covenants (a
collection of revelations given to the prophet and first president of
the church—Joseph Smith) states that "And all saints who remember
to keep and do these sayings...*shall find wisdom and great treasures of knowledge, even hidden treasures.*"

I had always tried to follow this scripture that provides well-
proven advice for better health and dates back to the 1833 revelation. The "Word of Wisdom," as it is known, advises moderation
in diet with the counsel to eat meat sparingly; to consume a diet
high in fruits and vegetables; and to avoid smoking, caffeine, and
alcohol—unusual advice in the 1830s. I even recall, in researching
out the harmful effects of smoking cigarettes as a medical student,
an advertisement in the *Journal of the American Medical Association*
(JAMA) showing a doctor in a white coat smoking a cigarette with
the caption: "Smoke Lucky Strike (cigarettes) for your good health."

In addition to the direct health benefits, I was fascinated by the promise of finding "hidden treasures of knowledge" by those who follow the teachings.

Some of the great discoveries in medicine occurred by chance from doctors or patients noticing a side effect from a medicine they were taking or an observation by the doctor of unanticipated benefit to another system in the body. Sometimes, as Plato stated in New Republic, "necessity is the mother of invention."

At least four hidden treasures of knowledge or impressions came to me during my career that have changed the way I practice eye surgery and have influenced other eye surgeons around the world from what they have told me.

The first occurred as just a stroke of luck or an impression I had during an operation where I wondered what the eye pressure level was upon completion of cataract surgery. With the technology now available to measure the eye pressure immediately following cataract surgery, I thought, *We measure everything else so precisely in medicine, I wonder why we don't measure the eye pressure right after completion of our operations?* The current standard of care is what I would later call "the Goldilocks Method." At the end of an operation, the surgeon taps on the eye with a Q-Tip or Weck-Cel (tiny microsponge) or their fingertip and thinks, *Hmmm, not to firm, not too soft, the eye pressure must be just right.* Well, after doing this and verifying it with a tonometer (a device to test pressure of the eye much like checking air in a tire), we found during a study that the eye pressure many times immediately after surgery was not safe or in a safe range. I was even referred two patients who had lost nearly all their vision due to their doctor not checking the eye pressure after their surgery and the subsequent optic nerve injury from the pressure being left too high for too long right after cataract surgery.

Not only did we find about 30 percent of patient's eye pressure was outside the normal safe range immediately after surgery but that the eye pressure the next day when measured in the clinic was typically within five points of where we left it at the conclusion of their surgery in the operating room. At first, when presenting this finding at scientific meetings, no one said much or acknowledged that this was important. My first paper on the topic was rejected by a respected journal for what seemed to be no reason (possibly because eye surgeons would be held to a new standard to check pressure after every cataract operation). In any case, by continuing to present our research and getting repeatable results, the academic world began to take notice. Exciting to make that contribution, and hopefully no other patients suffer needless loss of vision when the rest of the ophthalmology world takes my message to heart and adjusts eye pressure immediately after cataract surgery. In addition our research seems to not only prevent the no. 1 complication of high pressure but also showed that the no. 2 complication following cataract surgery of cystoid macular edema or CME is dramatically lessened if eye pressure is immediately adjusted at the conclusion of cataract surgery.

My next discovery occurred when a patient who had undergone prior LASIK eye surgery began to develop corneal ectasia similar to early keratoconus (a progressive steepening of the cornea with astigmatism of the front of the eye). Scientists discovered when concentrated riboflavin (vitamin B2) eye drops were applied to the scraped surface of the cornea followed by exposure to a medical grade ultraviolet light source, cross-linking and therapeutic stiffening and flattening of the bulging cornea occurred. This cornea cross-linking prevented further progression of this disease and could lessen the need for a cornea transplant.

A company called AVEDRO manufactured the first FDA-approved calibrated UV light source for treating keratoconus and postrefractive surgery ectasia. Before this procedure was covered by insurance, the charge for treatment was $3,500 per eye.

One of my patients that I had performed prior LASIK surgery on years before and had premium intraocular lens implants subsequently developed early ectasia and glasses or contact lenses did not help.

I suggested the AVEDRO treatment, and when we told her of the price, she began crying and asked, "Don't you have anything cheaper and less painful? I'm retired and on a fixed income. I can't afford $3,500, let alone $7,000 for both eyes to be treated."

My heart went out to her. "I suppose you could just take a ribo-flavin supplement and go outside in the sun without sunglasses for fifteen minutes a day" (for the UV effect), I suggested.

"How much riboflavin should I take?" she asked.

"How about fifty milligrams per day (the most I had remembered seeing on the package of B-complex vitamins?"

"Okay, I can do that," she said.

"Let's try it out, and I'll see you back in six months."

Six months later, Mrs. Anderson returned and, strangely enough, had the exact same flattening of her steep cornea that the patients treated commercially with the $3,500 AVEDRO treatment received. *That's amazing*, I thought to myself.

"Oh, and, Dr. Jarstad, my vision seems much clearer too."

"Maybe we're on to something. Let's keep you on the B2 for another six months. Any side effects?"

"No, just turns my pee bright yellow," was her response.

Other patients were treated including a radial keratometry patient whose daily fluctuating vision resolved after six months of treatment, and we reported our findings at the International CXL (cross-linking) symposium in Zurich, Switzerland, in early December of 2017 and won "Best Paper of the Conference" for the prestigious two-day symposium among two hundred scientific papers from forty-four countries.

The third hidden treasure occurred following an emotional telephone call from a respected family practice doctor near my Federal Way Clinic about the year 2009.

His daughter married a brilliant young computer specialist and was living in Manila, Philippines. This doctor tearfully explained that his daughter's first child, a son, was born two months premature and had developed retinopathy of prematurity (a condition where high doses of oxygen are required to allow survival but can cause abnormal blood vessels to sprout and bleed from the developing retina). My colleague stated that the doctors in the Philippines were considering a vitrectomy operation to remove blood clots, along with laser, to treat the sprouting blood vessels but that the child would likely develop cataracts and amblyopia (a lazy eye) from surgery. He stated, "You've done a lot of research. Do you know of anything in the research pipeline that might help our grandson?"

I told the physician about Avastin, a vascular endothelial growth factor inhibitor that was successful in treating and reversing abnormal blood vessels in diabetics that might just work for his grandson.

"Yes, but do you know any retina specialists in the Philippines?"

"I do know Dr. Vincente Santos in Manila. I will give him a call. I was just there lecturing not too long ago. He's the best retina surgeon in Manila."

I called Dr. Santos. "Vic, this is John Jarstad."

"Hi, John, what's new?

I explained the situation, "Vic, have you ever used Avastin?"

"Of course, John. We have it here and use it all the time in our diabetic patients."

"Have you ever used it in a child with retinopathy of prematurity?"

"I don't think anyone has ever tried it."

"Would you consider it in my colleague's grandson?"

"Well, I could. He's got nothing to lose." But, John, what dose would I use?"

"I don't know, but how about half the adult dose?"

Dr. Santos agreed to see the newborn and treated him with half the adult dose, and the abnormal blood vessels disappeared; the child did not require surgery and developed normal vision.

Necessity is the mother of innovation, and now Avastin injections into the eyes of premature babies with retinopathy of prematurity is an accepted standard treatment.

The fourth hidden treasure occurred in patients taking the high dose dietary riboflavin as part of my cornea cross-linking study—it also cured their migraine headaches.

One of the early-study patients reported at their three-month follow-up visit: "Doc, is this riboflavin supposed to cure my migraine headaches?"

"What? Tell me more!"

"I haven't had any since beginning the study for my eyes."

After this remarkable coincidence, I began treating patients with classic or ophthalmic migraine—a migraine of the eye with zig-zag light flashes but without the headache—and found that the first seventy-five of seventy-six patients treated with 400 mg of dietary riboflavin were cured.

Certainly, these four examples of "hidden treasures of knowledge" have blessed the lives of my patients.

In addition to these four "hidden treasures," perhaps my greatest invention occurred in 1993 when Mr. Andy Corley, the president of Eyeonics (early manufacturer of the Crystalens), visited my office in Federal Way and asked if I were to design the ideal lens implant delivery device, what would it look like? After sketching my idea (an inexpensive, disposable device like a 3-cc plastic syringe with a tapered tip so it could fit through a 2–3-mm incision and most importantly spring-loaded so it had some back pressure as to not suddenly shoot through the eye and could be used with one hand so the surgeon could steady the eye with forceps in the other hand), the Bausch + Lomb passport (now Crystalsert) lens injector was born. I'm excited that with few changes, my lens injector design is still used today.

CHAPTER 48

MISSION WITH MITT ROMNEY TO INDONESIA

I received an exciting call from Charity Vision's founder, Dr. William E. Jackson, in the early Spring of 2017; and he asked if I would be interested in joining recent Republican presidential candidate Mitt Romney and his sons and their families on a medical eye mission trip to Indonesia later that spring. Since I was familiar with that beautiful region of the South Pacific and its people, spoke and understood enough Bahasa Indonesia to get by well, and was a former USCG-licensed charter boat skipper with years of experience at sea in the North Pacific, Dr. Jackson thought I would be good to have along.

Two tall ships would be outfitted and would travel from Bali to Lombok, Bima, and Komodo Islands to examine patients, fit eyeglasses, and do cataract and glaucoma screenings and surgery. All I had to do was get myself there, and the rest would be taken care of.

I arrived with a duffle bag full of Dollar Store reading glasses of various prescription powers, my eye examination equipment bag,

TonoPen, eye drops, antibiotics, and steroid drops for the ten-day mission.

Arriving later than the others, I caught up with them in the afternoon right before the ships would sail. These "tall ships," as they are known, reminded me of the *Black Pearl* from the movie *Pirates of the Caribbean* and looked to be in well-maintained shape. The group was split into two parties. Mitt and his wife, along with a son and a few of his grandchildren, would travel on the larger white hull sailboat and the rest of us on the *"Black Pearl."* Our captain was a stocky Australian woman who was a licensed shipmaster and knew her stuff so far as navigation was concerned. Dr. T. D. Gondhowiardjo, my lifelong friend and former chairman of the Ophthalmology Department at University of Indonesia in Jakarta and past president of the Indonesian Ophthalmology Association (IOA), would be my bunkmate in our berth which contained two small twin beds, along with a shower and sink.

We left port on the east side of Bali in the late afternoon and, after a dinner on board of local cuisine prepared by the chef, caught some sleep due to the gentle rocking motion of the waves and awoke early the next morning off the coast of Lombok Island.

While there, we screened several villagers and provided much-needed reading glasses. *"Lebbie satu attu dua"* (Which is better—one or two)? The Romney grandchildren assisted in vision screening and distributing the reading glasses and were real workers. I was impressed with their work ethic and perseverance in close to a hundred-degree weather. No complaints and cheerful, optimistic attitudes. Most of our work on Lombok was fitting glasses, and the vast majority of patients did not have surgical eye problems.

Our next stop was Bima. Here we screened in a school classroom and examined the entire school's children. Again, very few needed eyeglasses, but we did find several who had accommodative esophoria (cross-eyes) that were straightened out by simply providing them with the correct eyeglass prescription. We arranged surgeries here and performed cataract operations with the assistance of local nurses; and I even had Mitt and one of his grandsons assist me with an operation or two, irrigating the cornea so I could view the inside of the eye through the magnifying lens of the surgical microscope when the surface became cloudy due to the drying effect of the ambient air. When I noticed that Mitt's twelve-year-old grandson was a quick study, had steady hands, and had a real knack for medicine, I asked him if he would ever consider becoming an eye surgeon. "Nope, not a chance! I'm planning a business career," was his quick answer.

Our last stop was on Komodo Island. This beautiful desert isle with few inhabitants but plenty of the famous Komodo dragons was a welcome diversion from our week of work. These large reptiles with a poisonous bite that could kill a man in twenty-four hours from the infection they carried in their teeth were everywhere. Some six feet or longer. There was a photo area where the locals would take your photo behind the dragon and, with the angles and magnification, make it appear that one was actually riding on the back of the beasts when we were about six to ten feet behind them.

Following a hike up to a high promontory above the island, we took several photos including one I will treasure with Mitt, Anne Romney, and myself overlooking the harbor of Komodo Island.

I was impressed that Governor Romney, after his defeat by President Obama in the 2012 election, was able to regroup and sponsor such incredible effort in bringing together a team to serve the poor and needy of Indonesian's outlying islands.

One incident captured the true nature of now Senator Romney while at dinner one of the first nights aboard ship. Our crew from the "*Black Pearl*" transferred in small boats over to the larger ship, and as the entire Romney family gathered around a twenty-foot-square table, those of us who were the "hired help" were sitting off to the sides on barrels or the elevated gunwales of the tall ship after getting our dinner. As Senator Romney noticed me sitting by myself, he suddenly looked over and said, "John, what are you doing sitting over there by yourself? Come over here and sit next to me. I want to talk to you." With this kind invitation, I sat next to the former governor of Massachusetts, most recent presidential candidate, and future senator of Utah for the next hour; and he asked all about my education, research, and medical mission trips, and particularly found my trip to North Korea with my meeting with Kim Jong-un fascinating.

I tried to find some common topics that I had remembered from reading about his history and biographical information, recalling that both he and I had been on the varsity school wrestling teams. When I asked him about this experience, what weight he wrestled, his win-loss record, and other moves in the sport, he was very self-effacing in stating, "I wasn't a very good wrestler. Most of the time, my teammates would cheer for me to 'BRIDGE, ROMNEY! BRIDGE!'" ("Bridging" is a move a wrestler makes when his opponent puts him over on his back and the wrestler arches his back like a bridge to avoid losing by getting his shoulders pinned to the mat). I was impressed by his honesty and humility in relating this story.

The other thing that impressed me during our two weeks together was just how close the Romney family was, along with their teamwork and work ethic. The fact that almost all five of his sons, including one who is a physician, held advanced MBA degrees and were successful in their own right. It is a shame that this accomplished Harvard MBA attorney, successful husband, and father was not elected to lead our country as president, but how fortunate we are that his love of country, sacrifice, and dedication to the service of our country lives on as he serves as US senator from Utah.

Senator Mitt Romney, Ann Romney, and the
author—Komodo Island, Indonesia

CHAPTER 49

GOING DOWN WITH
THE SHIP (DUBAI)

D uring Labor Day weekend in 2018, I decided to sponsor a
day at Lake of the Ozarks (rated by *USA Today* newspaper as
America's number one recreational lake) on my Mastercraft
X-7 wakeboard boat and rented the condo next to the one I owned
at Land's End Development in Osage Beach, Missouri.

The technicians were excited to spend a couple of days at the
lake during the three-day weekend. The women stayed in one condo,
and we men in the one I owned.

Everyone brought pot luck BBQ items, and we did some "live
band karaoke" on Friday evening. The next morning, we headed out
on the lake. Everyone had an opportunity to wakeboard, waterski, or
tube behind the X-7.

On Labor Day at the end of another long day of water sports,
we started back to the condos for dinner during "rush hour" at the
lake. So many large boats including sixty-foot cabin cruisers, smaller

waterski boats, and everything in between began racing back to their condos or homes around the lake for dinner.

As we rounded the bend for the last mile or two before port, two large cruisers passed us, kicking up a huge three-to-four-foot wake on either side of our twenty-one-foot wakeboard boat. Since our boat draws only twelve to eighteen inches of freeboard, the large wakes came over the side as I tried to expertly "quarter the wakes" as I'd learned as a USGC-licensed shipmaster. Unfortunately, the waves were just too high and swamped us.

I had all my passengers put on life vests, and they offered to go over the side into the lake to reduce the weight on the boat and allow me time to bail out the water which was almost knee high. Just as the bilge pumps were almost finished, another large vessel passed closely by and swamped us. This time, the boat went under, and the engine was shut off to prevent water from coming into the cylinders.

A rescue boat soon arrived and offered to pick us up. I stayed with the ship in a futile attempt to pump out the water by hand. "Get off your boat!" the captain of the rescue boat yelled. "It's not worth dying over," he screamed. "Jump off now!" And with that, I climbed the mast up out of the water-filled small craft and jumped over the side.

I had forgotten that freshwater lacks the buoyancy of saltwater, and after jumping over, I went straight to the bottom, probably twenty feet down until my momentum stopped, and I swam for the surface. Going back up like a rocket, I hit my head on the swim platform of the rescue boat and was knocked out silly. The others pulled me on board, and soon after, the sheriff's patrol boat arrived, and a towboat was called to pull our sunken craft to shore.

After arriving back to the condo dock (thanks to the kindness of the rescue boat and sheriff), we prepared dinner and with me babbling on speaking nonsense and having one pupil slightly larger than the other, the technicians insisted I visit the ER at Lake Regional Medical Center where I was diagnosed with a concussion after the MRI of my head was negative. Part of the problem was that I was answering questions in an English accent and making no sense in asking the staff to call one of the fellow attending eye surgeons at

University of Missouri, repeating, "Call Dr. _____. They will know exactly what to do," as if that eye surgeon would have any influence on diagnosis or treatment of my concussion.

The next day after a fitful night's sleep back in Columbia, I boarded a plane to begin my journey to Dubai, United Arab Emirates, to give a keynote lecture on my research on high-dose dietary ribo-flavin and sunlight in the treatment of keratoconus and ectasia. Still suffering from confusion, I left my passport and wallet with all my travel documents at the TSA conveyer belt in London Heathrow. As I sat down to order food at one of the airport food establishments, I suddenly realized I had no wallet, credit card, or passport. Only my iPhone. As I retraced my steps, I thought I might have left it at TSA. Returning there, I asked if anyone had turned in a passport and wallet. "You must go speak to a supervisor," the efficient and curt agent replied. I walked over to the supervisor, and her first question to me was, "Please tell me your passport number" (like I could remember that with a recent concussion?). Her next question was for me to state my name and address. That, at least, I could remember. "Okay, right, yes, we have your items right here." As she opened a large wooden box with a lock on it, I was gratefully reunited with my passport, wallet, credit cards, and about fifty English pounds I'd packed from a previous trip. An answer to prayer. But disheartening that I was still fuzzy headed after my concussion.

After a nice lunch of my favorite shepherd's pie, I boarded the British Air connecting flight to Dubai.

I arrived in that incredibly clean city about six in the evening and paid sixty dollars for a five-minute ride to my hotel where the International Eye Research Meeting was to be held, beginning the next day. It was a lovely room overlooking the harbor and the ships unloading along with the tour boats.

I presented my keynote lecture and afterward made friends with a young lady medical student and her husband where we exchanged phone numbers and e-mail addresses because of her interest in my research. The next day was my birthday, and someone either from home or at the hotel sent a huge birthday cake to my room. No way could I eat that all by myself. Since it was lavishly decorated and I knew no one in town, I texted my new friends, and they arrived almost immediately to meet me in the hotel lobby to share in the cake. They were from Australia, and I shared my thoughts on applying to ophthalmology residency programs and fellowships.

The following day, I had a few hours after the conference to try the Dubai Ski Dome, the largest indoor ski resort in the world, right in the middle of the desert. The facility offered all the equipment, including ski jackets and pants along with helmets, and I scheduled a two-hour session for about fifty dollars. It was a blast skiing indoors at about twenty degrees when outside it was near a hundred degrees. Very refreshing and about halfway through my ski session, my cell phone rang. I had forgotten it was my birthday (September 7), and the entire University of Missouri Eye Department called to wish me a happy birthday. I panned the scene and used my camera to video a run for the audience. Since it was not crowded, I made run after run nonstop as is my custom and had a great workout meeting some interesting young men dressed in traditional head scarfs and robes who were from Saudi Arabia and young members of the Saudi royal family. We made a run together and discussed politics on the chairlift back up the indoor mountain. I was surprised at their knowledge of both American and international politics.

The next day, I boarded my flight home to England. As the plane was taking off, there was a significant rumble, and the overhead bin above me opened suddenly, and a large and heavy carry-on suitcase came crashing down right on top of my head. Insult to injury, likely another concussion!

I traveled home still fuzzy headed from the two concussions, which occurred all within a week's time.

It was fun to revisit London and from there, I attended the ARVO Eye Research meeting in Belfast, Ireland.

In Belfast, I presented a summary of our research into high-dose dietary riboflavin and sunlight in treating keratoconus, along with my research in immediate adjustment of eye pressure following cataract surgery to prevent cystoid macular edema. Both posters received rapt attention on the convention floor. I attended the Church of Jesus Christ of Latter-day Saints Ward in Belfast at the north edge of the city and met a couple from my old mission in England who knew several of the members I had worked with in Walsall. They offered to take me on a day tour to Carrickfergus, County Antrim, Northern Ireland, where my ancestors on me mum's side hailed from. It is a lovely small town situated on the coast just eight miles northeast of Belfast. It was so fun to visit the castle and have lunch in an ancient public house with a traditional lunch of what my ancestors may have eaten in the inn they may have visited.

From there, after the conference, I traveled south by motor coach to the Dublin airport, where I hired a rental car and met a young lady I had corresponded with and after meeting with my local bishop (who encouraged me to go ahead and begin dating since my divorce would be final in another month or two). We met and headed to Johnstown Castle and a concert performed by Celtic Women. I had entered the drawing for tickets to an exclusive event to be filmed for television to be shown in the USA on PBS later that fall and had to submit an airline ticket showing I would be in the area at the time of the performance. I met "Karen" at the airport, and we drove to the venue and arrived about two hours before the show. Much to my surprise, we were interviewed on TV and provided front-row seats to the left of the stage. I had the forethought to bring an American flag throw blanket which can be seen in the performance covering our knees.

It was a magical night with heavenly music. It was fun to meet someone who also spoke German as well as English; and after spending that night in separate hotel rooms, we had breakfast and drove back to Dublin, where we window-shopped and listened to some very accomplished street musicians playing U2 songs perhaps where the singer "Sting" got his start. From there, we had an Irish buffet lunch, and it was time to take Karen back to the airport to catch her flight back to Zurich.

Two hours later, I caught my connecting flight home. A stop in London for a day and a visit to Brighton and lunch with an old friend from my missionary days and then back to London for my flight home.

It was a whirlwind visit covering three countries, two scientific eye research meetings, and a concert all in under a week.

CHAPTER 50

A DIFFICULT DECISION: PEACE AND A SECOND CHANCE

A few years into my marriage, I became increasingly concerned about violent outbursts and symptoms occurring in my wife. I suggested we visit a counselor, and she suggested we see someone recommended by our church social services. After visiting weekly for a year together, since I was a physician, I asked to speak to the counselor, an older woman, and asked her what the treatment plan was? "Oh, there's no plan. I'm just trying to be your wife's friend."

Following this encounter and visiting another local counselor closer to our Federal Way home (rather than the sometimes-forty-minute commute each way to the first counselor in Bellevue, Washington) and feeling I had done my best to find help and noticing the adverse effect of spending three hours commuting and counseling each week had on our minor children, I decided that I would continue to pay for weekly visits for my wife; but I could not commit to these hours, starting a medical practice, and "being there" for my children (I would take each child to Denny's restaurant one night a week to work on mathematics homework or just to talk while ordering dinner). I had made it a habit during my busiest time at Mayo Clinic during my eye surgery residency to spend Saturday mornings each week with one of the four children on a rotational basis—called their "Special Day." This wasn't as much time as I'd hoped, but at least each one knew they could chose to do anything they wanted on their "Special Day" and that they would have my full attention. Going bowling, minigolf, to the pet store to look at hamsters or play with newborn puppies, to the Dairy Queen for an ice cream treat, or to a park just to talk about their week were activities each child looked forward to and that they remembered years later.

While not going into too many details and after providing seven years of weekly counseling sessions, my wife's multiple arrests for violent behavior or going to jail in handcuffs for motor vehicle infractions, along with my stressful job as an eye surgeon and business CEO, took its toll on me. Others in the community and our church community became aware of the problems, and it became increasingly clear that our marriage would not stand the test of time. As soon as our youngest child graduated with her photography degree and later an MBA degree and moved out of our home and when the opportunity to sell my practice developed, along with the job offer of an associate professorship at University of Missouri, I made the difficult decision to end our marriage and move on. I should point out that I have never been charged with any crimes, assault, and violence, or incarcerated. Violence, other than playing defensive back in football, was never in my nature.

I moved to Columbia, Missouri, in the fall of 2015 and lived alone that entire first year as we tried to sell our magnificent waterfront ten-thousand-square-foot mansion in the Seattle suburb of Federal Way. It was then that I realized I had made the right decision. The change in my environment—no longer walking on eggshells, worried about when the next violent eruption would occur—along with the calmness and peaceful solitude surrounding me, contributed to my productivity and success to a level I had never reached before. Scientific discoveries followed as I threw myself into my work, published groundbreaking medical journal articles, and found joy in teaching full-time the brilliant and motivated eye residents at University of Missouri in Columbia.

I could have been perfectly happy living there alone for the rest of my life with my work helping patients.

After our home sold in the summer of 2016, I found a very nice four-bedroom home in the Old Hawthorne subdivision near the golf course which would accommodate our pool table and my music equipment, along with each bedroom having its own full-bath suite. I moved from a comfortable rented townhouse in August of that year. The townhouse was an answer to prayer as I had looked for an entire three-day weekend just after I was offered the University of Missouri position and found nothing close to work or in a nice area. The morning I was to fly home, after much prayer, the thought came, *Go look online one more time.* It was then I saw the new listing at 5915, the same address as my father's Ski Hut Honda shop in Tacoma on Sixth Avenue. If ever there was a time to believe God answered prayers and that our ancestors can assist us from beyond, it was then.

My wife made a couple of attempts to visit, staying for a month or two the following year, but spent most of her time, instead of in Missouri with me, visiting the four children in Portland, Salt Lake City, and Los Angeles, but especially visiting Jessica and her six children—ninety minutes away in Blue Spring, Missouri.

After her final uncontrollable violent outburst in a hotel one morning after visiting the grandchildren, I came to the realization that things would likely never change in our marriage, and I decided it was finally time to seek a divorce and live alone perhaps for the remainder of my life as my closest friends assumed and gave their opinions for someone my age.

Once the divorce was finalized just before the end of 2018, I began to investigate some dating sites and was disappointed in meeting people who were not often as advertised online.

After communicating with some interesting women and getting to know them through texting and phone calls, I put together a list of the qualities I was looking for in a potential partner and second future wife someday. I decided that a professional woman who was cheerful and confident, who knew how to work either in her chosen profession or as a volunteer, who was intelligent, and who had a joy for life was at the top of my list. I went on first dates with a bank vice president, a top computer forensic accountant genius, and a PhD who was also an RN. And whilst all were fascinating, accomplished, and attractive women, only one seemed to click. It was then I discovered a website for "millionaires" or high-net-worth individuals. *Is there really such a thing?* I thought. *And would any turn out to be compatible?* One very interesting woman just slightly younger than me was from Paris, France, and had a home (more like a mansion) on the French Riviera. She was going to fly me over to meet up. She spoke fluent French, Russian, and English, and was a professor of linguistics at a major university in Paris. We spoke on the Internet and hit it off well. Another was a cosmetic manager of a large department store in Zurich, Switzerland, and we met for a concert at a castle in Ireland.

It was two months after my divorce when I noticed an amazing lady dentist who lived in South Florida on the West Coast in St. Petersburg. Not only was she beautiful and athletic (she'd won a bikini body building competition in her age group); but also she loved the same type of music I did, was learning the piano, and was a runner-up in *Dancing with the Stars* for the Florida Region.

The fact that she grew up in Seoul Korea and attended college in the Netherlands only added to my fascination. Dr. Kristine Marshall had "given me a rose" on the dating site, so I contacted her in my best translation of Korean to try to get a response. She answered me and, fortunately at the end of the translation, said, "If it's okay with you, can we speak English?"

I had immense respect for the Korean people and their discipline and dedication, along with their high moral values and work ethic. At first, she was reluctant to converse much, stating that her Yorkshire terrier of thirteen years, Charlee, had died unexpectedly just that weekend and then asking if we could talk another time. This hit home to me because I had lost my Lhasa apso, Chip, just three years before and empathized completely at the devastating loss of a near-lifelong companion. Once I expressed my sorrow for her loss and explained my similar loss, she decided she did want to meet me.

"I'm scheduled to fly to India next Monday to give a keynote lecture at the All-India Ophthalmology Meeting in New Delhi," I told her. "The following week, I'm going to Indonesia to speak at their National Eye Research Meeting, but could we meet up a week or two after that?"

"How about this weekend?" she offered. "Well, as long as I can get back to Missouri by Monday at noon when my flight leaves for New Delhi, I think that would work! I would really like to meet you."

I arrived at the Tampa airport, and Dr. Marshall picked me up in her Mercedes convertible. We talked the entire way and most of the night. The next day, she took me to visit her dental office in the Bliss building. "Hey, when was the last time you had your teeth cleaned?" she asked. "I just got a reminder postcard in the mail, so I'm about due." "Why don't I do a deep cleaning and scaling as long as you're here?"

I was impressed with her gentle and thorough technique, as well as how quick and efficient she was.

We went out for lunch and cooked dinner together. I flew home, and we kept in touch. A month later, Dr. Marshall called me and let me know she and three girlfriends were going skiing in Colorado and wondering if I might be able to check and see if I could find a nearby condo or hotel to rent so we could meet up at Copper Mountain to make a few ski runs together? I checked on the Internet, and there was only one hotel with a single room available that next weekend. I booked it and told her I would text her when I arrived Friday afternoon.

To my surprise, when I asked her where she and her roommates were staying, it was the same exact hotel. She was in 536, and I would be in 436 just one floor below. We met and skied two days in a row, and the third day was Sunday. I told her I would not want to ski on Sunday. Normally, I strive to keep the Lord's Day holy, and the only two times I made an exception, I broke my leg one time and my humerus bone the next. Fortunately, there was a blizzard, and most of the resort was closed, so we did some window-shopping and had lunch in the lodge.

That last day, we noticed a jewelry store going out of business sale sign with "50 to 80 percent off" in the window. On a whim, whilst Kristine was looking at necklaces in another part of the store, I asked the cashier what was the largest diamond engagement ring they had in stock. He said they had sold quite a lot of the inventory, but they did have one that was about one carat, and it was flawless. It would be on sale from an original price of over $12,000, and he could let me have it for around $3,500. I had Kristine come and take a look at it. She tried it on, and it fit just perfectly. "Okay," I said as she left. "Please wrap this up for me as quick as you can." I paid for it and put it in my ski jacket pocket for later.

The next day, Monday, our final day on the slopes, we met for breakfast and headed up to the slopes. There was six inches of fresh powder snow and a clear blue sky. We went to the top of the Rendezvous lift, and I told Kristine I wanted to get a photo of her with the backdrop of the mountain peaks behind her. After a few photos, I asked a gentleman behind me if he would be so kind to take our photo together. As soon as he was all set, I dropped down to one knee and pulled out the ring and proposed telling Kristine that I loved her and wanted to be with her forever. "Will you marry me?" She had the perfect answer: "I was hoping you would ask!"

Soon after, we began to plan a wedding. I was thinking maybe in the fall about six months away which would provide me time to sell my house in Missouri along with time to find a new position in Florida. She asked if we could get married in April. "My sister and her family visit each April from Holland around my birthday (April 23), so if we got married then, they could all come." "That's two months away!" I said. "But, hey, we are older and both have been alone for several years, so why not?"

So on April 22, 2019, we were married in St. Petersburg, Florida, at the city hall. It almost didn't happen.

As we arrived to fill out the papers, we were told that everything was in order so there would be a three-day waiting period and we could come back and get our license. *Three days!* That wouldn't work! Her sister and family would be returning to Holland in two days, and I had a flight the same day to go back to work. Kristine was devastated and crying. I was shocked because we had a wedding dinner planned for that evening, and I had already booked our honeymoon hotel reservation. As she left in tears, the inspirational thought came to me to "go talk to a supervisor! DO IT NOW!"

As Kristine was walking toward the elevator in her wedding dress, I excused myself and walked back to the license window. "Is there anyone I could talk to like a supervisor?" I asked. I explained the situation, and soon an older kind woman appeared and explained that the only way we could be married that day would be if we could have an attorney sign a statement for exceptional circumstances and have a judge sign a waiver. I asked if she knew any attorneys or judges nearby. She said, "Judge Thomas Jagger is in this same building, and he might be able to see you if he's not booked up." She called up, and after several minutes, she came back with her thumbs up. "I can't guarantee anything, but the district judge will see you now upstairs." I quickly caught up with Kristine, who was waiting by the elevator. I told her we were going upstairs and made a silent prayer with all my energy of soul that the judge could help us. He was our only chance, and I prayed that I didn't want to go to a hotel together not married. Judge Jagger ushered us into his chambers and said, "Okay, kids, what's your story?" After explaining our situation, that Kristine's sister's family had traveled all the way from Holland and her brother from Houston, Texas, and that I had to return to work in two days, he said, "Okay, I've heard enough. Hand me those papers. It's not like you two are young kids or doing something on a whim. Looks like you've both been around the block—so good luck!" And with that, we were back downstairs and were married that morning.

It was a simple yet nice ceremony. We had both written some vows to take care of each other, be our best friends, and help each other. To love each other forever. Once a few photos were taken, Kristine's sister's and brother's families treated us for brunch at a French restaurant on the beach drive, and then it was off to the hotel to check in and get dressed and organized for the wedding dinner.

So many of her friends from Tampa area arrived, and one gay couple who were patients of Dr. Marshall's dental practice provided four large bouquets with four dozen long-stemmed red roses that were magnificent and really added a magical touch to the evening. Another friend, a cake decorator produced individual cakes that looked indistinguishable from Tiffany jeweler's bright-blue-wrapped boxes.

The food was amazing and expensive. Kristine took care of everything. It was a magical day and night that would have been a personal tragedy for us if it had not happened. We will always be grateful to the city clerk supervisor and judge Thomas Jagger for allowing us to tie the knot and start a life together on a high note.

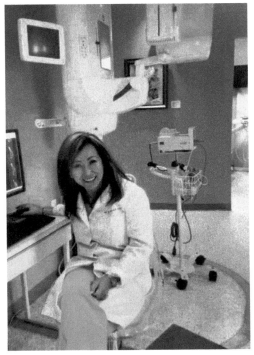

Dr. Kristine Marshall, DDS

CHAPTER 51

MISSION TO HONDURAS

The year 2019 turned out to be an incredibly busy year. In December 2018, I was contacted by old friends from Federal Way, Washington—Evelyn and Jose Castellar, who had a successful convention center in town and had moved to a villa and cocoa farm near La Ceiba, Honduras, right at the edge of the jungle. Evelyn and Jose are true humanitarians who have dedicated their lives in retirement to helping the "cloud people" on the edge of the Honduran jungle by constructing a medical clinic, dental clinic, and sports complex to bless the lives of the people in the area. "Projecto Honduras," as it is called, provides food, clothing, and medical and dental care to a people "no one else will help," according to Evelyn. She had no formal medical training, was not a nurse or physician, but took it upon herself to observe minor surgeries in the local hospital and became quite skilled over the years at diagnosing and treating common ailments with antibiotics and minor surgical procedures.

When the Castellars first contacted me, it was about making a trip to Honduras to perform cataract surgery along with the feasibility of creating an eye center to help patients who had no opportunity for eye care. I had hoped to visit in person to determine the needs; but instead, with my hectic schedule and all else that was going on, I decided to fund the construction of a free-standing eye clinic and surgery center based on a scaled-down version of my own clinic in Federal Way.

The Castellars had worked with another old friend of mine, Dr. Erick Hartman, an optometric physician from Tacoma whom I had known since I was in grade school. He was a member of the Projecto Honduras board of directors; and together, we planned for and built a two operating room facility with a small clinic and screened-in waiting area on the cocoa plantation.

The first time I visited, I was greatly impressed with the cleanliness and beauty of the small facility. The operating rooms were tiled with white marble, as were the walls. There was room for two surgery operating room stretchers and two microscopes so that two operations could be performed simultaneously. I have seen this setup used all over the world to create more efficiency, whilst in the USA, only one patient at a time can occupy an OR.

During that first visit, I offered to take along a resident or two from the University of Missouri. To my delight, Drs. Van Nguyen and Ryan Mercer, two of our best resident eye surgeons, agreed to go along on the mission. Van had worked with Pete Carroll, Seattle Seahawks coach when he was at USC and who originally planned on going into orthopedic surgery when the ophthalmology bug got him. I lobbied hard to have him join our Missouri program. Van's family emigrated from Vietnam, and he expressed interest even in early interviews about doing humanitarian missions back to his family's mother country someday.

Ryan, a devout Christian and excellent surgeon, was the type of resident one wishes all eye surgery residents were like—cheerful, thoughtful, compassionate with excellent hands and a brilliant intuitive mind. Both young eye surgeons were ideal for a mission trip.

We arrived in San Pedro Sula on a Friday at about noon and then took a three-hour bus ride to LaCeiba. Once there, Jose picked us up and drove us and our duffle bags full of donated glasses and supplies to the hacienda on the edge of the jungle.

We set up our screening equipment, including a portable slit lamp biomicroscope, and immediately began screening cataract patients. We also noted many patients with severe pterygia (a pterygium is a winglike growth over the cornea that can cause an opacity so severe as to make one legally blind). The equatorial sun and lack of wraparound sunglasses contributed to the epidemic nature of this condition. The treatment involved numbing the eye, peeling off the winglike growth, scraping the surface smooth, and then placing a graft of the lining of the eye tissue called the conjunctiva into the defect.

We found four excellent candidates for cataract surgery and thirty other patients with pterygia or droopy eyelids and even a man whose skin was so redundant that a rhytidectomy (removing an ellipse of thick skin above the eyebrow) was necessary along with blepharoplasty to allow him to see without going around holding up his eyelids anymore.

One gentleman required such an operation and was so happy to not have to walk around with one hand holding up the skin over one eye to see that his grateful reaction rivaled any of the happiest sight-restored cataract patients in our university or private practice experience.

Each evening after a long day of operations and fitting eyeglasses, we were fed by one of three chefs employed by the Castellars. The local food was prepared to perfection, and the accommodations were about the finest I had experienced in my twenty-five years of overseas medical mission work. The Castellars even had a pet howler monkey named "Buddha Monkey," that was a real character and took a special liking to Van and Ryan. It would climb up their backs and sit on their shoulders before climbing down and stealing food.

For snacks, the plantation grew cacao, the precursor to chocolate. It was sweet and addicting.

We played a pickup game of basketball under the covered full-court gym on the compound one night, pitting the doctors against the local youth; and there was also a full-sized soccer pitch. Truly an amazing place.

One memorable patient was a young fourteen-year-old girl who was legally blind from cataracts due to malnutrition. Her white cataracts prevented her from seeing the path down a rocky cliff to get to the village. She had been navigating this path to work in the fields from her hut on top of the mountain each day, feeling her way down in the morning and back up the rocky slope at night.

Because no one was certain exactly when her cataracts first developed and whether or not she was amblyopic (amblyopia is a lazy eye condition brought about by poor vision before age eight when the visual pathways have fully developed), we were unsure just exactly what this young teenage girl might see.

When we removed her patch the next morning, she looked over and said, "Hey, there's a monkey over there!" as she spotted mischievous Buddha Monkey across the room. At that point, her family and everyone in the room clapped and shouted for joy.

As we completed our final postop exams and prepared to head back to Columbia, Missouri, both Ryan and Van expressed their appreciation for coming along on their very first eye mission trip. They had both performed well in both the clinic exams and in the operating room, gaining valuable experience that would spark their future desire not only to continue humanitarian mission work but also to use the experience performing delicate eye surgeries on some very advanced and challenging patient's eyes in future operations.

Evelyn Castellar outside Projecto Honduras Eye Clinic

Missouri Resident Eye Surgeons Dr. Van Nguyen and Dr. Ryan Mercer in the Projecto Honduras Operating Room

CHAPTER 52

MISSION TO KYRGYZSTAN

I n late 2017, I received a call from Bill Jackson of Charity Vision in Utah, who inquired whether I would be interested in a teaching mission to Kyrgyzstan. He had made contact with a Dr. Malik Umar, who was one of the younger, recently trained eye surgeons and who was interested and had requested help in order to learn some of the newer techniques in cataract surgery. The medical university in Bishkek, the capital, had not had an American lecturer at the medical school since the Russians left in 1993 according to the doctors there, and they were keen on having me put together a series of lectures for the residents along with a talk one evening for all the ophthalmologists in the country. My son Robby, who had just begun working with Charity Vision, went along to document the trip and investigate what other items would be useful to donate to the eye surgery program there in the future.

I was told at the time that there were 99 eye specialists in the country, and I was surprised that 104 showed up for my lecture (evidently, some came from neighboring Kazakhstan along with some doctors not of our specialty).

I presented my talk on the "Four True Eye Emergencies: Advances in Cataract and Refractive (LASIK) Surgery, Robotic, Femtolaser-Assisted Cataract Surgery and Modern Eyelid Surgery, Macular Degeneration, and Diabetic Retinopathy." Each attendee was provided a certificate of training, which the organizers asked me to autograph for each individual attending the course.

A wet lab was conducted with a donated portable Zeiss microscope from Charity Vision to the university for the resident eye surgeons in training, and we also donated a ten-quart pressure cooker, along with a 220V hot plate for sterilizing the eye surgery instruments.

The minister of health welcomed us, and we had a private meeting in her office where we discussed the needs of ophthalmology in Kyrgyzstan and the possibility of assisting through Charity Vision or Latter-day Saint Charities. She welcomed us and gifted me a beautiful chess set in an intricate leather-covered wooden case. A true keepsake.

I was able to instruct Malik in the use of a new device for hard brittle cataracts called a "Mi-Loop" that could split a dense cataract into two halves to make it easier to remove using the older M-SICS (manual small-incision cataract surgery) technique. The portable ten-quart pressure cooker was ideal for their surgery center and saved hours of time sterilizing with an old copper tube boiler-type ancient model.

On our final day in Bishkek, we finished surgery early, and Dr. Umar took us to the mountains outside of town. I had no idea the altitude of the peaks south of town was so high (several over twenty thousand feet). Good skiing for a future visit. Can't wait to return.

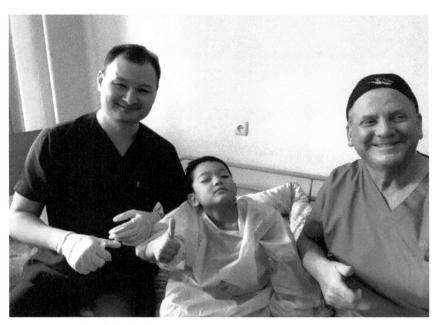

**Dr. Malik Umar, a young cataract patient, and
Dr. Jarstad in Bishkek, Kyrgyzstan**

CHAPTER 53

MISSION TO ECUADOR

In the summer of 2018, I was contacted by Global Medical Partners and the University of Missouri Medical School to see if I would be interested in serving a two-week short-term medical mission with their group of physicians on board the USNS *Comfort* (the sister ship identical to the USNS *Mercy*). Since I had experience on the *Mercy*, it was a no-brainer for me to volunteer. Plus, with my upcoming divorce which would be nearly finalized near that time in the fall, there would be no complaints from certain family members.

Dr. Maggie Cardonell, our pediatric ophthalmologist, was also very interested in going along with several men and women primary care physicians from MU Health; and she and I would work alongside the Navy cornea specialist Dr. W. Allan Steigleman (now a cornea specialist at the University of Florida in Gainsville after completing his military service) in performing cataract surgeries and any other eye procedures the local doctors needed us to do. We would also have the opportunity to teach some of the local ophthalmologists as well as those visiting surgeons from Mexico, Peru, and Colombia who were on board the USNS *Comfort*.

Dr. Cardonell and I assembled all the donated equipment we could possibly need and fit into four duffle bags and caught our flight with the Global Medical Team members to Miami and then on to Quito, Ecuador. Quito is situated at a high altitude (9,350 feet above sea level) and was a very fascinating place. The food was amazing, and the hotel we were assigned to for the one-night layover was great. Because of the high altitude, no mosquitos were a problem.

The next day, our team flew to Esmeraldas on the Pacific Coast where the *Comfort* was docked.

During our first day aboard, we noticed that one of the microscopes used for eye surgery was damaged and unusable because the beam-splitting prism inside the microscope housing was out of alignment, giving the surgeon impossible double vision. Dr. Steigleman apologized about the damaged microscope which had crashed into the operating theater wall during a hurricane prior to crossing the Panama Canal and trying to organize shifts so that the one good operating eye microscope would get plenty of use.

One thing I learned as a charter boat skipper and commercial fisherman in my life before medicine was that there were no repair shops miles offshore. I also learned how to fix things at sea.

Dr. Cardonell and I located a loose prism set on board in the optometry unit and found if we used a six-prism diopter loose lens taped onto the ocular of one side base up and a second six-prism diopter loose lens taped on the other side base down, the images fused and the microscope worked beautifully.

This allowed us to use two operating rooms and perform twice the number of operations we might have otherwise been limited to with a single microscope.

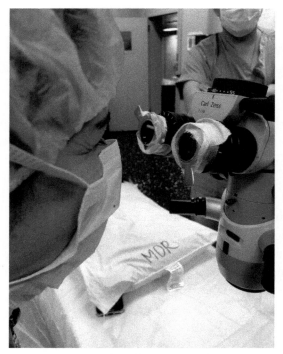

**Dr. Maggie Cardonell with taped on prisms
to repair surgery microscope**

Together, Dr. Cardonell and I worked on a little girl with con-genital ptosis (drooping of the upper eyelid); and because she had no eyelid muscle function at all, we performed a tarsal sling operation using a permanent suture we attached to the upper border of the eye-lid and then undermined the long needle to a location up under the eyebrow to allow the opening of her eye with her purposely raising her eyebrow (as in using a surprised look). The operation worked perfectly!

Another memorable patient was a gentleman who came with his family five hours by car from the border with Colombia. The account of his surgery was posted by the Navy public relations staff on the US Navy's military website. The patient was told his cataract was too far advanced to be removed safely using the current technol-ogy. We decided the referring doctors were right, and thank goodness for Mayo training in "old-school" extracapsular cataract surgery where the lens is removed in one piece through a larger incision. This operation went well, and the next morning, the patient was already seeing 20/25 out of his formerly blind eye.

Other memories aboard the USNS *Comfort* included sleeping in a three-tiered "rack," as the bunks are referred to on the Navy ships; flying by Huey helicopter back to Quito over the steep Andes Mountains (barely making it over at such high altitude peaks) and seeing the isolated little Ecuadoran farms from the air; shopping for souvenirs including a handmade guitar, which for $30 included my name engraved with a wood-burning pencil; and having a couple of great meals in downtown Quito restaurants with our dedicated team of doctors and nurses.

It was exciting to work with the best eye surgeons from both the US Navy and the local countries. Hopefully, we were able to make an impact on the lives of the patients and their families whom we had the pleasure of serving at no cost to them in restoring their sight. The local doctors were very proficient in their style of surgery, particularly the surgeon from Mexico, who we had teach some of the other local doctors too.

Recently, I noticed several Internet articles detailing our USNS *Comfort* mission. It was fun to be back aboard the *Mercy*-type hospital ship and exposed again to the discipline and organization of the US NAVY (which, for me, provided an opportunity to experience what I missed by not accepting the offer to attend the prestigious Uniformed Services University Medical School which I was accepted to in the 1980s).

Ecuador team with a happy cataract patient (L-R: Dr. Steigleman, Dr. Jarstad, cataract patient, Dr. Lopez, and Dr. Cardonell)

CHAPTER 54

THE JOYS OF TEACHING!

One of the joys of being an academic teaching professor has been the satisfaction of seeing my residents, medical students, and fellows succeed. Feelings similar to an anxious parent wishing the best success for their children, as a teaching professor, it brings me great satisfaction knowing I may have had a small part in shaping the careers of future eye surgeons and leaders in ophthalmology. In this way, passing the torch onto the best of the next generation of outstanding eye surgeons.

These are three of the 280-plus residents, fellows, and colleagues I have trained.

Dr. Devy Mandagi of Jakarta (now perhaps the highest volume cataract surgeon in Indonesia); Dr. Teguh Susilo, one of the very few fellowship-trained retina specialists who recently opened his own "HINC Vision Eye Clinic" and eye-surgery center in his home town of Surabaya, Indonesia; and Dr. Helena Ndume of Namibia, who was honored by the United Nations with the first Nelson Mandela prize for her charity work in providing over thirty thousand cataract patients with complimentary surgery—all epitomize the best in technical skill and compassionate treatment I have tried to emphasize in training these and the other outstanding eye surgeons below.

Patients often ask me if I was to have cataract surgery, who would I select to perform my own operations? I would feel safe and comfortable with any of the doctors I have personally trained.

Speaking of which, here are some of the many residents and fellows I have trained in cataract and LASIK eye surgery:

University of South Florida, Tampa

Dana Schneider, MD
Chris Barron, MD
Gonzalo Ortiz, MD
Whitney Whitfield, MD
T. Bradford Gillette, MD
Phillip Brunetti, MD/MS
Sara Bijan, MD
Vania Rashidi, MD
Keith Zimmermann, MD
Oliver Filatowski, MD
Sahas Narain MD/MS
Jacob Liechty MD/MS
Sabah Amir, MD/MBA
Sabrina Khalil, MD
Thomas Wepplemann, MD, PhD, MPH
Nabeel Zafrullah, MD
David Drucker, MD
Vishnu Adi, DO, MPH
John Cheung, MD
Jeslin Kera, MD
Kimberly Menezes, MD
Yasmin Ayoubi, MD

Fellows

Sara Bijan, MD

Mark Hankins, MD
Chris Donovan, MD
Alireza Baradaran Rafii, MD

University of Missouri

Residents

Erica Ballard (Embry), MD
Jason Rodier, MD
Philip Wilson, DO
Benjamin Buckner, MD
Mack Savage, MD
Austin Strohbehn, MD
Lindsey McDaniel, MD
Trevor Rosenlof, MD
Samuel Thomsen, MD
Ethan Crider, MD
Ryan Mercer, MD
Salman Sarwar, MD
Riley Scott Bylund, MD
Azeem Khan, MD
Vaishnavi Balendiran, MD
Sudhinder Koushik, MD
Kathleen Kwedar, MD
James Landreneau, MD
Van Nguyen, MD
Andrew Plummer, MD
Brian Kirk, MD
Marwa Thomas, MD
Jessica Ferrell, MD
Samuel Barry, MD
Andrew Polk, MD
Lauren Wiggins, MD

Fellows

Anthony Grillo, MD
Krishna Shanmugam, MD
Filbert Nguyen, MD
Samantha Herretes, MD
Whitney Potter, MD

University of Washington

James Britt, MD
Richard Hopp, MD
Carol Cooper, MD, PhD
Starla Fitch, MD
David Boes, MD
Aaron Weingeist, MD
Janet Carroll, MD
Michael Lee, MD
Elizabeth Choy, MD
Roger Badoia, MD
Thomas Matsko, MD
Robert Nash, MD
Brian Roth, MD
Ronald Zamber, MD
Janet Barrall, MD
Teresa Thornberg, MD
David Boes, MD
Todd Schneidermann, MD
John Barleen, MD
John Skerry, MD

Sam Ratulangi University Manado, Indonesia

Teguh Susilo, MD
Devy Mandagi, MD
Olga Poluon, MD

Michael Je, MD
Roy Umboh, MD
Anne Umboh, MD
Norman Tansuria, MD
Rilya Manoppo, MD
Freddy Kasih, MD
Roland Saiyang, MD
Renie Indrian, i MD
Airin, MD
Daniel Siegers, MD
Marcella Dualong, MD

University of Indonesia, Jakarta

Iksan Revino, MD
Yunia Iriwati, MD
Sjakon Tahija, MD

University of Zimbabwe

Tomas Milosev, MD
(Yugoslavia)

Helena Ndume, MD (Namibia)—recipient of the UN's first Nelson Mandela prize for thirty thousand charity cataract operations

Solomon Guramatunhu, MD (attending physician)
Roy D'Souza, MD (attending)

Angola

Fifteen residents

Madagascar

Twelve residents

University of Philippines

Sixteen residents

University of Southern Philippines

Thirty-six residents

Bacolod City Philippines

Thirteen residents

Baler, Aurora, Philippines

Sam Ratulangi Medical Manado Indonesia

Fifty-one residents

Jogykarta Indonesia

Thity-six residents

Bandung Indonesia

Three residents

Kyrgyzstan

Three residents
Malik Umur, MD (attending)

Last but not least:

Pacific Northwest University
Allison Jarstad, DO. (Yes, my daughter.)

CHAPTER 55

ACADEMIC PROMOTION AND SOUTH FLORIDA

S oon after marrying Dr. Kristine Marshall, I was nominated for an early rank advancement from associate professor to professor (the highest level of academic rank) at the University of Missouri. Prior to the COVID-19 pandemic, we were able to have a commuter marriage for our first eighteen months together, alternating flying to each other's homes on alternate weekends. As I applied for a position at the University of South Florida in Tampa, the new department chairman, Dr. Ramesh Ayyala, a charismatic man almost my age who shares so many common interests and also lived in England, training near where I lived (outside Liverpool), offered me a position as a professor and to assist in teaching the residents. It would be about six months before I would sell my Missouri home, reach my five-year retirement mark, and be able to join Kristine in St. Petersburg.

The frenetic pace of the work here is stimulating, and we tend to see the most complex patients and the most difficult types of surgeries. It's been intellectually stimulating and has given me new life as a teaching and research professor.

Some of my inventions I hope to bring to fruition are a pocket-sized cataract phaco machine—the "Pocket Phaco," and in conjunction with Dr. Ayyala's idea to combine it with a laser module to be developed for third-world use at a lower cost is one we will be working on with a team of researchers.

Another of my inventions is the Jarstad—Stone Cataract Teaching Head. This device created in partnership with my neighbor and long-time friend, Paul Stone, simulates the most difficult part of a cataract operation—the capsulotomy. Paul found a model of a crash test dummy for a lifelike head that an acrylic stand fits inside and by using white clay sandwiched in between two thin sheets of blue cellophane film from the "Party Store," provides as close to real life simulation for our resident surgeons to practice operating successfully on a model just before going into the operating room and performing the same maneuver on a live patient.

EPILOGUE

After returning to Seattle from Indonesia following one very successful medical mission trip, we felt somewhat like returning and conquering heroes and settled back in to our daily routine. Traveling abroad has always helped me appreciate my home, clinic, and outstanding employees, led in Federal Way by my head nurse and surgery center director Linda Stuart, RN, and clinic nurse Carol Johansson, LPN. Linda worked with me and looked out for me ever since the day I first began my private practice at St. Francis Hospital in Federal Way and was always compassionate, and one of the most brilliant nurses I have ever worked with. Carol was my surgery scheduling nurse and was extremely accurate and precise. Like Linda, Carol is an outstanding worker and one of the most dedicated, helpful persons I have ever met.

Shortly after returning home, I was asked by Michelle Davis, one of my employees, to speak at a Young Single Adult fireside on my medical mission experiences. It was held in the Covington, Washington, Church of Jesus Christ of Latter-day Saints Stake Center. Perhaps upward of a hundred young adults attended.

I gave a slideshow and video presentation of the first modern cataract surgery performed in Zimbabwe, Africa. I took the zebra skin Dr. Solomon Guramatunhu gave to me. It was spiritually exhilarating to once again fulfill the promise of my patriarchal blessing (a patriarchal blessing is given to members of the Church of Jesus

Christ of Latter-day Saints typically after baptism into the faith or during teenage years. It provides inspired counsel, along with promises, that can be obtained during life upon conditions of faithfulness. It also identifies the tribe of Israel a member is born into or adopted into according to revelation and inspiration received by the patriarch of each stake or LDS diocese), which I received at age fourteen and states, "Thou shalt find joy in the Lord in testifying of Him." I shall now close the same way I close my fireside talks—with my testimony (see Appendix "Our Savior's Personality").

Before I conclude, let me just say to the reader that writing this book has been an incredible journey for me. I don't know what my future holds at this point. Or even how much future I have left. As I enter my upcoming retirement age, I feel fortunate to have lived longer than I thought I might. I feel grateful to Heavenly Father for the many varied and intensely spiritual experiences I have been blessed with. After fifty plus volunteer medical missions all over the world, I can echo the statement of the prophet Joseph Smith who said, "A man filled with the love of God is not content with blessing his family alone, but ranges through the whole world, anxious to bless the whole human race." It's been my incredibly good fortune to be able to serve so many wonderful, deserving, and grateful patients with no thought of repayment.

There is also gratitude in my heart for the necessary challenges and trials that I have suffered through, as they have taught me patience and faith. Through all this, I have been sustained by a loving Lord, who has always been there for me, including in my darkest hours. If there is any wisdom I could impart from my many foolish mistakes in life, it would be this:

Keep trying! Success often came not only one step but more often two or three or ten steps beyond failure. **KEEP TRYING!** Or as Sir Winston Churchill stated, "Never give up. Never, never, never give up!

It is my hope that the reader will forgive the foibles of my penmanship, grammar, and ramblings, and will judge me by the intent of my heart: To go about doing good, to help and serve as many of God's children on this earth with every last ounce of energy, and to share my skills and talents with as many of my Heavenly Father's sons and daughters as possible that I might be an instrument in His hands in returning sight to the blind and hope to the downcast.

Selemat Jalan or until we meet again. God be with you.

John Steven Jarstad, MD

Selemat jalan and terima kasih (Goodbye until we meet again and thank you) from the medical mission team at Pulau Karimun (Karimun Island) Indonesia on January 26, 1994.

The Dharmais Perdami Katarak Safari team performed over four hundred sight-restoring eye operations in a cooperative effort between the foundation of Indonesian president Suharto, the surgeons of the University of Indonesia, and Deseret International volunteer surgeon John S. Jarstad, MD.

APPENDIX

OUR SAVIOR'S PERSONALITY

A Physician's Testimony

By John S. Jarstad, MD

> Tell me the stories of Jesus, I love to hear
> Things I would ask Him to tell me if He
> were here.
> (the Church of Jesus Christ of Latter-day
> Saints *Children's Songbook* 57)

I love that primary song. What would we ask Him to tell all of us if He was here today?

Brothers and sisters, I ask for your faith and prayers that the gift of the Holy Ghost may be here with us today that my speaking and your listening may be guided by the Spirit as I bear witness of the Savior, whose birth we commemorate just over two thousand years ago this month.

Much has been written about the Savior, Jesus Christ. And there are many wonderful talks about his life. Today, I would like through the scriptures to maybe help us all get to know Him and His personality just a little better.

Luke, a fellow physician and one of the twelve apostles, will serve as my main reference today. We learn much about the Savior's early years from him.

> And in those days there went out a decree from Caesar Augustus that all the world should be taxed. And all went to be taxed, every one to his own city. And Joseph also went up from Galilee

314

out of the city of Nazareth, into Judea unto the city of David, which is called Bethlehem: because he was of the house and lineage of David. To be taxed with Mary his espoused wife, being great with child. And she brought forth her first born son and wrapped him in swaddling clothes and laid him in a manger because there was no room for them in the inn.

And there were shepherds abiding in the field keeping watch over their flock by night. And lo the angel of the Lord came upon them and the glory of the Lord shone round about them and they were sore afraid. And the angel said unto them Fear not for behold I bring you good tidings of great joy which shall be to all people. For unto you is born this day in the city of David a Savior which is Christ the Lord. And this shall be a sign unto you ye shall find the babe wrapped in swaddling clothes lying in a manger. And suddenly there was with the angel a multitude of the heavenly host praising God and saying Glory to God in the highest and on earth peace good will toward men. (Luke 2:11–24)

So we learn that He was born in Bethlehem, that He was born of Mary, and that Joseph was not His true father. From the very beginning, we learn that He faced irony many times during His life—the Son of God, the Savior of the world born in a stable. He was the greatest helper of human kind, yet no one would help His earthly parents find room at the inn (Luke 2:7). Later, the lawyers and teachers in the temple asked, "Is this not the carpenter's son" (Mark 6:3)? They knew neither Him nor His Father.

I'm grateful that He chose to be born in humble circumstances, that anyone can identify with Him.

We know that He grew in wisdom and stature and in favor with God and man (Luke 2:52).

Now at those times, there was a very strict class distinction. **Jesus was identified as a tradesman's son**. As our prophet President Hinckley has said, "What a beautiful thing that is" (*Ensign* April 1998). He had to work for a living. He was taught in Joseph's carpentry shop how to hew, plane and join, and sand and polish wood; how to fit and build chairs, tables, doors, and furniture; and especially how to repair the broken ones.

There is just something **pure and honest** about someone who works with his or her hands to make a living.

We learn from the scriptures that **he was brilliant of mind** and intellectually He had no equal. In the New Testament, we are amazed by his quick wit and one-line gems.

The Pharisees asked, "Can anything good come out of Nazareth?"

And his answer was, "Come and see" (John 1:46).

He was physically and mentally strong. He fasted for forty days and then afterward withstood the temptations of the devil and paid Him no heed (Luke 4:1–13). Everywhere He went, he walked. Miles and miles each day.

A professional colleague and friend of mine who served as a mission president in the Philippines wrote a wonderful article called "Life in the Time of Christ and His Physical Attributes" (Roger Hiatt, MD, *The Journal of Collegium Aesculapium*, July 1984). He said,

> According to historical records and our beliefs, he was a Jew. Jewish men of his day and time were small and short, standing between 5'3" and 5'7" tall. And averaged between 120 and 150 lbs. Could I ask everyone who is between 5'3" and 5'7" please stand up. That is how tall the historical records say our Savior was. Lentulus a predecessor of Plato described him to the Roman senate as being "somewhat tall" and of a "ruddy countenance" such that the beholder may both love and fear. His hair is long in the order of the Nazarenes and the color of a fully ripe filbert

(hazelnut) to the level of his ear, whence down-
ward it is more of an orient (or darker) color,
curling and waving on his shoulders. His forehead is plain and delicate, the face without spot
or wrinkle, beautiful with a comely red.

His nose and mouth are exactly formed. His
beard the color of his hair, thick and forked. In
reproving terrible, in admonishing courteous, in
speaking very modest and wise; in proportion
of body well shaped. None has seen him laugh,
many have seen him weep. A man for his surpass-
ing beauty excelling the children of men.

Isaiah said, "There hath no beauty that we should desire him"
(Isaiah 53:2). Yet he was without blemish. His features were striking,
and His bone structure and skin without blemish was perfect. But
he was ordinary enough looking that Judas had to point him out of
a crowd (Luke 22:47), and Mary mistook him for a gardener (John
20:15).

I believe He chose not to look like a movie star, so that He could
identify with those of us who may feel plain or even homely. So that
when we meet Him, we will not be able to say, "If I was as beautiful
as you were, I could have done so much more with my life."

All of his senses were perfect. We know that His vision was
perfect because He saw Zacchaeus far away in a tree (Luke 19:2–8).
His hearing was perfect. He heard the pleas of the blind or lame in
a cacophony of voices (Luke 18:35–43). His sense of touch was so
refined that He could feel the woman touch the hem of His gar-
ment in a crowded throng (Luke 8:43–48). That He was perceptive
beyond other mortals is evidenced by the fact that He understood
human nature so well that He often could tell exactly what people were thinking. As when He saw through the deception of the
Pharisee's question about whether to render to Caesar the things that
be Caesar's and unto God the things that are God's (Luke 20:20–26).

His personality was perfect (Luke 6:40). He was honest and
pure. Undefiled by forbidden foods or actions. He could look him-

self in the mirror each day and could sleep soundly and peacefully each night as evidenced by the story of Him falling asleep on the rolling ship the night before He walked on water (Matthew 8:23–27).

He was cheerful. He bade others to be of good cheer (Matthew 9:2; Mark 6:50; John 16:33; Acts 23:11). He was complimentary and knew how to pay compliment as when he described John the Baptist as **"among those born of women none is greater"** (Luke 7:28). And it's recorded that Jesus marveled at the faith of the centurion whose slave was dying and that Jesus need only give the word and his servant would be healed (Luke 7:2–10).

He stood up for what He knew was right and was firm and strong when He needed to be—like when He overturned the moneychanger's heavy tables and scales and drove them out of the temple (Matthew 21:12; Luke 19:45–46).

He knew who he was and wasn't afraid to tell others:

> And he came to Nazareth, where he had been brought up and as his custom was, he went into the synagogue on the Sabbath day, and stood up for to read. And there was delivered unto him the book of the prophet Isaiah.
>
> And when he had opened the book, he found the place where it was written, the spirit of the Lord is upon me, because he hath anointed me to preach the gospel to the poor; he hath sent me to heal the broken hearted; to preach deliverance to the captives and recovering of sight to the blind, to set at liberty them that are bruised.
>
> To preach the acceptable year of the Lord. And he closed the book and he gave it again to the minister, and sat down. And the eyes of all them that were in the synagogue were fastened on him. And he began to say unto them, this day is this scripture fulfilled in your ears. And all bare him witness and wondered at the gracious words, which proceeded out of his mouth. (Luke 4:16–21)

He was an example of grace and poise. When He had just finished telling the story of Naaman, the Syrian leper who was cleansed by bathing in the Jordan River seven times and pointing out that no Israelite lepers were cleansed, they carried Him to the brow of a cliff intending to throw Him over the edge; but Luke 4:30 says, "He passing through the midst of them went His way."

He was such a great teacher that people were "astonished and amazed' at His doctrine. He taught with power (Luke 4:32).

He understood fishing and where to lay down the nets—so much so that Peter James and John were astonished at the huge catch. He calmed them by telling them, "Fear not from now on you will catch men" (Luke 5:10).

He loved all people and ate frequently with publicans and sinners (Luke 5:27–32). He taught unconditional love. To love one's enemies as well as friends and pray for them (Luke 6:27, 35). To be merciful, nonjudgmental, giving, and forgiving. He taught in parables using common everyday examples because he knew we would forget: motes, beams, trees, fruit, rocks, sand, birds, bread, coins, bottles, garments, flowers, fish, serpents, eggs, scorpions, camels, buildings, weeds, money, pearls, suppers, weddings, workers are just a few of the subjects of the Savior's parables (see *parables* in the Bible dictionary).

He was practical and innovative. When His disciples were hungry, they picked corn even though it was on the Sabbath (Luke 6:1–5). He quoted David who ate the shewbread of the temple under similar circumstances. He healed a man with a withered hand on Sunday too (Luke 6:6–10). When He perceived the Pharisees about to condemn, he read their thoughts and asked, "Is it lawful to do good or evil on the Sabbath? To save a life or destroy it" (Luke 6:8–9)?

He was prayerful. When it came time to select his chosen twelve apostles, Luke says, "He went out into a mountain to pray and continued **all night** in prayer unto God" (Luke 6:12).

He was compassionate. When his disciples suggested sending people away to get food, He had a better idea, and a miracle fed the five thousand. When they were going to send little children away, He made them the greatest in heaven (Luke 9:47–48).

He gave clear answers. When told His family was waiting, He answered, "My mother and brethren are those that hear the word of God and do it" (Luke 8:21).

Now was he part human? Yes. Did He get frustrated, anguished, or tired? I'm sure He did yet without sin. We know that in Luke 13:34, He cried, "O Jerusalem, Jerusalem, Thou which killeth the prophets and stonest them. How often would I have gathered thy children together as a hen gathereth her children and ye would not."

Here was the Son of God who could heal, could provide salvation, is the light of the world, is the bread of life; and yet ironically, no one appreciated Him. They didn't accept Him. They tried to kill Him and frequently asked Him to leave. In the midst of the *tempest*, He asked His disciples, "Where's your faith (Matthew 8:23–27)?

One story that really hits home for me is the story of the ten lepers who are all healed and only one returns to give thanks. And Jesus said, "Was there not ten cleansed? But where are the nine" (Luke 17:17)? What's interesting is that those statistics of one in ten patients saying thanks are pretty accurate today too.

He is loyal. He promises, "Whosoever shall confess me before men, him shall the Son of man also confess before the angels of God" (Luke 12:8).

He had priorities straight. "Beware of covetousness. A man's life doesn't consist of his possessions" (Luke 12:15). "Seek ye first the kingdom of God and all else will be added unto you" (Luke 12:31).

He realized the seriousness of his calling. "But I have a baptism to be baptized with; and how am I straightened till it be accomplished" (Luke 12:50).

He cared for the poor and lonely. Using Luke 14:7–14, He might have said today, "When you have a feast or a BBQ, don't always invite only your family, friends, or rich neighbors who will feel obligated to ask you back. But invite the poor, maimed, lame, and blind, and you'll be blessed because they can't repay you. You will be repaid at the resurrection of the just."

He understood business and accounting principles. He tells the story of the unjust steward settling bad debts for eighty cents and fifty cents on the dollar (Luke 16:1–12), and the parable of the talents is a classic lesson on investing (Luke 19:11–27).

He teaches us it is okay to be confrontational if we're forgiving. "If your brother trespass against Thee rebuke him" (in other words, you don't have to be a pushover). Then if he repents, forgive him—even up to seven times in the same day (Luke 17:3).

There were some people He just didn't' like. The Pharisees were one.

> And he spoke this parable unto certain which trusted in themselves that they were righteous, and despised others: The Pharisee prayed with himself, on a prominent street corner in a loud voice: "God I thank Thee that I am not as other men are, extortioners, unjust, adulterers or even as this publican. I fast twice a week and give tithes of all I possess." The publican on the other hand stood afar off from the street corner and would not lift up so much as his eyes unto heaven, but smote upon his breast saying, God be merciful to me a sinner. (Luke 18:9–14)

Sisters, you would love this.

He did things right away when asked. When a blind man called out, He said, "What would you like me to do for you?" And the man's answer was, "Lord, that I might receive my sight." And Jesus said unto him, "Receive thy sight. Thy faith hath saved Thee" (Luke 18:40–42).

Earlier, we talked about how the Lord's perfect vision helped him spot Zacchaeus far away in a tree. The other thing about this story is that the Lord forgave this well-known sinner. Several in the crowd may have murmured, "Oh, great, He's going to eat and be the guest of a well-known sinner."

Now this is what the people didn't know: "Behold Lord, the half of my goods I give to the poor; and if I have taken anything from any man by false accusation, I restore him fourfold." And Jesus said unto him, "This day is salvation come to this house" (Luke 19:1–10), signifying that Zacchaeus was forgiven.

He was very observant. I'm certain he had a photographic memory. He noticed things other people might miss. Before his triumphal entry, He knew exactly where a colt would be tied up. At Passover, He knew exactly where a room large enough for the Last Supper would be ready and furnished (Luke 19:29–35).

He was well respected by the doctors (teachers) and lawyers from age twelve but also the religious scribes. After teaching of the resurrection, they said, "Master Thou hast well said" (or in other words, "Thou art well versed"). And after that, they durst not ask him any more questions at all (Luke 20:39–40).

He was calming and reassuring to His friends. "When you hear of wars and commotion, be not terrified. Settle it in your hearts. Don't even meditate beforehand what you shall answer. I will give you the speech and the wisdom to overtake your adversaries" (paraphrase of Luke 21:9–15).

"Take heed to yourselves" (in other words, "Take care of yourselves") lest your hearts be overcome by the cares of this world (Luke 21:34).

He was great at delegation. He sent Peter and John ahead to go prepare the Passover (Luke 22:7–13).

He was the ultimate example of service. When asked who was the greatest at a feast, He pointed out that it was those who were waited upon; but He mentioned, "You notice I'm the waiter" (paraphrase of Luke 22:24–30).

He prayed for his friends. That their faith would not fail (Luke 22:32).

He was very forgiving. Now some would say when they make a mistake, "I'm so disappointed. I'm sure the Lord is so disgusted and so disappointed with me."

Remember, He's used to it. Peter denied even knowing Him three times, yet the Lord chose Peter His rock to later lead the church as His chief apostle (Luke 22:54–62).

He had compassion even for his enemies. When Peter smote off the ear of the high priest's servant who was coming to arrest Him, Jesus immediately healed him (Luke 22:50–51).

He knew when to speak and when to remain silent. When Pilate asked Him, "Art Thou the King of the Jews?" He answered, "Thou sayest it" (Luke 23:3), or as we might say today, "You said it." While before wicked Herod, who ordered John the Baptist beheaded, "He answered him nothing" (Luke 23:9).

He was faultless according to the roman soldier at the crucifixion. He even forgave his killers (Luke 23:47).

I believe He had a sense of humor. Peter denied Him three times, so Jesus later asked him three times to feed His sheep (Luke 22:54–62; John 21:15–17).

He really knew the scriptures. On the road to Emmaus, He caught up with two traveling disciples and had a little fun with them. The conversation may have sounded something like this:

> "Hey, why are you two so sad?" He asked.
>
> "Where have you been?" they answered. "Are you a stranger to Jerusalem and didn't you know what's happened here the past few days?"
>
> And He went along with them. "What things?"
>
> "Why, about how Jesus of Nazareth was a prophet mighty in word and deed and how He was condemned to death and how we were all so trusting that it was going to be He that should have redeemed Israel, and today is the third day since this was done. And rumors say a few women and disciples came to His tomb and didn't find Him." (paraphrase of Luke 24:13–24)
>
> O fools and slow of heart to believe all that the prophets have spoken. Then beginning at Moses He expounded unto them, in all the scriptures the things concerning himself." (Luke 24:25–27)

After he took bread and broke it and blessed it, they recognized Him, and He vanished.

"Did not our hearts burn within us as He talked with us and opened the scriptures?" they later exclaimed (Luke 24:32).

Finally, He gave the disciples infallible proof of the resurrection and made a point to eat fish and honeycomb with them (Luke 24:36–43).

He was kind, compassionate, and tenderhearted. In the *Book of Mormon*, we read that after His resurrection, He appeared in the Americas to the descendants of the Nephites and Lamanites (3 Nephi 11–26). He called their little children to Him, and overcome with emotion, He took each one and blessed them and then prayed for them. We read in 3 Nephi 17:16 that "Eye hath never seen neither hath the ear heard before so great and marvelous things as we saw and heard Jesus speak unto the Father on behalf of these little children." Filled with compassion, our Savior had all those who were blind or deaf or lame or sick come forward, and He healed them every one (3 Nephi 17:6–10).

Spiritually, and that is where we all want to know Him, **He reigns supreme**. In the premortal existence, He was our Father's favorite Son. He was his right hand. How did He attain this position? Through diligence and obedience according to the scriptures. We read in Hebrews 5:8–9, "Though He were a Son yet learned He obedience by the things which He suffered. And being made perfect, He became the author of eternal salvation unto all them that obey Him."

We, too, have the opportunity to become more like Him. To me, this is the real miracle of Christmas—that our Heavenly Father has given to us the gift of life on this earth; the gift of free agency to make choices (many times, they're hard and even ironic choices); and the gift to gain a physical body and learn to control it, feed it the right foods (physically and spiritually), take good care of it, and discipline it and the spirit within. **And most of all the gift of a way back.**

The Parable of the Chocolate

When I was a young boy, I remember having a fascination about chocolate. You might say I was a borderline chocoholic. If anyone here has ever been addicted to something—whether it be smoking, food, coffee, drinking, drugs, videos or Internet, sports, or ballet—you'll know the feeling I had about chocolate. When can I get some chocolate? How can I earn money to buy chocolate? How can I be nicer to people so they might offer me some chocolate? And will anyone find me out?

I guess it started at an early age when my parents left me alone with my two uncles. They took two of my sisters and me to a carnival and bought us each some of those little chocolate "Ice Cubes" from Bavaria. At first, we all tried to say no, because our mom was health conscious and didn't want us to eat too much "junk food." Eating too much chocolate was too rich for our young taste buds, and we felt really sick afterward. But after practically force-feeding them to us, years later, we all began to crave them.

When I told my mom about this, she was shocked and didn't believe me. "Oh, honey, your uncles would never do that," she said.

Years passed, but subconsciously, I must have vividly remembered those bright shiny silver and blue wrappers of the Bavarian Ice Cube chocolates with the red lettering, wondering if I'd ever be able to try them again. Once in a while, I'd see them in a store near the checkout counter and try to remember what they tasted like.

Later, when I was a teenager in high school, it seemed like everyone I knew liked chocolate. One of my friends even got a box of fifty different varieties of chocolates, some with the little alcohol centers from her dad every Christmas.

She was always offering me one of those little miniature bottle chocolates, but I never took her up on the offer.

About a year before my mission call, I remember going with a few friends in my car to see a movie: **Willy Wonka and the Chocolate Factory**. Have any of you seen it? What's it about? Right! CHOCOLATE! It was so hard to sit there through that movie. I wanted to get up right then and go to the concession stand for a giant box of Milk Duds or M&M chocolates. But I was an athlete at the time, and our high school coach warned us about eating chocolate before a meet and breaking our training diet.

When I did get my mission call, I was surprised to learn I would be going to England and to the Birmingham mission with Bourneville, England, right in our area. Did you know that the Cadbury chocolate factory in Bourneville upon which the movie *Willy Wonka* is based was just a few miles from our mission home?

Well, fortunately, I was not addicted to chocolate on my mission. I didn't have time for it. Working hard and praying hard and seeing a few heavier-set English kids with messy chocolate all over them helped me avoid even looking at it. When I returned home, I don't think anyone imagined I could have a weakness for chocolate.

Then I met my wife and after we were married, I found out that she enjoyed chocolate too. In fact, we both found that it even helped us stay awake to study better in college.

What's the point to this long rambling story? Well, after thinking I had perfect willpower and then slipping up a couple of times over the years and indulging in nibbling small bites of Bavarian chocolate, I realized it could become habit forming for me and even addicting. After trying to break the chocolate habit several times on my own, unsuccessfully, I finally went to the Lord in utter hopelessness for help. It was only through fasting, prayer, and trusting completely in the Savior's power of redemption that I was able to completely overcome those cravings for foreign chocolate.

I know if the Savior can help me overcome my craving for chocolate, He can help any one of us with any weakness we may be struggling with.

Brothers and sisters, we have been given many gifts this Christmas season, but the greatest of all gifts has come to us from our Heavenly Father. The gift of a Redeemer, a Savior, an Advocate to plead our cause to the Father. Someone who will be there waiting for us at the gate when it is our turn to come home.

"For the time will come when every soul who forsaketh his sins and cometh unto me and calleth on my name and obeyeth my voice and keepeth my commandments shall see my face and know that I am" (D&C 93:1).

And the reassuring guarantee: "That the keeper of the gate is the Holy One of Israel and He employeth no servant there" (2 Nephi 9:41).

Of these things I testify with every fiber of my being by the power of the Spirit and in the sacred name of our Savior and Redeemer. In the name of Jesus Christ. Amen.

JOHN S. JARSTAD, MD

Funeral Address for My Father—John Otis William Jarstad

THE PLAN OF SALVATION

By John S. Jarstad, MD
June 19, 1999

On behalf of the Jarstad family, I would like to express my appreciation to all of those who have participated in the services today. It is a fitting tribute to Dad that so many of you are here. We would also like to thank the doctors, nurses, and family members who helped and visited Dad during his lengthy illnesses, and those of you who sent cards or offered prayers on his behalf.

Dad influenced many people during his lifetime, and this past week, I received tributes from two people on opposite sides of this earth who could not be here today. One is a devout Muslim and brilliant scientist from Indonesia, Tjahjono Gondhowiardjo, who met Dad and said he was a strong principled man with a life full of humanity and friendships, who raised good children, and who was sure to be at Allah's side. The other is a full-blooded African tribesman and Christian, Dr. Solomon Guramatunhu, a surgeon from Zimbabwe who remembers Dad for his great humanitarian spirit, compassion, and dignity in serving the people of Zimbabwe on one of our medical missions. As you can see, Dad liked people and had the ability to make friends quickly and easily. He made a lasting impression on those he met.

In the few remaining minutes, I would like to present a few thoughts on Dad's faith, hope. and beliefs that may bring comfort to those of us left behind.

A fitting analogy to Dad in the Bible was Job, who asks, "If a man die, shall he live again" (Job 14:14)? There is no question of greater importance at a time like this. Those of us who are healthy and live in comfort and security seldom give any thought to death. Our minds are on other things. Yet there is nothing more

328

certain, nothing more universal, nothing more final than the closure of mortal life. No one can escape it, not one. All have walked their way to—as Shakespeare described it—"the undiscovered country from whose bourn no traveler returns" (Hamlet).

But Jesus Christ changed all that. Only a God could do what he did. He broke the bonds of death. He, too, had to die; but on the third day, following his burial, He rose from the grave, "the first fruits of them that slept" (1 Corinthians 15:20), and in so doing brought the blessing of the resurrection to every one of us. Concerning this wondrous thing, the apostle Paul declared, "O death where is thy sting, O grave where is thy victory" (1 Corinthians 15:55)?

Dad grew up in a strongly religious Lutheran home. Prayers were said, gratitude for blessings given, loyalty, and honesty expected. Dad often repeated the words of his father Otto Jarstad, who said, "Never steal anything, not even a nickel." Later in life, Dad added to his strong Lutheran beliefs the teachings of the modern prophets from the Church of Jesus Christ of Latter-day Saints. He particularly respected our current prophet Gordon B. Hinckley (a former journalist) and President Spencer W. Kimball, a courageous man of just over five feet tall, who gradually lost his golden radio voice to throat cancer. I'll always remember Dad watching President Kimball on TV during a general conference broadcast in October of 1974. The prophet was giving a speech in his raspy voice about the importance of cleaning up dilapidated properties. He could have been talking about our backyard. In that speech, he stated,

> The Lord created for us this beautiful world and gave a commandment to till the ground and dress the land and make it habitable. We recommend to all people that there be no undue pollution, that the land be taken care of and kept clean, productive, and beautiful.

President Kimball went on to say,

> We are concerned when we see numerous
> front, side, and backyards that have gone to
> weeds, where ditch banks are cluttered and
> trash and refuse accumulate. It grieves us when
> we see broken fences falling barns, leaning and
> unpainted sheds, hanging gates, and unpainted
> property. And we ask our people again to take
> stock of their own dwellings and properties.
> We look forward to the day when, in all of our
> communities, urban and rural, there would be
> a universal, continued movement to clean and
> repair and paint barns and sheds, build side-
> walks, clean ditch banks, and make our prop-
> erties a thing of beauty to behold.

Before President Kimball finished speaking, Dad stood up,
changed quickly into his work clothes, went out into the backyard, and began cleaning up and following the prophet's advice.
"That's great, Dad," I said, "but couldn't you wait until Monday?"
What an example of obedience. Moreover, anyone who knew Dad
knew he loved to plant flowers and helped to landscape all of his
children's yards. He took President Kimball's message to heart
the rest of his life. He would have loved seeing all the beautiful
flowers here today.

The logical follow-up questions to "If a man dies, will he
live again?" are the questions regarding the purpose of life that
Dad believed were answered through the Church of Jesus Christ
of Latter-day Saints teachings:

- Where did we come from?
- Why are we here?
- And where are we going after this life is over?

Dad believed we lived in spirit form before we were born as the book of Job states, "There is a spirit in man and the inspiration of the almighty giveth them understanding (Job 32:8)." Also we read that Jeremiah was told, "Before I formed Thee in the belly I knew Thee and before Thou camest forth out of the womb, I sanctified Thee and I ordained Thee a prophet unto the nations" (Jeremiah 1:4–5).

He also believed the words of the English poet Wordsworth, who said, concerning our existence before mortal birth, "Our birth is but a sleep and a forgetting: The soul that rises with us our life's star, hath elsewhere its setting and cometh from afar: Not in entire forgetfulness, and not in utter nakedness, but trailing clouds of glory do we come from God, who is our home" (*Ode to Intimations of Immortality* 1807).

So Dad believed that God knew each one of us before we were born and that there was a purpose to life. The task for us was to learn what our purpose is and to be challenged each day with the uncertainty of what life will throw at us.

Will it be a fastball up and away, or will it be a curveball down and in when we are nearly down and out? How we respond to those challenges determines our success or failure in the here and now. Also, as experience is gained and patterns develop, habits of character become internalized, and we become completed (Greek = *perfect*) beings.

I'm sure as we all prepared to journey to earth, God may have said in much the same way we tell our children as they first venture off to start school, "Now be careful and watch out. There will be pain and suffering, vexing irony and injustice, and perplexing times when there will seem to be no answers." And we all probably said, "Okay, Father. We can handle it. No problem." Does that sound familiar to you, fellow parents of teenagers?

But how can you adequately explain to a small child about chronic, unrelenting, and terminal pain; soul-piercing unfulfilled dreams; humiliating and devastating irony; and injustice? Painful firsthand experience was the only way. A worthy goal for many of us will be to drink out of the bitter cup of life without becoming bitter.

Yes, life has experiences to offer, and Dad certainly learned from the school of hard knocks more than once. After a failure, though, he picked himself up and started over again, trying something new.

So our Heavenly Father sent us to this earth to test us and to prove us. He wanted to see if we would follow His rules and commandments after being separated from Him, learn by experience, and most importantly learn to love. I know that my dad learned to love.

So Dad's spirit is no longer with his body. As a medical doctor, I have seen clinically several times that death is the separation of the spirit from the body.

I would now like to explain so the grandchildren can understand something about death.

GLOVE ANALOGY: This is a glove like the kind of glove Grandpa would wear when he helped people in the yard. My hand represents the spirit. The glove represents the body. Without the spirit inside, the body doesn't move. And it's cold. But with the spirit, life is given to the body, and it can be useful in serving others. At the time of death, our body and our spirit separate, and the body remains here, but our spirit self returns to the God, who gave it life. We learn from the scriptures that there is a place prepared for us after we die to await the resurrection. If we have done well, that place will be a place of peace and joy, a paradise of rest and reunion with our loved ones.

How do we know if we have done well? Christ said, "By their fruits ye shall know them. Do men gather grapes of thorns or figs of thistles" (Matthew 7:16–20)? In other words, look at what Dad accomplished; the service he rendered to others; the sacrifices and generosity he gave to his family, friends, and total strangers; the legacy of compassion, philanthropy, and good works he left behind for his children and grandchildren to follow. Look at all the good people who have gathered here today. You are the crown jewels and gems of humanity. I don't see any thorns or thistles here.

Two months ago, we celebrated Easter Sunday. The central point of the gospel or "good news" is that Jesus—after lying in a tomb and having all His followers experience that terrible sense of loss, dejection, hopelessness, and misery—arose from the dead on that first Easter morning. To the utter amazement of everyone, an angel appeared and said to the followers, "Why seek ye the living among the dead? He is not here but is risen" (Luke 24:5–6). These simple words "He is not here, but is risen" have become the most profound in all literature. They are the declaration of the empty tomb. They are the fulfillment of all He had spoken concerning rising again. They are the triumphant response to the query facing every man, woman, and child who was ever born. Jesus appeared and spoke to Mary, and she replied. He was not an apparition. This was not idle tales of imagination. He was real as real as He had been in mortal life. He did not permit her to touch Him, for He had not yet ascended to His Father in heaven. That would happen shortly. What a reunion it must have been to be embraced by the Father, who loved Him and who also must have wept for Him during His hours of agony.

Jesus next appeared to two men on the road to Emmaus. He conversed with them and ate with them. He met with his twelve apostles behind closed doors and taught them. Thomas missed the first visit and was invited to feel of His hands and His side later on and exclaimed, "My Lord and my God" (John 20:28). He later spoke to over five hundred at one time (1 Corinthians 15:6). Who can dispute the documentation of these facts? There is no record of anyone ever retracting his or her testimony of these experiences. While there is plenty of evidence that they bore witness of these events throughout their lives, even giving their own lives in affirming the reality of the things they experienced, their word is clear, and their testimony is secure. Men and women throughout the centuries have accepted that testimony by the millions. And countless numbers have lived and died in affirmation of its truth which has come to them by the power of the Holy Spirit and which they could not deny. This is important to us because Paul said, "As in Adam all die so in Christ shall all be resurrected" (1 Corinthians 15:22)." Dad believed in Christ and in the glorious hope of the resurrection.

I want to talk lastly for a minute about hope. In a wonderful tribute to Dad by John Wallingford, the sports editor of the *Bremerton Sun*, where Dad was himself sports editor years ago, Mr. Wallingford mentions Dad's unusual energy and optimism. He quotes dad's brother Glenn, who is with us here today, who calls Dad "the best brother (he) could ever have." Our everyday use of the word *hope* includes how we hope to arrive at a certain destination by a certain time. We hope for the visit of a loved one. These are some of our proximate hopes. Ultimate hope is a different matter. It is tied to Jesus and the blessings of the great atonement, blessings resulting in the universal resurrection, and the precious opportunity provided thereby for us to practice emancipating repentance, making possible a perfect brightness of hope. Speaking of this hope, one of the ancient American prophets from the *Book of Mormon* has said,

> Now after you have gotten into this straight and narrow path, I would ask if all is done. Behold ye have not come this far except it be through the word of Christ with unshaken faith in Him relying wholly upon the merits of Him who is mighty to save. Wherefore ye must press forward with a steadfastness in Christ, having a perfect brightness of hope and a love of God and of all men. Wherefore if ye shall press forward feasting upon the words of Christ and endure to the end, thus saith the Father, ye shall have eternal life. (2 Nephi 31:19–20)

I want each of you to know that Dad had this hope even to the very end. He never gave up. One of our treasured but painful

334

memories during his last week was Dad's plea for us to do something more, that maybe if we could just try a different approach or something new, he might completely recover and be able to walk again. In frustration, he asked my wife, who was frequently by his side, "C'mon, PS, just pick me up right now, strap me to your back, and carry me out of here." When that didn't work, he was ready to go home and began to call for his papa, sisters, brother, and mom.

I remember my dad as someone who was the best friend a kid could ever have—who played ball in the backyard with us; took us along fishing when we were old enough; gave us real jobs and responsibilities at an early age; trusted us with dangerous machinery, automobiles, and boats a little too soon; and professionally filmed all our childhood antics, athletics, and events. He was a man of integrity, brilliance, humility, hope, and love. May we all strive to honor his memory by the lives we live from this day forward, is my prayer. In the name of our Savior Jesus Christ. Amen.

References:

1. Hinckley, Gordon B., "He Is Not Here, but Is Risen," *ENSIGN* report of the 169th Annual General Conference of the Church of Jesus Christ of Latter-day Saints, May 1999, pp. 70–72.
2. Kimball, Edward, Teachings of Spencer W. Kimball. Bookcraft 1985

"You Raise Me Up" by Josh Groban

To My Dad
By Stephanie Jarstad
Christmas 2003

When I am down and, oh, my soul, so weary;
When troubles come and my heart burdened be;

Then I am still and wait here in the silence,
Until you come and sit awhile with me.
You raise me up, so I can stand on mountains;
You raise me up, to walk on stormy seas;
I am strong, when I am on your shoulders;
You raise me up, to more than I can be.
You raise me up, so I can stand on mountains;
You raise me up, to walk on stormy seas;
I am strong, when I am on your shoulders;
You raise me up, to more than I can be.
There is no life—no life without its hunger;
Each restless heart beats so imperfectly;
But when you come and I am filled with wonder,
Sometimes, I think I glimpse eternity.
You raise me up, so I can stand on mountains;
You raise me up, to walk on stormy seas;
I am strong, when I am on your shoulders;
You raise me up, to more than I can be.
You raise me up, so I can stand on mountains;
You raise me up, to walk on stormy seas;
I am strong, when I am on your shoulders;
You raise me up, to more than I can be.

My Father the Hero

By Allison Jarstad
2002

My greatest teacher has been my father. Through his loving advice, counsel, and example, he has made an impacting influence upon my character and on my life. As I look up to him more and more, he has become a role model and friend to me.

Growing up without much money, my dad worked an after-school job throughout his high school years. Managing homework and a job may seem difficult for a high school student, but it is nearly impossible for a champion cross-country runner and a three-sport athlete, like my father. As I experience adversity, loss, and stress as a scholar athlete, I look to my supportive father for guidance, because he understands the challenges I face and motivates me to attack them with all of my effort. He takes time from his busy schedule to watch all of my races, games, or meets so that he won't miss any moment of my success or glory.

Because he wanted his children to have a better childhood than he did and because he enjoys serving others, he unselfishly worked with amazing dedication and drive to graduate from the Mayo Clinic Residency Program and become an ophthalmologist. Even when life is hard, he does not give up, for he has set his priorities and has goals that he pushes himself to reach. This example motivates me to dream big. He has taught me that I can accomplish anything and to never settle for less than my best. Specifically, this advice has helped me become a school record holder in the pole vault and a two-time state qualifier in cross-country.

More important than athletics and school, however, my father has taught me that integrity is the key to success. Not only is it vital to be honest to others in order to be respected, but it is also imperative to be honest with one's self. He has taught me to love myself and expresses his growing love for me every day. My father stands up for what he knows is right, and because I look up to him, I push myself to take on his positive traits.

My father has not only provided a stellar example of what one can achieve through dedication and sweat, but he has also taught me to persevere through defeat and to remain humble and grateful in victory. I love my father and the woman he has helped me to become.

Curriculum Vitae
John Steven Jarstad, MD

Qualifications

Education
MD University of Washington School of Medicine 1984

BS Brigham Young University 1980

HS (Honors) George R. Curtis High, Tacoma, Washington, 1974

MBA Course—Regis University, Denver, Colorado, completed first quarter (3.7 GPA)

Post Graduate Training
Board Certification—American Board of Ophthalmology 1989

Residency Mayo Clinic, Rochester, Minnesota, Ophthalmology 1985–1988

Internship Mayo Clinic, Rochester, Minnesota, (Internal Medicine, ENT, Neurology) 1984–1985

MS Fellowship NIH Nuclear Medicine and Ophthalmology 1984

Academic Appointments and Experience
Professor—University of South Florida 2020 to present

Professor—University of Missouri 2020

Associate Professor—University of Missouri Columbia 2015–2020

Medical Director—CEO, Evergreen Eye Centers Inc. 1989–2015

Visiting Professor—University of Indonesia Department of Ophthalmology 1994–2003

Visiting Professor—University of Philippines Department of Ophthalmology 2001

Visiting Professor—Fatima Medical College Department of Ophthalmology 2001

Visiting Professor—University of Nigeria, Lagos, Review Course 1996

Visiting Professor—University of Zimbabwe 1993–1996

Clinical Faculty—University of Washington Department of Ophthalmology 1989–1996

General Ophthalmology—Idaho Falls, Idaho, 1988–1989

Honors and Awards

Best Cataract Surgeons in America 2022—American College of Elective Surgery

America's Top Ophthalmologists—Consumer Research Council 2002–2005

Outstanding Intellectuals of the Twenty-First Century—IBC Cambridge, England, 2002

Who's Who among Business and Health Professionals 1994–2002

Washington Academy of Eye Physicians and Surgeons Humanitarian of the Year 2001

King County Council Commendation for International Humanitarian Work 2001

Sister Dora Award for Cost-Efficiency in Cataract Surgery—St. Francis Hospital 1995

Lecturer's Medal—University of Indonesia School of Medicine 1994

Surgical Innovator's Award—Jarstad Refractive Cataract Surgery Incision Marker

- American Surgical Instrument Company (ASICO) 1993

Federal Way Favorite—Outstanding Community Volunteer 1991

Outstanding and Effective Teacher in Ophthalmology—Mayo Medical School 1987

Inventions/Patents

Inventor Jarstad Refractive Cataract Surgery Incision Marker

- American Surgical Instrument Company (ASICO model #AE-1527) 1993

Design Consultant Chiron Passport

- Foldable Silicone Intraocular Lens Implant Delivery System, 1994, Chiron Ophthalmic

Design Consultant AMO Prodigy

- Silicone IOL folding device (oval modification) Allergan Medical Optics 1989

FDA Basic and Clinical Studies

Phase 1 Clinical Investigator/Clinical Study Director

- Wyeth 41,195 Topical Mast Cell Stabilizer Drug Trial 1987, Mayo Clinic
- ARVO Proceedings 1987

Phase 1, 2, 3 Clinical Director Medical Monitor, Design Team, Mentor O&O

- *SIS* Phacoemulsification System First IRB approved use and first human trials 1993–1996

Phase 1 Clinical Investigator Optical Radiation Corporation Memory Lens

- First US Surgeon to implant ORC foldable Acrylic IOL in human trials 1994

Phase 1 Clinical Investigator Spectrum Biomedical—Optical Coherence Device for Noninvasive Serum Cholesterol Monitoring 1993

Phase 1, 2, 3 Clinical Investigator AMO 100D Teledioptric IOL for Macular Degeneration

- Galilean Telescope IOL for Severe Macular Degeneration 1990

Phase 3 Clinical Investigator AMO First Foldable Silicon IOL for Human Trials 1987

- This lens became the AMO SI-18 and became the number one IOL line in US history.

AMO SA 40N ARRAY Multifocal IOL 2/1998

- Among first surgeons to implant foldable Multifocal IOL

TEAM Member NIH Gamma Camera Imaging of Ocular
Melanoma with Radiolabelled
- Monoclonal Antibodies 1984

Speakers Bureau / Consultant
- Allergan
- American Medical Optics (SI-18, AMD-100, SA-40 Multifocal)
- Mentor O & O (SIS and Odyssey Phaco Machines)
- Pharmacia (Healon, Healon GV)
- Chiron (Refractive Cataract Surgery and Marker)
- Bausch & Lomb
- Iris Medical (Solid-State Diode Ophthalmic Lasers)
- Allergan Medical Optics
- Ophthalmology Management Journal
- Deseret International Foundation

Affiliations
Past President—Washington Academy of Eye Physicians and Surgeons 2000–2001
Executive Committee—Washington Academy of Eye Physicians and Surgeons 1999–2002
American Academy of Ophthalmology
American Society of Cataract and Refractive Surgeons
American Medical Association
Washington State Medical Association (Interspecialty Council 2000–2001)

Community Service
Chief of Medical Staff—St. Francis Hospital, Federal Way, Washington, 2004–2005
Co-Director for all outpatient surgery—Tampa General Hospital-USF, 2021 to present
Cochairman—St. Francis Hospital Annual Benefit Gala 2002–2004

Ophthalmology Board—Deseret International Foundation 1992–Present

Country Representative—Indonesia and Nigeria, Deseret International Foundation

District Chairman—Boy Scouts of America 1997–2000 (Quality District 1998–2001)

Executive Board—Boy Scouts of America Pacific Harbors Council 1997 to present

Endowment Committee—BSA Pacific Harbors Council 1999 to present

Kiwanis—Chairman Eyeglass and Hearing Aid Drive 1993 to present

Stake Mission President—Church of Jesus Christ of Latter-day Saints 1986–1988, 1996–1997

Family/Interests

Married to Dr. Kristine Marshall, DDS

Fishing, Music, Cinematography—Video Editing

German, Bahasa Indonesian, Norwegian, Korean, Russian

Publications and Presentations

Jarstad, J.S. "High-dose dietary Riboflavin and direct sunlight exposure in the treatment o keratoconus and post-refractive surgery ectasia. International Journal of Pathology. ISSN: 2324-8599, 2018 September 7, 2018 Eye and Vision Congress, Dubai, UAE.

Jarstad, J. S., R. A. Boudreau et al. "Bringing the ASC Mind-set to the Hospital." *Ophthalmology Management*, Vol. 4, pp. 74, 2001.

McDonald, M, R. B. Foulkes, N. R. Hogan, J. S. Jarstad, and S. E. Wilson. "Dialogue: Can ablated corneal tissue be harmful to refractive surgeons?" *Eye World*, Vol. 6, Number 6, 2001.

Beirne, M. N. and J. S. Jarstad. "Getting Started—New Options in Punctal Occlusion." *Review of Ophthalmology*, August 2001.

Jarstad, J. S. "Complications of PRK Surgery." Annual Meeting—Indonesian Association of Ophthalmologists, Bali, Indonesia, 1995.

Jarstad, J. S. "Should Patenting of Surgical Procedures and Other Medical Techniques by Physicians Be Banned?" Letter to the Editor, *Ocular Surgery News*, December 1, 1994.

Jarstad, J. S. "The Excimer's New Clothes." Letter to the Editor, *Ocular Surgery News*, August 15, 1994.

Jarstad, J. S. and P. W. Hardwig. "Swan Syndrome—Intraocular Hemorrhage from Wound Neovascularization Months to Years after Anterior Segment Surgery." *Canadian Journal of Ophthalmology*, Vol. 22:271–275, August 1987.

Jarstad, J. S. "Optimization of Surgical Technique with the Array Multifocal IOL using a New Marker for Refractive Cataract Surgery." **Abstracts—American Society of Cataract and Refractive Surgeons' 1999 Annual Meeting.**

Jarstad, J. S., R. A. Boudreau, and L. R. Stuart. "Twenty-Five Cataracts, One OR, Eight Hours—How We Did It!" **Instructional Course—American Society of Ophthalmic Administrators' Annual Meeting 1999.**

Jarstad, J. S. "Smart Scheduling." *Ophthalmology Management*, April 6, 1999.

Jarstad, J. S. "Need More Days in the Week?" *Ophthalmology Management*, June 2, 1999.

Jarstad, J. S. and A. P. Weingeist. "Reusable or Disposable? *Ophthalmology Management*, October 19, 1999.

Jarstad, J. S. and A. P. Weingeist. "A Five-Year Prospective Randomized Study of Reusable vs. Disposable Supplies in Cataract Surgery." **Abstract—ASCRS Annual Meeting 1999**.

Jarstad, J. S. "Cataract Surgery Efficiency." *Ophthalmology Management*, April 15, 2003.

Jarstad, J. S. "Secure Business E-Mail, Encryption, and Privacy. New E-Mail Initiative Helps Physician Offer Secure and

Private Communication." *Ophthalmology Management*, June 11, 2003.

Jarstad, J. S. "Attendees Share What They Learn at AAO." *Ophthalmology Management*, January 2002.

Jarstad, J. S. "Saturation-Dosing" for Dry Eye/NTIOLs = Higher Reimbursement." *Ophthalmology Management*, October 2000.

Jarstad, J. S. "Ophthalmologist's Seeing Stars." *Puget Sound Business Journal*, March 3, 1997.

Jarstad, J. S., D. J. Shetlar, W. M. Bourne, J. P. Marcoux, L. Borrmann, J. Lue, E. Duzman, J. Leon, and P. W. Welsh. "Evaluation of Two Mast Cell Stabilizers for Ragweed Conjunctivitis with Graded Ragweed Provocation Testing." *Suppl to Investigative Ophthalmology and Visual Science*, Vol. 28, No. 3 p. 38, 1987.

Boudreau, R. A. and J. S. Jarstad. "Practice Management Pearls in Ophthalmology." Invited Lecture. **Tenth National Congress and Twenty-Ninth Annual Meeting of Indonesian Ophthalmologists Association**, June 7, 2003, Jogykarta, Indonesia.

Jarstad, J. S. "Eighteen Years of Cataract Pearls." **Cataract and Refractive Surgery Symposia, Tenth National Congress and Twenty-Ninth Annual Meeting—IOA**, June 9, 2003.

Jarstad, J. S. "Refractive Surgery Pearls." **Cataract and Refractive Surgery Symposia, Tenth National Congress and Twenty-Ninth Annual Meeting IOA**, June 9, 2003.

Jarstad, J. S. "Treatment of Cataract and Refractive Surgery Complications." Keynote Address, **Tenth National Congress and Twenty-Ninth Annual Meeting— Indonesian Ophthalmologists Association**, June 10, 2003, Jogykarta, Indonesia.

Purba, D., W. Gunawan, B. Harmani, J. S. Jarstad, Sudjarno, P. Djonggi, H. M. Lee, and S. Sudarman. "Posterior Segment Complications in Cataract Surgery (CME, Endophthalmitis, Dropped Nucleus, Posterior Uveitis,

Retinal Detachment, Phaco Post Vitrectomy)." **Symposium on Cataract and Refractive Surgery, Tenth National Congress and Twenty-Ninth Annual Meeting IOA**, June 10, 2003, Jogykarta, Indonesia.

K. Hassan and J. S. Jarstad. "Review of Oculoplastic Surgery—Ptosis." *Lagos Review Course*, University of Nigeria Department of Ophthalmology, Lagos, Nigeria, November 9, 1996.

Jarstad, J. S. and J. R. Jarstad. "Top Ten List for Improving OR Efficiency in Cataract Surgery," University of Philippines Department of Ophthalmology, **Grand Rounds Invited Speaker**, June 10, 2001.

Jarstad, J. S. and J. R. Jarstad. "Ophthalmic Emergencies." Fatima Medical College Department of Ophthalmology, **Grand Rounds Invited Speaker**, Manila, Philippines, June 9, 2001.

Jarstad, J. S. "Management of Cataract and Refractive Surgery Complications." Washington Academy of Eye Physicians and Surgeons Annual Meeting, September 15, 2003.

Jarstad, J. S. "Single Stitch vs. No-Stitch Cataract Surgery—A Prospective Study of 200 Randomized Cases." Washington Academy of Eye Physicians and Surgeons Annual Meeting, 1991.

Jarstad, J. S. "Music in the OR—A Prospective Double Masked Study of Four Types of Music As It Affects OR Efficiency." Presentation at Pharmacia Booth, AAO, 1994.

Gondhowiardjo, T. D., J. S. Jarstad, and R. A. Boudreau. "Performance Standards in Cataract Surgery—A Computerized and Predicted Approach." *Indonesian Journal of Ophthalmology* (submitted for publication on November 12, 2003).

Radio, Television, and Print

Interview National Public Radio, "PRK—Is Something Better Almost Here?" 1996.

Interview KING 5 News, "Multifocal IOL—New Technology" 1998 Lori Matsukawa.

Interview *Tacoma News Tribune* of John S. Jarstad, MD, in "Gift of Sight Restored to Thousands," April 2, 1998, Rita Happy.

Interview Federal Way Mirror, "The Gift of Sight (Reporter Has Sight Restored with Successful PTK)." Linda Dahlstrom, Features Editor, 1997.

Interview KCPQ 13 Health Beat, "Macular Degeneration," 1996.

Interview Channel 4 News Idaho Falls, Idaho, "Salmon Man Has Sight Restored with Successful Cornea Transplant," 1988.

Article from *People's Voice*, Harare, Zimbabwe, January 25, 1993.

US eye specialist donates equipment

Herald Reporter

A TOP United States eye specialist, Dr John Jarstad, has donated medical equipment worth $1 million to be used in eye operations.

The equipment includes lens implants which take the place of the cloudy cataract. The cataract is the commonest eye disease in Zimbabwe and in the United States, said Dr Jarstad.

This new equipment will reduce a huge bill of about $68 million incurred by Zimbabwe annually when sending people for eye surgeries in South Africa.

The chief Government ophthalmologist in the Ministry of Health and Child Welfare, Dr Solomon Guramatunhu, said the equipment would help reduce the bill by between 80 and 90 percent.

He said cataract with lens implant was now done in the country and some cornea transplant carried out on a monthly basis with special equipment donated from the US and flown freely to Zimbabwe by Air Zimbabwe.

Dr Guramatunhu said the eye department was waiting for the delivery of a special laser machine for treating patients with diabetic eye disease.

Dr Jarstad, who was in Zimbabwe during the last two weeks, left for the US on Friday after having done about 50 eye operations.

Article from People's Voice, Harare, Zimbabwe January 25, 1993

EYE TO EYE

Telephone No.: 730011

Telegraphic Address
"MEDICUS", Harare

References:

MINISTRY OF HEALTH
P.O. BOX 8204
CAUSEWAY
ZIMBABWE

26 March 1993

Dear Dr Jackson

On behalf of the people of my country let me take this opportunity to express thanks to all of you at Deseret International for what you and your volunteers have done for Zimbabwe. Aptly the term "Christlike curing" was recently used to describe your approach.

Your ongoing efforts to assist us in those areas of health that we had discussed with you, have brought produced very effective results. Let me officially acknowledge some of the contributions made by Deseret in less than 3 years.

* The cataract surgery program has gone from a conservative and chronic one, to one that can stand on its own and has received the highest praise. Since this was one of our nations greatest needs this means that thousand of lives will be changed by the good work of your volunteers. To date through I.O.L Placements Two thousand four hundred and seventy -five corneal transplants have been completed to date.

* One of your recent doctors contributed to the understanding of optimetrics by our medical staff, and provided his skills in teaching at our newly established optics centre. It did not go unnoticed that at the same time his co-instructor was receiving a stipend for his time and efforts, whilst he was working freely. The prospects of working to bring about additional advances in:-

     modernizing eye care
-    further assistance with our optics programme
-    initiating arthroscopic surgery at the Medical School during this year are exhilarating. These will represent a huge step forward.

It is rare to find individuals or foundations who are as dedicated and who ask for so little in return. Most of the world operates on a quid pro quo basis and a "return on investment" of some kind. You have only asked our cooperation and support. We look forward to continued association with the folks of Deseret.

God bless you in your work, and consecrate us all to furthering the health of the people of Zimbabwe.

DR T J STAMPS MP
MINISTER OF HEALTH AND CHILD WELFARE

JOHN S. JARSTAD, MD

DESERET INTERNATIONAL FOUNDATION, INC.

890 QUAIL VALLEY DRIVE
PROVO, UTAH 84604
801 221-0919
FAX 801 374-8961

5 April 1993

Dr. John S. Jarstad, M.D.
34509 9th Ave., South #101,
Federal Way, Washington 98003

Dear Dr. Jarstad:

We just wanted to send you a letter of appreciation for your recent wonderful work in Zimbabwe. Many lives have been lifted up and much good has been accomplished because <u>YOU</u> took your time, assets, and talents to the people there. On behalf of the Foundation it is my privilege to express our deep affection to you for your contributions of medical assistance and materials which you have given these people.

We know that you took donated supplies with you to Zimbabwe. I am enclosing the following two forms for your use. They are self-explanatory and are, of course, voluntary as far as your completing them is concerned. They can be used by you for Income Tax purposes under charitable contributions and they allow us to track the amounts and types of medical supplies and Physician expenses incurred by our Medical Staff.

Simply fill them out, make a copy for yourself, and mail them back to us as soon as you can. Thank you, once again, for the wonderful work you have done.

Sincerely,

Joel E. Leetham
Executive Secretary

TAX EXEMPT #77-0222786

348

MAYO
CLINIC

7 August 2019

200 First Street SW
Rochester, Minnesota 55905
507-284-2511

Jay C. Erie, M.D.
Department of Ophthalmology
507-284-3701

Dear University of Missouri School of Medicine:

It is my pleasure to write a strong letter of support for the promotion of Dr. John Jarstad to Professor of Clinical Ophthalmology. I am currently Professor and Emeritus Chair in the Department of Ophthalmology at Mayo Clinic in Rochester, Minnesota, and have known John since he was a resident in our training program in the 1980s.

While John was a very busy surgeon in the State of Washington, he was also very active as a clinical investigator in numerous intraocular lens studies and in speaker bureaus. Despite heavy clinical demands, he remained true to his passion for teaching surgery to residents as a Clinical Assistant Professor at the University of Washington Ophthalmology Department and as an Adjunct Professor at Pacific NW University College of Osteopathic Medicine.

John's interest and success in teaching surgical techniques to residents in the U.S. and internationally led him to Mason Eye Institute, where he teaches cataract and refractive surgery. In his short time in Columbia, John has successfully expanded resident education to include a new phacoemulsification surgical curriculum and the use of various specialty intraocular lenses. He teaches all residents at all levels, ranging from basic examinations to advanced skills. Additionally, he advanced the research arm of ophthalmology for residents and medical students by mentoring multiple students in research projects.

John's clinical work is accelerating at Mason Eye Institute, with recent valuable clinical research in dietary riboflavin in corneal cross-linking, miniaturized phacoemulsification machines, intraocular pressure control, and cystoid macular edema prevention after cataract surgery. His innovative work has been recognized at numerous national and international meetings, including the American Society of Cataract and Refractive Surgery.

Dr. Jarstad has improved and continues to improve resident education at Mason Eye Institute and is most deserving of promotion to full Clinical Professor. He has my highest recommendation.

Jay C. Erie, MD

Professor and Emeritus Chair
Department of Ophthalmology, Mayo Clinic
Rochester, MN

JOHN S. JARSTAD, MD

Randall J Olson, MD
Professor and Chair of Ophthalmology
and Visual Sciences
CEO, John A. Moran Eye Center
65 Mario Capecchi Drive
Salt Lake City, UT 84132
Phone: (801) 585-6622
Fax: (801) 581-8703

July 29, 2019

Frederick W. Fraunfelder, MD, MBA
Chair, Roy E. Mason & Elizabeth Patee
Mason Distinguished Professor of Ophthalmology
Assistant Dean of Academic Affairs
Mason Eye Institute, University of Missouri

RE: John S. Jarstad, MD, Candidate for Professor of Clinical Ophthalmology

Dear Dr. Fraunfelder,

It is a pleasure to write this letter of recommendation for Dr. John Jarstad in consideration of his promotion to the rank of Clinical Professor at the University of Missouri in the Department of Ophthalmology.

First, some of my background before I submit my recommendation. I have served for 40 years as Chair of Ophthalmology at the University of Utah, and also as the Chief Executive Officer of the John A. Moran Eye Center. I have had the opportunity to know Dr. Jarstad for at least 20 years and had a chance to spend time with him in his extremely well-run clinical operation in the Seattle area. He already had a reputation as an outstanding surgeon, and I was pleased to hear that he wanted to give up that very successful practice in order to pursue an academic career. I have seen him in many ono-on-one teaching situations as well as presenting lectures. He has excellent skills, and he is extremely well-regarded in the country among anterior segment surgeons.

Dr. Jarstad is a very busy anterior segment surgeon who does both corneal refractive surgery as well as straight forward and complex cataract and refractive surgery. He is the Director of the Anterior Segment Division in your department and presently is Vice Chair of the Department for Clinical Affairs. His engagement in teaching is notable not only for the depth of what he does, but also for the fact that he has taken his passion so far that he has developed a highly regarded teaching capsulorrhexis cataract surgery simulator to help residents learn this skill set. This shows that he wants to go the extra mile in regards to allowing residents and students with whom he works to learn superior surgical skills. He has mentored over 100 residents, including residents from many international countries around the world.

He has always been well-known for his volunteer work long before he started an academic career, and has been on more than 50 humanitarian missions to 25 countries in helping patients around the world. While provision of care was important, he is a big believer the most important

Randall J Olson, MD
Professor and Chair of Ophthalmology
and Visual Sciences
CEO, John A. Moran Eye Center
65 Mario Capecchi Drive
Salt Lake City, UT 84132
Phone: (801) 585-6622
Fax: (801) 581-8703

part that he does is teaching others so they can provide services on their own. This has allowed him to be involved in a host of different activities where he has tried to impart his knowledge broadly throughout your community and the campus as well as internationally.

On the research front, Dr. Jarstad is particularly well-known for his work in cross-linking. His work in association with avoiding the complication of corneal haze has been well-recognized and been verified in the British Journal of Ophthalmology. He has a very long track record of working with pharmaceutical industries in translational medicine and helping to bring other treatments forward. He was very involved in the early days of injectors for foldable lenses, and his discovery that enhanced dietary riboflavin with direct sunlight can result in cross-linking has been extremely well-regarded and was awarded the top research paper for 200 entries in the International Cornea Cross-Linking Symposium in Switzerland in 2017. His entrepreneurial attitude is further shown in his development of a miniature phacoemulsification machine that Bausch & Lomb has agreed to produce for the Third World that is so small it could fit in your pocket. This provides a critical need in regards to international work, and he is, indeed, lauded and should be lauded for this particular development. He is also doing work in regards to posterior capsular opacification, and his knot for iris repair has been well-regarded.

On the speaking front, he has had an opportunity to speak throughout the world and given Distinguished International Lectures multiple times in Indonesia, Philippines, India, Dubai, and London. This shows, indeed, that he not only has local and national but international respect.

I know Dr. Jarstad, in our last Cataract and Refractive Surgery Session, received the Best Paper of Session and many felt one of the best papers given at the meeting where he was recognized as best of the best for his outstanding work. He's given a host of different papers throughout the country, and Newsweek in 2011 recognized him as one of the Top 15 Leaders in Laser Eye Surgery. As evidence of this, he has multiple inventions and patents that he has been directly involved in.

For service he served as the Past-President of the Washington Academy of Eye Physicians and Surgeons, as well as on the Executive Committee of the Washington Academy of Eye Physicians and Surgeons for three years. His community service is extremely broad and represents his interest in a vast array of activities in the community including in his church. It is evident that he is very keen to help in a host of different areas and relationships.

He does list 33 publications both in peer-reviewed and non-peer-reviewed journals. There is a very long list of important presentations around the world that shows that he is highly sought after for his work. He also lists his involvement in several published books.

In summary, we have in Dr. Jarstad a renaissance person who clearly takes his responsibility as a clinical master in complex anterior segment problems including cataract and refractive surgery to

JOHN S. JARSTAD, MD

Randall J Olson, MD
Professor and Chair of Ophthalmology
and Visual Sciences
CEO, John A. Moran Eye Center
65 Mario Capecchi Drive
Salt Lake City, UT 84132
Phone: (801) 585-6622
Fax: (801) 581-8703

heart and is recognized as an international leader in the field. He loves teaching, and it is a passion for him to pass this information onto others. This is confirmed by his interest not only in inventions but the number of people with whom he has worked and trained and his leadership position in the Department of Ophthalmology. He has also been involved in translational-type research and is sought after as a speaker nationally and internationally.

In summary, we have an individual who has a very broad set of skills and is being considered for advancement to the rank of Clinical Professor. Certainly, in my review of the guidelines for your university, he meets these criteria and should be considered for advancement to the rank of Professor. I am confident that at our university, he also would have no trouble being advanced to the rank of Professor due to his many accomplishments.

Sincerely,

Randall Olson, MD
Professor and Chair, Department of Ophthalmology
& Visual Sciences
CEO, John A. Moran Eye Center

RJO:sb

Employees of Evergreen Eye Center 2006
Cindy Armstrong (Lead Technician, Retina Angiographer)
Roxanne Berhorst (Burien office—Reception)
Kristin Boudreau, MS (Credentialing, Collections, Industrial Engineer)
Rick Boudreau, COE (Certified Ophthalmic Executive—Administrator)
Michelle Callen (Billing Office)
Gary Chung, MD (Eye Physician and Surgeon—Cornea Specialist)
Michelle Davis Sheldon (Surgery Center Reception)
Linda Day, MD (Eye Physician and Surgeon—Retina Specialist)
Jane Dickinson (Lasik Coordinator)
Stasi Dorscher, COT (Certified Ophthalmic Tech—Human Resources)
Lisa Dunajski-Veeder (LASIK Coordinator)
Polly Emerson, COT (Certified Ophthalmic Technician)
Wendy Faulconer (Ophthalmic Technician)
Bradley Frederickson, OD (Optometric Physician)
Angie Gleed (Administrative Assistant)
Claudia Griffith (Billing Office)
Barbara Jarstad (Patient Transportation, Clinic Design Team)
Karen Jarstad (Patient Transportation, Video Editor, Public Relations)
Carol Johansson, LPN, COT (Scheduling Nurse—Lead Technician)
Michelle Jordan (Patient Reception)
Shereen Kaip (Surgery Center Patient Coordinator)
Candi Koehn (Clinic Patient Reception)
Debbie Markler, RN (Surgery Center)
Marie McWilliams, COT (Ophthalmic Technician)
Diane Meldrum (Patient Reception)
Irene Mendoza (Patient Reception)
Lisa Newell, COA (Ophthalmic Technician)
LaNelle Ramey, RN (Surgery Center Scrub Nurse)

Debbie Rioux (Billing Office)

JoAnn Robinson (Billing Office Accounts Payable—Assistant Administrator)

Dean Rockey, MD (Eye Physician and Surgeon "Hero")

Nyla Sheldon, COA (Ophthalmic Technician)

Brandi Small, COA (Ophthalmic Technician)

Kara Smith (Patient Reception)

Laurel Stone (Clinic Technician/Assistant to Physicians)

Linda Stuart, RN (World's Best Surgery Center Director)

Heather Sturhan, COA (Ophthalmic Technician)

Mary Sundnes, COT (Ophthalmic Technician)

Robert Tester, MD (Eye Physician and Surgeon—Principal in LLC)

Valentina Werth, COA (Ophthalmic Technician)

Deana Whitesel (Billing Office)

Cynthia Whitten (Patient Reception)

Brianne Willner (Patient Reception)

Geri Jo Wolanski (Surgery Center/Administration/Billing)

Rohana Yager, COT (Ophthalmic Technician)

TRIBUTES TO CHILDREN RAISED

Jessica Ruth (Jarstad) Washburn

Jessica attended school in Minnesota, Idaho and graduated as Valedictorian of Federal Way High School in Washington State. She was accepted to Columbia University New York but decided to attend and graduate from Brigham Young University, Provo, Utah in Art History.

She Married Alan Washburn an Electrical Engineer and they are the parents of six children. Jessica, an accomplished newborn and family professional photographer, became a successful chocolatier and opened Bliss Chocolatier in 2020. Along with her youngest sister Stephanie Jessica won the "Baking it" show on NBC TV (Available on Peacock, Apple TV with SNL co-hosts Andy Samberg and Maya Rudolph) winning first prize during the holiday series in 2021.

John Robert Jarstad.

"Robby" attended school in Minnesota, Idaho and graduated from Federal Way High School in Washington State. Robby was an accomplished bass guitar player and toured with Ivy League and Post Meridian on Van's Warped Tour, before completing a master's degree in Public Administration at American University in Washington, D.C., where he met his wife Ying "April" Li—also a graduate of American University in the same master's degree program. Robby was employed by Charity Vision and currently works in the financial industry. His wife April is a lead customer relations supervisor for NuSkin company.

Allison Rae Jarstad, D.O.

Dr. Allison Jarstad attended school in Washington graduating from Federal Way High School and was a high school record holder in the girl's pole vault as the first girl athlete to go over 10 feet at the high school and at the South Puget Sound League Track Meet. She was a member of the girls track and cross-country team that qualified for the state meet. She was a Division 1 NCAA women's pole vault Mountain West scholar athlete. She attended Pacific Northwest College of Osteopathic Medicine, Yakima, Washington where she was valedictorian and "Student Doctor of the Year." She completed her residency in ophthalmology at State University of New York – Upstate in Syracuse, New York (the same University where her grandfather John O.W. Jarstad completed the master's program in Radio and Television Broadcasting). She completed fellowships in Cornea and Refractive (LASIK) Surgery at University of California – Irvine and an International Fellowship in Ophthalmology at Stanford University, Palo Alto, California and is a practicing cornea surgeon.

Stephanie Ann (Jarstad) Moikeha

Stephanie graduated from Federal Way High School where she was an accomplished gymnast (State qualifier in the balance beam) and captain of the varsity swimming and diving team.

With severe scoliosis prior to a 13 hour operation to straighten her spine, some competitors commented that she had an unfair advantage of a quarter turn on her dives due to her condition. Stephanie graduated from Brigham Young University, Provo, Utah with a Bachelor of Fine Arts Degree in Photography. A professional photographer, Stephanie does wedding and engagement photos at Stephanie Jarstad Photography, Portland, Oregon.

ABOUT THE AUTHOR

John Steven Jarstad, MD, FAAO, FRSM-UK, is a board-certified ophthalmologist (eye surgeon) and professor of clinical ophthalmology at University of South Florida in Tampa. He has served as medical director and founding partner Evergreen Eye Centers in Federal Way, Washington; chief of the medical staff at St. Francis Hospital; co-director of all outpatient surgery at Tampa General Hospital-USF affiliated hospitals; a full-time faculty member at the University of Washington School of Medicine; associate professor at the University of Missouri; and an invited visiting professor in over twenty-five countries lecturing and demonstrating the latest in eye surgery techniques.

A Seattle native, Dr. Jarstad has repeatedly been voted one of America's top ophthalmologists by the Consumer Research Council. Two of his research studies in eye surgery were selected *best in the world* in cornea cross-linking and in cataract surgery.

Dr. Jarstad is the inventor of the Jarstad Refractive Cataract Surgery Marker, the Bausch & Lomb Passport Lens injector, and the Jarstad Cataract Surgery Simulator. He was a medical student research fellow at the National Institutes of Health and has served as a phase 1, 2, and 3 investigating scientist for several FDA-sponsored clinical research studies and as a medical monitor for new surgical devices in ophthalmology.

After serving a two-year volunteer mission for the Church of Jesus Christ of Latter-day Saints to England, Dr. Jarstad graduated from Brigham Young University in premed zoology, received his MD degree from the University of Washington-Seattle, and was an intern and clinical fellow in ophthalmology at the prestigious Mayo Clinic in Rochester, Minnesota.

Jarstad has served as a volunteer in the Church of Jesus Christ of Latter-day Saints as a high priest, seventy, ward mission leader, a stake mission president, bishopric counselor, and senior stake high councilor. He was a board member of Deseret International and Charity Vision and has served on the Vision Committee of the Church of Jesus Christ of Latter-day Saints Charities at church headquarters in Salt Lake City along with over fifty short-term humanitarian missions in Africa, Central America, South America, and Asia, including a four-month deployment on the USNS *Mercy* Hospital Ship and two weeks on the USNS *Comfort*.

Dr. Jarstad and his wife, Dr. Kristine Marshall-Jarstad, a cosmetic dentist, reside on Treasure Island in St. Petersburg, Florida, USA.

Proceeds from this book are donated to further the worldwide humanitarian work described herein and to provide sight to the blind.

Charityvision.net, donate.churchofjesuschrist.org, and Department of Ophthalmology—Eye Care for All c/o USF Morsani Eye Institute 13330 USF Laurel Drive, Tampa, FL 33612-4742.

CPSIA information can be obtained
at www.ICGtesting.com
Printed in the USA
BVHW010538010423
661520BV00021B/1060